Soviet and
Eastern European Trade
and Aid in Africa

PRAEGER SPECIAL STUDIES IN
INTERNATIONAL ECONOMICS AND DEVELOPMENT

Soviet and Eastern European Trade and Aid in Africa

Baard Richard Stokke

FREDERICK A. PRAEGER, Publishers
New York · Washington · London

The purpose of the Praeger Special Studies is to make specialized research monographs in U.S. and international economics and politics available to the academic, business, and government communities. For further information, write to the Special Projects Division, Frederick A. Praeger, Publishers, 111 Fourth Avenue, New York, N.Y. 10003.

FREDERICK A. PRAEGER, PUBLISHERS
111 Fourth Avenue, New York, N.Y. 10003, U.S.A.
77-79 Charlotte Street, London W.1, England

Published in the United States of America in 1967
by Frederick A. Praeger, Inc., Publishers

Library of Congress Catalog Card Number: 67-25250

Printed in the United States of America

TO MY PARENTS

AND TO FRANÇOISE

FOREWORD

This study is the product of research done for a doctoral dissertation submitted to the Graduate Institute of International Studies of the University of Geneva in the fall of 1967. It was completed prior to my employment by the Stanford Research Institute, and any views and conclusions expressed in the study are my own and not necessarily shared by that Institute.

ACKNOWLEDGMENTS

In the preparation of this study I received help, encouragement, advice and criticism from many people to whom I wish to express my gratitude.

I would like to extend my warmest thanks to Professor Rodolphe Nötel of the Graduate Institute of International Studies and of the United Nations Economic Commission for Europe. His friendly direction and scholarly criticism enabled me to bring this study to its completion. Throughout the research I enjoyed many interesting and fruitful discussions with Professor Norman Scott, who helped me to place the subject matter in its perspective. Thanks are also due to Professors Gerard Curzon and Gilbert Etienne, who offered useful suggestions for improving the original draft. During the early stages of the research, Professor Michael Kaser gave me liberally of his time. My gratitude also goes out to all my contacts in Africa and in the centrally planned economies for invaluable advice and help in verification. Mrs. Helena Pizurki carefully and patiently edited the manuscript, and Chief Librarian Norman Field graciously extended to me all facilities of the excellent United Nations Library in Geneva. To all of these individuals collectively I owe credit for any merits this study may have. Upon myself alone I place the onus for errors committed and conclusions drawn.

Finally, I should like to express my gratefulness to Professor Jacques Freymond, Director of the Graduate Institute of International Studies, who encouraged my efforts at all stages of my graduate studies.

CONTENTS

LIST OF TABLES

ABBREVIATIONS

CMEA	Council for Mutual Economic Assistance
ECA	Economic Commission for Africa (United Nations)
ECAFE	Economic Commission for Asia and the Far East (United Nations)
ECE	Economic Commission for Europe (United Nations)
EEC	European Economic Community
FAO	Food and Agricultural Organization (United Nations)
GATT	General Agreement on Tariffs and Trade
IBRD	International Bank for Reconstruction and Development
IMF	International Monetary Fund
NCNA	New China News Agency
OECD	Organization for Economic Cooperation and Development
OEEC	Organization for European Economic Cooperation
P.R.C.	People's Republic of China
TAB	Technical Assistance Board (United Nations)

UNCTAD   United Nations Conference on
                  Trade and Development

. . = Figures not available

-- = Magnitude nil or less than half the unit used

For typographical reasons, titles of all Russian
books, periodicals, newspapers, etc., have been
transliterated into English according to the
British Standards Institute System.

Soviet and
Eastern European Trade
and Aid in Africa

INTRODUCTION

This study presents an analysis of the economic
relations which have developed between Africa and
the centrally planned economies since the mid-1950's
to the present. It sets forth in macro-economic
terms the scope, growth, volume, and effects these
relations have had and promise to have on the development of industry and agriculture in the constituent countries of the African continent.

Although one decade is hardly long enough a
period to enable us to draw abiding conclusions, or
to extract pertinent data for trend analysis, one
would be interested to know how the Soviet and
Eastern European trade and aid endeavors in Africa
are actually progressing--what have been the failures
or success, i.e., what are the current results from
the ten-year experience of economic relations between
Africa and the Soviet Bloc?

In a study of this nature it immediately becomes clear that we are dealing with two separate,
though interconnected, subject matters: (a) trade
and (b) financial and technical aid. Wherever trade
is concerned, we shall seek to uncover growth and
commodity trends, pricing policies, and the degree
of trade creation--or diversion--that has followed
from this commodity exchange, and how far the expansion of trade, both as to its volume and partners
on both sides, has been accompanied by changes in
the degree of bilateral balance of the trade flows.
Finally, in order to determine future prospects for
the expansion of trade over and above present levels,
an answer must be found to the question as to whether
this is complementary to or competitive with local
production.

As to economic aid we would naturally like to
know how foreign aid is organized in the centrally
planned economies--in other words--what is their
"aid technique"? Do they extend project aid or
program aid[1] and has the past decade seen any changes
on this point? How much aid has been promised, what
has been delivered and what remains to be delivered?
All these are problems which must be solved if the
reader is to have a comprehensive picture of
Africa's economic relations with the Soviet Bloc.

But most importantly, the study of a decade of
African economic intercourse with the centrally
planned economies should permit us to make a value-
judgment and to determine which of the two modes of
development assistance--trade or aid--has contributed in the most effective manner to the economic
growth of the recipient countries and which one of
the two promises to do so for the future.

PERIOD OF STUDY

In this examination we shall be dealing with
the period 1955/56-1965/66. Obviously, categorizing
events and developments into periods is usually an
arbitrary and unscientific pastime, for events do
not jump from one to the next, but merge into one
another in a never-ending stream. Yet, for practical
reasons some limitations on time are necessary. The
choice of the period upon which this study is based
has been determined by both chronological and practical considerations.

The choice of 1955/56 as a starting point was
prompted by the fact that this was the year when the
Soviet Union, followed by her Eastern European
partners, began in earnest to direct her attention
to Africa. Prior to this time only few or insignificant contacts had been made.

The second date is less arbitrary, for practical
reasons alone have directed the choice of 1965/66 as
a cut-off point. Anything less than ten years would
not have given a proper perspective to this study,

while anything over ten years could not have been
properly documented. Some of the conclusions
reached will naturally go beyond the ten-year
period, but we have chosen to terminate the examination of African economic relations with the Eastern
trade area one decade after their initiation.

LIMITATIONS OF SCOPE

It should be noted from the outset that this
work will be concerned with economic facts and
analysis and not with political commentary. True,
since economic and political induction are branches
of science frequently sprung from the same stem, in
the study of a subject potentially as sensitive to
political analysis as the present, it may at times
be difficult to distinguish between the two. Nevertheless, throughout the examination a conscious
effort has been made at least to separate economic
evaluation from political appraisal. Not to have
alluded to political motivation, even obliquely,
would have deprived the research of a perspective--
an essential perspective--but certainly not one
constituting the _raison d'être_ of this study.

For the same reason this work contains no discussions of military aid, confining itself solely
to trade, financial and technical assistance and
cultural cooperation wherever this has strong
economic implications. From a research point of
view it is well-nigh impossible to obtain exact,
adequate and reliable information on military relations between Africa and the planned economies.
Thus, even casual allusion to military aid could
expose the study to the deliberate and disingenuous
inaccuracies of same documentation.

DEFINITIONS

By virtue of the subject matter, area limitations become immediately apparent. "Africa" in
this context will largely include those countries
on the continent which maintain economic relations
with the centrally planned economies.[2]

The latter group, as we have used the term, includes all present members of the Council for Mutual Economic Assistance with the exception of Outer Mongolia. For reasons of textual variations we shall alternatively employ the expressions: "the centrally planned economies," "The Soviet Union and Eastern Europe," "the Soviet Bloc," "the Eastern trade area," "the Eastern group," etc.; but in all cases it should be noted that we are dealing with the same group of countries: Bulgaria, Czechoslovakia, Eastern Germany, Hungary, Poland, Rumania and the Soviet Union. This terminology, however, should not be taken to mean that the centrally planned economies constitute a completely unified, homogeneous area. Great diversity exists among its members and in their relationships with the Soviet Union. But all of these countries do owe some allegiance to the U.S.S.R. and tend to support Soviet policy on several basic issues.

Finally a word on currency denominations. For reasons of uniformity we have, whenever possible, converted all currencies into current U.S. dollars at prevailing IMF or equivalent dollar rates of exchange with no attempt to adjust values or changes in prices. In cases where denominations other than this have been used, the relevant exchange rate is indicated.

The Soviet ruble constitutes here a special case. This was revalued, effective January 1, 1961.[3] Consequently, for all trade and credit agreements concluded prior to that date rubles have been converted to dollars at the "old" rate, i.e., 4:1 or $0.25 per ruble. Following the revaluation we have operated with an exchange rate of 90 kopeks per dollar, or $1.11 per ruble.

NOTE ON SOURCES AND STATISTICS

Any work on relations between developing countries and the centrally planned economies is bedeviled by numerous difficulties regarding reliability of source material. For one thing, neither recipient nor donor governments publish complete information on their trade and aid agreements. Important agreements are usually announced publicly at the time of signature, but there is no reporting on progress or regular information on implementation. Less important agreements are often not even announced officially and their existence is known only through a chance newspaper article or a radio broadcast, or perhaps through a speech by an official of the recipient country.

Unfortunately, information of this kind is not entirely satisfactory. Sometimes the existence of an agreement is reported, but the size of amounts involved is known only to signatories. Sometimes it is not perfectly clear whether the reports concern agreements actually concluded or simply offers made. Sometimes projects are reported, but one is left in the dark as to whether they are financed by credits or not.

Nevertheless, research on African economic relations with the Eastern trade area has been considerably facilitated in the course of the past five years. Valuable information can now be obtained from the Soviet foreign trade publication Vneshnyaya Torgovlya[4] which publishes regularly lists of trade and aid agreements with developing countries; and the annual Vneshnyaya Torgovlya Soyuza SSSR za (e.g., 1965) god[5] likewise gives statistics on Soviet foreign trade. Other centrally planned economies, in particular Czechoslovakia and Eastern Germany, also have helpful publications in the foreign trade field.[6]

Partly due to more accessible information from the Soviet Bloc countries, several international organizations have expanded their coverage of trade with this area. Particularly valuable here has been a new publication of the United Nations Economic Commission for Africa, Foreign Trade Statistics of Africa, Series A and B,[7] which gives data on commodity structure and direction of African foreign trade from 1960 onward.

Moreover, agencies of the United States Government, in particular the International Trade Analysis Division of the Department of Commerce, have also gathered substantial information on Soviet and Eastern European trade and aid agreements by a systematic scanning of hundreds of newspapers and specialized periodicals. Their reports have been a useful source for what follows. In addition, by examining national foreign trade statistics and balance of payments reports of the recipient African countries, we get an idea of existing trade flows and of the size of credit commitments--and indications as to how these credits have been distributed.

Other helpful and reasonably reliable sources on aid projects and trade flows are to be found in African and Soviet Bloc newspapers and periodical literature. For the researcher, two short-cuts facilitating the access to this information exist: Africa Research Limited (A.R.L.) publishes monthly its Africa Research Bulletin, which in the "Economic, Financial and Technical Series" carries relevant extracts from African newspapers on domestic and external economic developments.[8] The Mizan Newsletter performs excellently the same service regarding Soviet and Chinese writing on Africa and the Middle East.[9] As far as possible, every piece of information has been doublechecked, i.e., items appearing in the Soviet and Eastern European press have been confirmed with corresponding announcements in African media, or in Western compendia such as the Board of Trade Journal (London) and Marchés Tropicaux et Méditerranéens (Paris).

As regards statistics, wherever possible, trade and aid flows between individual African countries and the centrally planned economies (in Chapters 4 to 7) have been reconciled with global data appearing in Chapters 8 and 9. Tables on individual country trade flows were compiled largely on the basis of United Nations statistical publications and supplemented by national trade statistics of the Eastern group or of Africa. In some cases where the coverage of United Nations statistics appeared to be

incomplete, or not sufficiently up-to-date, preference was given to data derived from Soviet and
Eastern European statistics. These are more complete than those of African partner countries in
that they include deliveries of material and equipment for aid projects. Also, Soviet statistics
record imports from country of origin, disregarding
intermediate trading partners. Data taken from
national statistics of the centrally planned economies have <u>not</u> been adjusted to a c.i.f. basis; hence
comparison of information from different sources in
same years should be made with caution.

These caveats will undoubtedly prove distressing
and possibly confusing to readers who prefer to deal
with hard facts and figures that can be taken at face
value. Here we can only advise that there is more of
this to come. The subject of some aspects dealt with
in this study cannot honestly be presented in other
than conjectural terms and, while the statistics may
be useful for gaining some sort of perspective, it
is well that they be observed in their true light.

PLAN OF STUDY

It might at this point be helpful to say a few
words about how this study was planned and the
reasons why such a plan was chosen.

In the field of development literature several
competent works have already appeared on African
economic relations with the Soviet Bloc.[10] However,
as is the fate of any study on contemporary affairs,
most of these works are today either out of date, or
they were studies written before new and valuable
material--particularly pertaining to the African aspects of these relations--became public. For this
reason we have refrained from giving detailed background descriptions and have instead concentrated on
(1) providing the reader with a perspective on
African-Soviet Bloc economic interchange, (2) apply-
ing recently available material to an examination of
each pertinent African country and its relations with

the centrally planned economies, and (3) evaluating
the primary effects of this interchange on the
African economies.

As such, the study took its final form in three
main sections. In Part I we uncover the background
and motivations for these relations (Chapter 1) and
continue from these to discuss the development of
trade (Chapter 2) and financial and technical aid
(Chapter 3). Part II contains the body of the study
and comprises in four chapters (4 to 7) an area and
a country survey describing how Africa's trade and
aid relations with the centrally planned economies
have developed from their inception up to the
present. Part III concludes the study on trade
(Chapter 8) and on financial and technical aid
(Chapter 9). Summing up this information, an
attempt is made (in Chapter 10) to establish a
present assessment and to project the course these
relations are most likely to take in the future.

NOTES TO INTRODUCTION

1. Some readers might object to the term
"program" used throughout this study, and an interpretation might be in order. We understand "program"
to mean all activities included in the Soviet and
Eastern European aid effort, wherever these activities have been the object of prospective (long-term)
planning.

2. An important reservation and, indeed, one
that affects all discussion of economy and trade of
the African continent, is that arising from the in-
clusion of the Republic of South Africa. By many
standards, including those on which the international
trade statistics of the United Nations are based,
South Africa must be considered an industrialized
country--the only one in Africa. In consequence,
some of the general statements about the continent
would no longer be valid if the Republic of South
Africa was included, and this country is consequently
not treated in the following analysis.

3.   _Pravda_, November 15, 1960.

4.   Published by Vneshtorgizdat, Moscow.

5.   _Ibid._

6.   In particular _Czechoslovak Foreign Trade_
and _Der Aussenhandel und der Innerdeutsche Handel_.

7.   U.N. Doc. E/CN.14/STAT/Ser. A and B
(Addis Ababa, 1960-66).

8.   Published in Exeter, England.

9.   Published by St. Anthony's College (Oxford)
Soviet Affairs Study Group and the Central Asian
Research Centre, London.

10.   See in particular Joseph S. Berliner,
Soviet Economic Aid (New York: Frederick A. Praeger,
Inc. for the Council on Foreign Relations, 1958) and
U.N., ECA, _African Trade with the Centrally Planned
Economies_ (E/CN.14/STC/5, September 1962)(Addis
Ababa, 1962). A recent book treating this aspect is:
Marshall I. Goldman, _Soviet Foreign Aid_ (New York:
Frederick A. Praeger, Inc., 1967).

PART I

THE TEN-YEAR EXPERIENCE

CHAPTER **1** FOCUSING

THE PROBLEM

The past ten years have seen an impressive increase in economic relations between Africa and the
Soviet Bloc. From almost nonexistent trade in
1955/56, commodity exchange with the centrally
planned economies had, by 1966/67, come to represent
one twentieth of Africa's turnover of foreign trade.

But this is merely one part of the picture.
The growth of Soviet and Eastern European financial
and technical aid has been equally rapid--so rapid,
in fact, that by mid-1967 this group had committed
more than 20 per cent of all external development
aid to Africa from all sources. Moreover, as this
aid has been granted in the form of long-term
credits, it should--other things being equal--
significantly increase trade between the two areas,
particularly since the credits are financing extensive programs of equipment deliveries and of
technical assistance for which primary products are
being taken in repayment.

These illustrations leave little doubt that relations with the centrally planned economies have
made and will continue to make an impact on the direction and nature of economic growth in Africa. The
present--ten years after the inception of these re-
lations--offers an opportune moment to undertake a
study of the character of this interchange and to
determine whether it has, in effect, materially
accelerated the development of the African economies
that have been parties to it.

It would be impossible to state whether the
Soviet Bloc is purely politically motivated in its
expansion of trade and extension of financial and
technical aid to Africa or whether economic considerations are the predominant. Probably both
factors enter into the decision-making, for in no
other field have political and economic strategies
of the Eastern trade area undergone such far-reaching
changes in the past years as they have in attitudes
toward the newly independent nations. The prominent
part which the latter play today in Soviet Bloc
political thinking and involvement in world affairs
makes it easy to forget that only a few years ago
the very existence of a "third world" outside the
two great power centers was firmly denied by the
Soviet leadership.[1]

It is clearly outside the scope of this study
to detail the reasons for the change. It may serve
our purpose, however, to point out that it was
brought about as a result of two interdependent postwar developments--the unexpectedly rapid process of
decolonization and the growing importance of newly
independent nations as a tangible factor in world
politics. A third factor which has become prominent
in the past five years is the ideological conflict
within the Communist Bloc and the subsequent Soviet
desire to solidify its loyalties in the developing
world.

Parallel with, but also prior to, this development were changes in economic thought manifested
within the Eastern trade area. The impression was
that there existed a significant and powerful body
of expert opinion inside the centrally planned
economies that saw the diplomatic détente with the
West as an opportunity to secure some economic gains
in world trade and which wanted to concentrate on
this objective. In other words, while it was obviously politically advantageous to increase ties
with, and possibly dependence of, developing
countries on the Soviet Bloc by trading with them,
there were also strong economic motives for an increase in raw material imports from the "new"
countries.

As economic gains from political inroads were progressively recognized, trade missions were sent by the Soviet Union and the Eastern European centrally planned economies to any country willing to receive them. The welcome turned out to be particularly warm in the less-developed world. This was due not only to the fact that the Eastern trade area expressed a willingness to supply much-needed capital equipment and consumer goods in return for products which were doing badly on the world markets, but they also offered the newly independent nations an opportunity to diversify the direction of their foreign trade.

All this, however, is anticipating what is to come. To obtain a meaningful picture of the growth and of the nature of African economic ties with the centrally planned economies, it will be necessary to consider the economic structure of Africa and the position of the Soviet Bloc in world trade and then to examine the trade and aid flows in this perspective.

Any ranking or comparison of countries on the road to economic development will of necessity be arbitrary, but even so it is difficult to see how Africa could fail to wind up toward the bottom of the list. There is low production per capita and low productivity per area in the agricultural realm. A large part of the continent is still devoted to subsistence production. The dominant economic activity is subsistence agriculture and production of agricultural and some mineral raw materials; energy production and manufacture rate poorly. There is a shortage of skilled and semi-skilled labor, of managers and entrepreneurs. The needs in education are great--most countries still have relatively few high schools and only a small number of college graduates. Rates of illiteracy, incidences of disease (particularly deficiency diseases), infant mortality and early adult death are high. The infrastructure often remains grossly inadequate despite considerable improvements which have come about in the postwar period.

Latest available estimates reveal that in 1963, the average annual income per capita, for Africa as a whole, was approximately $122; but even this low figure should not be taken as an indication of living standards since in Africa as much as 60 per cent of the population live outside the money economy. In this connection it may be interesting to note, for the sake of comparison, that also, in 1963, annual per capita income in Latin America was approximately $350; in Western Europe $1,100; in the Soviet Union $820; and in the United States close to $3,000.[2]

This is a bleak description, but it still does not provide the full picture. In its Economic Survey of Africa Since 1950 the United Nations Secretariat distinguishes two archetypes between which most of the developing economies lie.[3] This distinction is interesting because it has a particular relevance to Africa. In both cases there is a modern and a traditional economy--or--each national economy has a dual facet, a money and a subsistence sector.

The first type is largely export-oriented. It is characterized by an exchange economy brought about by foreign capital and enterprise. It operates with high capitalization and advanced techniques, mainly in mining and agricultural enterprises.

As regards the second type, commercialization has been brought about mainly by transformation of part, or parts, of the traditional economy, usually by peasant production of crops for export and local consumption. We find here relatively little foreign investment in large-scale enterprises, and the movement of labor to the modern economy sector remains small.

It is therefore obvious that it is the first type which will have any chance of contributing materially to future economic development of the African continent. A typical feature of this type of economy, which is common to most African countries, is a high degree of production centered on primary commodities, these being either agricultural or mineral. Statistics showing a breakdown of gross

TABLE 1

AFRICA

Percentage Shares of GDP--Primary Products and Manufacturing

African Countries	Year	Agriculture	Mining	Total Primary Products	Manufacturing
Algeria	1958	21	3	24	11
Congo (K)	1959	28	19	47	13
Egypt (U.A.R.)	1961	25	1	32	17
Kenya	1964	42	-	43	10
Malawi	1963	47	-	47	6
Morocco	1964	32	6	38	14
Nigeria	1963	62	1	63	5
The Sudan	1963	55	-	55	5
Tanzania	1964	57	2	62	4
Uganda	1963	61	2	63	7
and for comparison					
India	1963	45	1	46	19[a]
South Africa	1963	9	12	21	28[a]
United Kingdom	1963	4	3	7	35
U.S.A.	1963	4	1	5	29

[a] includes construction.

Source: U.N., Yearbook of National Account Statistics, 1965, Table 3, pp. 457-58.

19

domestic product (GDP) by types of activity are
available for a few countries only (generally those
more advanced in development), but even these amply
demonstrate the preponderance of the primary sector.[4]

The importance of foreign trade to the continent thus became evident. Since most African countries devote a large part of their economic efforts
to the production of agricultural or mineral raw
materials for export, they naturally cover their
needs for manufactured goods by imports.

About two thirds of African exports consist of
agricultural products, while minerals and some fuels
represent most of the remainder.[5] The structure of
imports is only slightly more variated. In spite of
the fact that their dominant economic activity is
agriculture, foodstuffs figure prominently in the
import statistics of almost every African country.
Other important import commodities are manufactured
goods, of which machinery and equipment represent
approximately one third.[6]

There is of course nothing inherently wrong in
being heavily dependent on exports of primary products for financing imports. A country like Denmark,
for instance, due to close proximity to major markets
and wide variations within a few product ranges, has
been well able to rely on her predominant exports of
dairy products and meats to sustain her economic
growth and high standard of living. In Africa, however, where many countries are dependent on exports
of a very narrow range of primary commodities, for
which demand may be inelastic, we see a relative decline in import earnings and, as a result, a general
deterioration of the terms of trade.

This retrogradation has occurred for a variety
of reasons, the most important probably being notable
changes in the pattern of consumer tastes and dietary
standards in Western Europe and North America--which
together constitute Africa's most important export
market. We can illustrate this by pointing out the
structure of African exports which in the last few
years by and large has centered on the following

TABLE 2

Terms of Trade of Developed and Less-Developed Areas and of Africa, 1956-66

(1958 = 100)

	1956	1957	1959	1960	1961	1962	1963	1964	1965	1966
Developed Areas	97	96	102	103	104	105	104	104	104	104
Less-Developed Areas	104	100	99	99	97	96	97	97	97	97
of which: Africa	104	99	99	97	93	90	92	94	92	93

Source: U.N., Monthly Bulletin of Statistics, Vol. 20, No. 10 (October, 1966), Special Table A-3, pp. xii-xiii.

commodities: cocoa, coffee, cotton, groundnuts and
minerals. There has, of course, been a variety of
other products, but none have figured as prominently
in African export statistics as these. As regards
cotton, it has met, in the course of the last years,
with an increasingly heavy competition from synthetic
fibers, a competition which is likely to become more
important; while consumption of cocoa and groundnuts
has declined, thus causing a decline in price levels.[7]
Minerals therefore remain the only stable factor, but
prices for commodities within this group have also
fluctuated widely in the past few years. However,
lower prices have not caused a decline in output--
thus, the situation in Africa today is that the continent is being faced with larger yearly crops for
which we have seen declining price trends and also
products which are becoming increasingly difficult
to market due to competitive sources of supply.

The dichotomy might best be summed up by quoting
the United Nations Economic Commission for Africa,
which stated that "the African countries are hetero-
geneous in population, area, resources and, by and
large, in their prospects. They are homogeneous in
their backwardness, their common dependence on a very
narrow range of primary products and--above all--in
their desire to set out on the path of economic development."[8]

In the Soviet Bloc almost "complementary" developments have taken place. Since the mid-1950's,
the more advanced centrally planned economies have
seen an opportunity to make wider use of the international exchange of goods and of the subsequent
specialization of production as a means of ensuring
a more rational use of their resources. Consequently,
cost considerations are, with increasing frequency,
taken into account in foreign trade planning. This
development has been sufficiently elaborated elsewhere,[9] and mention of it here will be constricted
to illustrating the economic rationale for trade with
Africa. Because of the unequal economic structure in
Eastern European countries as contrasted with the
Soviet Union, each area will be discussed separately,
starting with the U.S.S.R.

At the time of the revolution, Russia was pre-
dominantly an agricultural country. As soon as the
Communists gained full control, they decided that
the Soviet Union should become an industrial power,
as well as a political force, second to none. In
the pursuit of this goal the Soviet Union maintained
a high rate of investment over a long period of time,
concentrating her efforts on the construction of
plants and on the equipment for heavy industry. Accordingly, within a period of some thirty years, the
Soviet Union rose from her status as an agriculturally
oriented country to become the second industrial power
in the world.

In the course of this development, some economic activities (particularly in the field of agriculture and food production) progressed far less
rapidly than did capital equipment-producing industries, and today the former are faced with increasingly
serious resource limitations. This is because within
limits the supply of land is fixed and raw materials
sectors have to expand output by exploiting less accessible, poorer and less productive soils. Institu-
tional factors, such as collectivization, have likewise retarded growth in agriculture. As industrial
production grew, it became evident that in the Soviet
Union extraction of certain raw materials required increasingly larger capital supplies. In the metallurgical field, for example, many ores were of low grade,
which made it difficult to achieve an increase in production. The cost factor is aggravated by the vast
distances within the country itself, and low productivity continues to hamper certain extractive industries. In addition, there have been incidents of
gross inefficiency in the development of Soviet capital
industry. The latter has suffered from poor planning,
material shortages and an almost nonexistent quality
control at the early stages, resulting in the need for
the import of quality or precision machinery. This was
supplied partly by Eastern Europe and it can be stated
without exaggeration that, since the end of World War
II, the Soviet Union has systematically tapped the
machinery-producing resources of her satellites--to
the extent that for all these countries the U.S.S.R.
has remained their major consumer of capital equipment. In return, food, grains and some raw materials
were supplied.

We can see here a curious duality in the Soviet foreign trade picture. On entirely rational economic grounds, the country today can import raw materials and certain beverage crops from the developing world, while supplying it with technical know-how and capital equipment--and at the same time, the Soviet Union continues to import capital equipment from Eastern Europe, while supplying this area with primary products. It would appear, therefore, although this cannot be documented, that the Soviet Union finds itself in the position of a middleman who imports high-quality capital equipment from Eastern Europe, exports her own lower-quality equipment to the developing world and imports primary products from this area, which might then be resold in Eastern Europe at a possible price advantage.

So far, we have only briefly touched on comparative cost considerations in Soviet foreign trade. This is because these may be given differing weights from one country to another; and, in spite of a somewhat laggard production in certain extractive industries, the U.S.S.R. is under no compulsion to attach much attention to cost considerations in the planning of external trade. At any rate its economic importance is insignificant in the case of a country of the size and with a natural resource endowment as that of the Soviet Union. But it does take on greater importance for Eastern European countries, where the relative dependence on trade is heavier. Here we find a far more uneven picture of natural wealth. Up to the early 1950's, the Balkan States were dependent on a low efficiency agriculture, while the industrial base was rudimentary and the standard of living primitive. Other countries, however, were by no means backward agrarian areas. Eastern Germany had been an integral part of the most developed industrial country in Europe, and Czechoslovakia, though small, was highly developed with a fairly diversified economy. The remaining countries of that area, though less advanced, had also achieved a certain degree of industrialization.

After World War II, means of production were nationalized, financial and distribution systems were put under State control, and collectivization of

agriculture was introduced. The aim appeared to be
to recreate in each of these countries the Soviet
Union structure in miniature and, consequently, emphasis was placed on rapid industrialization. The
primary sector was heavy industry, with agriculture
running a poor second. The rate of capital formation was drastically stepped up to some 20-30 per
cent of the Eastern European countries' net national
product devoted to gross fixed investment and of this,
on the average, roughly 50 per cent was channelled
into industry. To give this some perspective, it is
estimated that the postwar Eastern European rate of
investment was approximately three or four times that
of the prewar level.

Wherever such tremendous pressure on accelerat-
ing the rate of investment exists, there is usually
a squeeze on consumption of consumer goods, and it
is hardly surprising that, as in the Soviet Union,
agriculture fared badly. This was due mainly to the
fact that this sector was used as a major source of
investment funds and, therefore, forced deliveries
of low level farm produce at prices uneconomic to the
producer, seriously hampering the growth of output.
The picture was further darkened by forced collectivization, and Eastern Europe, which before the war
exported appreciable quantities of agricultural produce, notably grain, is today a net grain importer.
The total population to be fed is only a little higher now than in 1939, but a much higher percentage is
employed in industry, and improvements in dietary
standards for the working population still leave much
to be desired.

All these factors: diminishing supplies and
the deteriorating quality and quantity of consumer
goods, recurring food shortages as well as the sheer
human strain of industrialization and collectivization, probably all contributed to disturbances in
Eastern Germany in 1953 and in Poland and Hungary in
1956. Following these uprisings the rate of industrial growth was moderated, a larger slice of national
income was allocated to consumption and more investments directed toward light industry and agriculture.
These branches, however, have been slow in developing

not only in terms of quantity but, what is even more
important, in the quality of their output, which
again tended to encourage a pattern of trade involv-
ing exports of equipment against imports of consumer
goods and foodstuffs.

This is where we find the economic rationale
behind the commercial relations initiated by the
Soviet Bloc with Africa during the early 1950's.
Africa had surplus commodities to sell--commodities
for which her traditional markets became less and
less accessible. The Eastern trade area, and in
particular Eastern Europe, being faced with a growing demand for consumer goods and foodstuffs, could
absorb some of the African products and, at the same
time, provide the continent with much-needed capital
goods. Thus a viable commodity exchange developed.

Pursuant to this followed, a few years later,
the commencement of the Soviet and Eastern European
programs of financial and technical aid to Africa.

However, care should be taken here not to consider Eastern European inroads in Africa simply as
part of the Soviet African strategy. Intra-Soviet
Bloc relations have changed considerably since 1956
and, as a result, the centrally planned economies in
Eastern European countries have been able to give
practical considerations to their own interests and
to respond to political and economic incentives
emanating from their relations with Africa, although
these may be quite distinct from those of the Soviet
Union. To a much greater extent than the latter,
Eastern European countries have a genuine interest
in expanding commercial ties with Africa and their
relatively important role in African trade transactions has been more significant than that of the
Soviet Union. Moreover, in the past few years
Africa has become increasingly important as a battle-
field in the Sino-Soviet ideological duel and, while
economic motives may remain all-important, the Soviet
Union has seen a political advantage in concentrating
mainly on extending financial and technical aid, where
concrete results can more easily be shown than in
trade relations.

The expansion of trade and extension of economic aid, instead of imposing a burden on the centrally planned economies, may well result in a net economic gain over a period of years. As Soviet Bloc countries further develop their industrial capacity (followed by increased demands for basic products) and as the local supply of these basic products is gradually depleted (although more so in Eastern Europe than in the U.S.S.R.) it will become increasingly advantageous for that area to export capital goods and to import raw materials.

The implications of these trade needs are significant, even though they should cause only a small shift in the foreign trade pattern of the centrally planned economies. This is particularly so since they are coming at a time when many developing nations need the kind of capital goods and assistance the Eastern trade area is able to provide.

Obviously, the translation of a development desire into action--a thing most African governments are now eagerly seeking to do--requires large-scale investments and imports of investment goods. Thus the problem, as seen from the African side, has been to find countries willing to deliver, in return for traditional African exports, large quantities of capital goods and expert help without which industrialization and over-all economic development of the continent are unlikely to materialize.

NOTES TO CHAPTER 1

1. J. Stalin, Economic Problems of Socialism in the U.S.S.R. (Moscow: Foreign Language Press, 1952).

2. U.N., ECA, Industrial Growth in Africa (E/CN.14/INR/1/Rev.1)(New York, 1963), Annex I, p. 83.

3. U.N., Department of Economic and Social Affairs (E/CN.14/28)(New York, 1959), p. 12.

4. A qualification must be added to Table 1.
In countries with a relatively significant manufacturing sector (Congo K, Egypt, Morocco), this tends
to be largely geared to the processing of primary
products, or consists of small-scale, labor-intensive
"cottage" industries. Even so, Table 1 probably substantially understates the importance of agriculture
in the average African economy. This may be explained
by the fact that the major part of agricultural activities is still of the subsistence type, which is
given only a nominal valuation in the compilation of
GDP statistics.

5. See Table 6.

6. Ibid.

7. For a discussion of synthetics and primary
products, see UNCTAD, Synthetics and their Effects
on Agricultural Trade (E/CONF.46/59, March 6, 1964)
(Geneva, 1964), pp. 1-17.

8. U.N., ECA, African Trade with the Centrally
Planned Economies (E/CN.14/STC/5, September, 1962)
(Addis Ababa, 1962), Section 3, p. 5.

9. See: Joseph S. Berliner, Soviet Economic Aid
(New York: Frederick A. Praeger, Inc. for the Council
on Foreign Relations, 1958), pp. 119-36; and U.N., ECA,
Economic Planning in Europe (Geneva, 1965), pp. 43-55.

CHAPTER **2** DEVELOPMENT
OF TRADE

In more respects than one are relations between
Africa and the centrally planned economies marked by
paradoxes. They are tenuous, yet rapidly consoli-
dating, impressive in terms of contacts established,
yet relatively minuscule in size. On the one hand,
it would be a grave error of judgment to overstate
the importance to Africa of trade with the centrally
planned economies, for trade relations--on both
sides--are rather limited. In 1965, for example,
when upward of twenty-nine African countries traded
with the seven planned economies, turnover of this
commerce did not amount to more than about 5 per
cent of global African trade.[1] Furthermore, from
incomplete statistics for 1966 and 1967 it can only
be concluded that this level has been maintained.

However, the relatively modest nature of these
relations should not blind us to the fact that they
have grown to their present level from a very low
base, and over a relatively short period--only one
decade. The impact of this growth is compounded by
the fact that over the past ten years, the centrally
planned economies have managed to break into a market
which was--and to a large degree still is--essentially
colonial in character, a market where major manufacturing enterprises and financial institutions are
those of the former metropolitan country and where
economic relations between former colony and mother
country have been established to the point of taking
precedence over all other external economic activity.
Moreover, following independence, these relations
were further consolidated by the integration movements

in Western Europe; and the Common Market, the United
Kingdom and North America remain by far the most important of Africa's external economic contacts.[2]

What then is the nature of the growth in economic intercourse between Africa and the Eastern
trade area? As this has developed to date, it is a
diverse medium composed of a variety of elements.
Its central feature is the expansion of trade, the
other major part being the construction of agricultural, infrastructural or industrial installations
financed by the centrally planned economies. However, the division between these two components is
not as clear-cut as it may appear to be. What we
have is an interconnection, whereby the expansion
of trade has given rise to a program of financial
and technical aid financed by credits extended by
the centrally planned economies. Since the credit
program causes an increase, first in Soviet and
Eastern European exports, and then in imports of
African commodities in repayment for the loans, the
two components cannot be entirely separated. As
subsidiary activities, several African countries
have extensive programs of cultural and scientific
cooperation, as well as educational exchange with
the centrally planned economies. In practice, however, when turning to concrete descriptions of these
forms of interchange, we find that in the case of
Africa's economic relations with the Soviet Union
and Eastern Europe--these are always initiated
by the establishment of commercial trade links--
financial assistance and cultural cooperation usually
follow two to three years later. For this reason it
is logical that we turn our attention first to trade
between Africa and the Soviet Bloc, and in the following chapter, to a discussion on financial and
technical aid.

Due to more abundant resources and greater
flexibility in organizing these it has, in most
cases, been up to the centrally planned economies
to initiate the relations. Thus, it might be help-
ful--at this point--to give a summary description
of their foreign trade apparatus, before launching

into a discussion of trade and aid as this has developed over the past decade.

TRADE ORGANIZATION
IN THE CENTRALLY PLANNED ECONOMIES

Foreign trade in the Soviet Union and Eastern
Europe is based on state monopolies, usually vested
with each country's Ministry of Foreign Trade. This
has as its main objective to implement the foreign
trade plan which is part of that country's state
plan. Usually, the foreign trade plan is broken
down into two parts: the import and the export
plan. These are then established in terms of values to be realized in foreign exchange so that the
balance of payments is ensured. These plans, of
course, have to be closely correlated with the national production plans, material inputs, retail
trade, and investment plans, etc.[3] It is broadly
true to say that the import plan is the primary element, with the export plan being essentially an indication of means available for financing required
imports.[4]

Other active participants in the process of
establishing foreign trade targets are the foreign
trade corporations. These operate as subsidiary
bodies to the national Ministry of Foreign Trade
and have, in their functional fields, a complete
monopoly position in conducting transactions with
foreign importers and exporters, although the last
few years have seen several departures from this
rule.[5]

A particularly important aspect of the monopoly
position of the foreign trade corporations has been
their power to negotiate both export and import
prices. It should be obvious, therefore, that the
question of tariffs becomes meaningless to other
countries when they trade with state monopolies.
Whether state trading countries maintain tariffs or
not, is irrelevant. Since the foreign trade corporation is the sole importer, it can pay whatever it
wants for imports, and as the sole seller, it can

demand what it wants for exports, and the domestic prices at which these are sold may have very little to do with foreign exchange prices paid to or requested from the foreign supplier.

Another argument in discussions concerning foreign trade corporations is that state trading of this nature promotes bilateral agreements and discourages multilateral trade. Particularly in relations with Africa--where the centrally planned economy is often faced with several possible sources of supply--it may be easy to give preference to the one which agrees to buy a product which the Soviet Bloc country is anxious to export.

Be this as it may--within limits set by commodity export and import plans, as well as geographical, currency area, or country breakdown--the corporations are expected to operate on normal commercial principles taking into account price, quality, delivery and payment terms, etc. The number of these corporations may vary with each country, but averages around 20.[6]

TRADE ORGANIZATION IN AFRICA

Until the late 1950's, few African countries had elaborated any coherent policy of foreign trade. This was mostly seen as supplying metropolitan countries with required raw materials, or, in some rare cases--semi-finished products. With the advent of independence came an acute awareness of the need to change the economic structure from low productivity primary production to industrialization. To this end development planning was employed, and, as part of the development, plans were drawn up of requirements and targets for foreign trade. Thus, foreign trade planning in Africa is more of a recent phenomenon, and by mid-1967, not more than about one half of the independent states on the continent had plans and projections for foreign trade that were sufficiently integrated with over-all development programs.[7]

In Africa, as in the centrally planned economies, responsibility for implementing foreign trade
plans is with increasing frequency being handed over
to specialized public enterprises which, in nature,
have much in common with the foreign trade corporations. Some of these existed prior to independence
in the form of marketing boards which were found in
several British colonies. These were given monopoly
rights for purchasing from local growers and selling
on foreign markets the country's most important agricultural products. The purpose of central trade
organizations of this nature was to stabilize national income and the income of the private individual
farmer. The Ghana Cocoa Marketing Board is a good
case in point.[8]

Moreover, with the elaboration of coherent development plans, governments in several African countries have found it necessary to pursue a policy of
limiting the share of foreign capital in external
commerce as a means of expanding the public section
of the economy. To this end trade corporations were
established, and these have been particularly useful
in trading with the centrally planned economies. The
experience in Africa has been that when a government
corporation of a centrally planned economy is the
single buyer in a market, one single government
agency on the selling side finds it easier to negotiate with it than a number of competing sellers.

By and large, state monopolies in Africa operate
in a manner not unlike that of their counterparts in
the Eastern trade area, and an organization such as
the Ghanaian National Trading Corporation was established in 1963 with the specific purpose of dealing
with the Soviet Union and the centrally planned economies in Eastern Europe.[9]

TRADE AGREEMENTS AND BILATERAL TRADE

The main element in African trade with the
centrally planned economies is a one-to-one bilateralism conducted under trade and payments
agreements. This system not only facilitates the

perspective planning of foreign trade, but it also
carries with it the assurance that authorities of the
partner country are themselves planning to accept a
certain level and composition of imports from--and to
supply a certain level and composition of exports to--
the other country concerned. Moreover, as we have
seen, African countries frequently operate major development schemes through state agencies, and the fact
that such agencies are often directly engaged in foreign trade increases the ease with which offers of secure export markets can be matched by similar undertakings to import.

Another argument in favor of long-term bilateral
trade and payments agreements has been that these
tend, as a rule, to have a trade-creating as well as,
or rather than, a trade-diverting effect;[10] long-term
import and export schedules tend to be complementary
in their commodity composition and imports are made
possible on both sides, which would otherwise have
been precluded by currency shortage.

The first part of this argument is highly questionable, and we shall later test its validity,[11] but
there can be little doubt that bilateral relations
have had a currency-saving effect, as relatively little
trade has been transacted on a convertible currency
basis. Indeed, the very purpose of bilateral trade and
payments agreements in African-Soviet Bloc trade has
been to avoid the use of convertible currencies for
settlement of debit accounts and to provide for bilateral balancing by other means. These may include extra
shipments of goods and--in very rare cases--triangular
arrangements on re-exports.[12] The kind of settlement
most preferred by members of the Eastern trade area, and
a variation of which is embodied in many of the trade
and payments agreements, is the provision for extra shipments of commodities.[13] Under this arrangement, when a
debit builds up, the country with the export surplus will
cut back on shipments as the country with the import surplus accelerates shipments.[14] The accounts are thus
automatically balanced with movement of goods, and no
foreign exchange is required. The weakness of this system is, of course, that one may be forced to accept goods
the partner country offers, but these may not necessarily
be what one ordered. Since many agreements are automaticall

renewed, the goods shipment method also operates to
condition targets for the next trading period. We
shall illustrate this with an example.

Balanced trade may have been agreed upon between
the Sudan and Czechoslovakia. In 1965, these two
countries traded at about $5 million each way, and
this agreement was renewed. But in 1966 the Sudan
exported $6 million worth of commodities, while
Czechoslovakia exported merely $4 million worth of
goods and services. In 1967 then, Czechoslovakia
would be scheduled to export $6 million and the Sudan
$4 million, or something in between so that the $2
million are paid by a Czechoslovak export surplus.
These targets, however, are not set down in any new
agreement, but in attached protocols.

The payments agreement normally has the same
duration and renewal provisions as the trade agreement. Its principal objective is to provide for
means of bilateral settlement and frequently trade
and payments agreements are comprised in one document. Except for a reference to world market prices,
few actual unit prices are mentioned in these agreements. In the trade and payments agreements a maximum or minimum amount will usually be stipulated as
a value indication of quantities involved. Unit
prices will then be the subject of decision for each
individual transaction between the foreign trade
ministry/marketing board of the African country and
the foreign trade corporation of the relevant centrally planned economy.

Frequently, the centrally planned economies will
make available short-term technical (swing) credits
in their trade with Africa. Usually these range between 2.5 and 10 per cent of annual trade turnover,
but so far they have seen relatively little use.[15]

On this basis--starting from only a handful of
trade links in 1954/55--altogether 71 "basic" trade
agreements[16] between 22 African countries and the
seven centrally planned economies, had been concluded by the end of 1965, and in 1966/67 we can pro-
visionally add another seven agreements to the list.
This accounts for about 71 per cent of a total possible 283 bilateral links.[17]

TABLE 3

AFRICA

Trade and Payments Agreements Concluded with the Centrally Planned Economies, 1953-65

African Trading Partner	Soviet or Eastern European Trading Partner							Totals
	Bulgaria	Czechoslovakia	E. Germany	Hungary	Poland	Rumania	Soviet Union	
Algeria	x				x		x	3
Cameroun							x	1
Congo-Brazzaville							x	1
Dahomey	x	x		x		x		4
Egypt (U.A.R.)	x	x	x	x	x	x	x	7
Ethiopia							x	1
Ghana	x	x	x	x	x	x	x	7
Guinea	x	x	x	x	x		x	6
Kenya							x	1
Libya							x	1
Mali	x	x	x		x		x	5
Morocco	x	x	x	x	x		x	6
Niger	x				x		x	3
Nigeria	x	x					x	3
Senegal							x	1
Sierra-Leone							x	1
Somalia		x					x	2
Sudan	x	x	x	x	x	x	x	7
Tanzania (Tanganyika)	x						x	2
Togo	x						x	2
Tunisia	x	x	x	x	x		x	6
Uganda							x	1
Total of 22 countries	13	10	7	7	9	4	21	71

Sources: See Table 4, p. 51.

36

TABLE 4

AFRICA

Trade and Payments Agreements Concluded with the Soviet Union and
the Eastern European Centrally Planned Economies, 1953-65[a]

African Trading Partner	Soviet or Eastern European Trading Partner	Nature of Agreement	Signatory Date and Validity[b]	Details of Commodity Composition	Payments Agreements and General Conditions	Source[d]
Algeria with:	Bulgaria	Trade and Payments Agreement	February 22, 1963 Automatic renewal	Exports: Canned goods, cereals, wine, phosphates, minerals; Imports: Textile machinery, tool machinery, chemicals, etc.;	..[c]	Board of Trade Journal, London: July 5, 1963
	Poland	Trade and Payments Agreement	January 26, 1963 Automatic renewal	Exports: Fruits and vegetables, wine, tobacco, cereals; Imports: Potatoes, sugar, butter, chemicals, and pharmaceuticals;	..	Board of Trade Journal, London: June 28, 1963
	Soviet Union	Trade and Payments Agreement	November 4, 1963	Exports: Agricultural products; Imports: Telecommunication equipment, tractors, lorries, and cranes;	MFN clause on all trading matters	Pravda, Moscow: November 6, 1963
Cameroun with:	Soviet Union	Trade Agreement	September, 1962	Exports: Coffee, high quality woods, etc.; Imports: Industrial machinery, cement, and chemical fertilizers;	..	Africa South of the Sahara, Paris: September 27, 1962

Continued

37

TABLE 4 (Continued)

African Trading Partner	Soviet or Eastern European Trading Partner	Nature of Agreement	Signatory Date and Validity[b]	Details of Commodity Composition	Payments Agreements and General Conditions	Sourced
Congo - Brazzaville with:	Soviet Union	Trade Agreement	December, 1964	..		Tass - Press Release, Moscow: December 16, 1964
Dahomey with:	Bulgaria	Trade Agreement	April 24, 1963	Exports: Groundnuts, palm oil, copra, cotton, bananas, manioc, tapioca, pineapples, etc.; Imports: Machinery, Diesel engines, electrical material, cement, chemicals, pharmaceuticals, sugar, preserves, etc.;	MFN clause on all trading matters. Imbalance in trade flows to be settled by payments in convertible currencies	..
	Czecho-slovakia	Trade Agreement	April 24, 1963 Automatic renewal	Exports: Palm oil, copra, groundnuts, cotton, tobacco, fruits, etc.; Imports: Machinery, electrical equipment, water-pumps, motor-cycles, agricultural machinery, tubes and pipe fixtures;	MFN clause on all trading matters. Settlement of balances in convertible currencies. Establishment of trade missions	Czechoslovak Foreign Trade, Prague: No. 6, June, 1963
	Hungary	Trade and Payments Agreement	February 13, 1962	Exports: Coffee, copra, palm oil, groundnuts, etc.; Imports: Meat conserves, sugar, cotton fabrics, rayon, chemicals, matches, machinery, bicycles, and motorcycles;	MFN clause on all trading matters. Settlement of balances in convertible currencies, or by additional trade. Credit Margin: $100,000	West Africa, London: December 29, 1962

Country	Agreement	Date / Validity	Exports / Imports	Terms	Source
Rumania	Trade Agreement	December 20, 1962	Exports: Cotton, groundnuts, copra, bananas, pineapples; Imports: Tool machinery, transport equipment, electrical equipment, tires, detergents, and pharmaceuticals;	..	Board of Trade Journal, London: March 20, 1964

Egypt (U.A.R.)
with:

Country	Agreement	Date / Validity	Exports / Imports	Terms	Source
Bulgaria	Trade and Payments Agreement	May, 1962 Validity: 3 years Automatic annual renewal	Exports: Raw cotton; Imports: Cheese, tobacco, bicarbonate of soda, wood, cigarette paper, insulated cables, etc.;	MFN clause on all trading matters. Annual value of commodity exchange: $11.5 million in each direction. Settlement of balances via clearing accounts	Bank for International Settlements, Basel: May 24, 1962
Czechoslovakia	Trade and Payments Agreement	June 18, 1960, and March 21, 1962 Validity: 3 years Automatic annual renewal	Exports: Raw cotton, rice, groundnuts, artificial silk fibers, cotton seeds, rayon, etc.; Imports: Cheese, sodium, wood, paper, bricks, porcelain and ceramics, glassware, engines, transformers, pumps, electrical machinery, etc.;	Settlement of balances in Pound Sterling via clearing accounts. Credit margin: E.£ 2 million	Board of Trade Journal, London: May 11, 1962
Eastern Germany	Trade and Payments Agreement	November 28, 1960 Validity: 3 years Automatic annual renewal	Commodity exchange not specified, but see Czechoslovakia;	MFN clause, which is not applicable to other members of the Arab League, nor other members of the CMEA. Absolute prohibition of re-exports. Settlement of balances in Pound Sterling	..

Continued

39

TABLE 4 (Continued)

African Trading Partner	Soviet or Eastern European Trading Partner	Nature of Agreement	Signatory Date and Validity[b]	Details of Commodity Composition	Payments Agreements and General Conditions	Source[d]
	Hungary	Trade and Payments Agreement	April 2, 1959 Validity: 3 years Automatic annual renewal	Exports: Raw cotton, fodder, yarn; Imports: Radio sets, valves, cranes, telephone equipment;	Annual trade turnover of about $20 million. Settlement of balances in convertible currencies via clearing accounts. Credit margin: E.₤ 1 million	..
	Poland	Trade and Payments Agreement	November 2, 1960 Validity: 3 years Automatic annual renewal	Exports: Cotton, textiles, citrus fruits, manganese ore, etc.; Imports: Industrial equipment, ships, chemicals, timber, tools, porcelain and ceramics, electro-metallurgical products, coke, coal, bicarbonate of soda, cardboard paper;	Total turnover for first 3 years set at $5.7 million. Settlement of balances in convertible currencies via clearing accounts	..
	Rumania	Trade and Payments Agreement	July 16, 1956 Automatic annual renewal	Exports: Raw cotton, cotton yarn; Imports: Paraphine, diesel oil, lubricants, bicarbonate of soda, caustic soda, paper, wool, industrial machinery;	MFN clause on all trading matters. Settlement of balances in convertible currencies via clearing accounts. Credit margin: E.₤ 500,000. Rumania will use Egyptian firms as representatives in Egypt.	..
	Soviet Union	Trade and Payments Agreement	March 27, 1954; August 18, 1953, and new agreements: June 23, 1962, Automatic annual renewal	Exports: Raw cotton, rice, semi-finished products; Imports: Tobacco, crude petroleum, benzine, paraphine, diesel oil, lubricants, steel industry products, machinery, automobiles, tractors, and agricultural machinery, etc.;	MFN clause on all trading matters. Settlement of balances in convertible currencies. Credit margin: E.₤ 1 million. Expected annual turnover; 1963-66: $166 million. Absolute prohibition of re-export of Egyptian products	Pravda, Moscow: June 24, 1962 Board of Trade Journal, London: June 28, 1963

40

Ethiopia[e] with:	Soviet Union	Trade Agreement	July 11, 1959 Validity: 3 years Automatic annual renewal	Commodity exchange not specified;	MFN clause on all trading matters	Vneshnyaya Torgovlya, Moscow: No. 8 and 9, 1959
Ghana with:	Bulgaria	Trade Agreement	October 5, 1961 Validity 3 years Renewed in 1964	Commodity exchange not specified;	Settlement of balances in Ghanaian Pounds. Credit margin: G.₤ 300,000. Prices to conform to world market levels	West Africa, London: January 18 and 25, 1964
	Czecho-slovakia	Trade Agreement	October 16, 1961, Validity: 5 years Automatic annual renewal	Exports: Cocoa, groundnuts, fish, oils, etc.; Imports: Complete industrial installations;	Compensation account. Settlement of balances via mutual agreement. Credit margin: G.₤ 250,000	West Africa, London: October 21, 1961
	Eastern Germany	Trade Agreement	October 19, 1961, Validity: 5 years Automatic annual renewal	Exports: Cocoa and other agricultural products; Imports: Engineering products, timber, textiles;	Settlement of balances in Ghanaian Pounds. Credit margin: G.₤ 500,000	West Africa, London: October 28, 1961
	Hungary	Trade Agreement	April, 1961 Validity: 3 years. Renewed in 1964	Exports: Bananas, cocoa, cocoa beans, cola-nuts, citrus fruits, industrial diamonds, manganese, aluminum; Imports: Machinery and transport equipment, telecommunication equipment, pharmaceuticals, etc.;	Compensation accounts. Settlement of balances in additional product delivery. Prices to conform to world market levels. Credit margin: G.₤ 200,000	West Africa, London: January 18 and 25, 1964

Continued

41

TABLE 4 (Continued)

African Trading Partner	Soviet or Eastern European Trading Partner	Nature of Agreement	Signatory Date and Validity[b]	Details of Commodity Composition	Payments Agreements and General Conditions	Source
	Poland	Trade Agreement	October 26, 1961. Validity: 5 years. Renewal for 1 year	Exports: Citrus fruits, cocoa, coffee, hides, palm oil, rubber, iron minerals, diamonds, etc.; Imports: Industrial equipment, photographic materials, paints, soap, cosmetics, cotton and linen fabrics;	Settlement of balances in Ghanaian Pounds. Credit margin G.₤ 500,000	Board of Trade Journal, London: May 25, 1962
	Rumania	Trade Agreement	September 30, 1961. Validity: 3 years Renewed in 1964	Exports: Cocoa, cotton, rubber, raw hides, palm oil, industrial diamonds; Imports: Industrial transformers, tool and agricultural machinery, etc.;	Settlement of balances in Ghanaian Pounds. Credit margin G.₤ 250,000	West Africa, London: October 7, 1961, and January 18 and 25, 1964
	Soviet Union	Trade Agreement	August 4, 1960 Automatic annual renewal	Exports: Cocoa beans, coffee, citrus fruits, palm oil, cotton, rubber, etc.; Imports: Airplanes, machinery and transport equipment, canned goods, etc.;	Settlement of balances in Ghanaian Pounds. Prices to conform to world market levels. Credit margin: G.₤ 4 million	Vneshnyaya Torgovlya, Moscow: No. 11, 1960
Guinea with:	Bulgaria	Trade and Payments Agreement	October 10, 1959 Automatic annual renewal	Exports: Cocoa, groundnuts, etc.; Imports: Machinery, electrical equipment, building materials, etc.;	..	West Africa, London: March 10, 1962
	Czechoslovakia	Trade Agreement	July 3, 1959, and June, 1961. Annual renewal	Commodity exchange not specified;	Increase in trade turnover by 20 per cent over the period 1961-63	Czechoslovak Foreign Trade, Prague: No. 7, 1961

Country	Type of Agreement	Date / Validity	Exports / Imports	Notes	Source
Eastern Germany	Trade Agreement	January, 1960 Validity: 5 years Automatic annual renewal	Exports: Oil-seeds, bananas, coffee, citrus fruits, etc.; Imports: Engineering industry products, pharmaceuticals, textiles, etc.;	Total trade turnover to increase by 30 per cent over 5-year period: 1960-65	Africa South of the Sahara, Paris: March 28, 1963; Marchés Tropicaux, Paris: November 30, 1963
Hungary	Trade Agreement	June, 1959 Automatic annual renewal	Exports: Palm kernels, iron ore, industrial diamonds, tropical fruits; Imports: Industrial and tele-communication equipment, chemicals and transport equipment;	..	..
Poland	Trade and Payments Agreement	June 20, 1960, and November 22, 1963. Annual renewal	Exports: Iron ore, bauxite, bananas, foodstuffs, oil-seeds, etc.; Imports: Transport equipment and agricultural machinery, textiles, radios, etc.;	..	
Soviet Union	Trade and Payments Agreement	February 13, 1959, and September 8, 1960. Validity: 5 years, renewable	Exports: Coffee, bananas, and other agricultural products; Imports: Complete industrial installations and model farms;	MFN clause on all trading matters	Vneshnyaya Torgovlya, Moscow: No. 10, 1960
Kenya with:					
Czecho-slovakia	Trade Agreement	January, 1964 Renewal clause	Exports: Fodder, maize, oil-seeds, coffee; Imports: Engineering equipment, industrial machinery, agricultural equipment;	..	Czechoslovak Foreign Trade, Prague: No. 7, 1964

Continued

TABLE 4 (Continued)

African Trading Partner	Soviet or Eastern European Trading Partner	Nature of Agreement	Signatory Date and Validity[b]	Details of Commodity Composition	Payments Agreements and General Conditions	Sourced
	Soviet Union	Trade Agreement	April 24, 1964 Automatic annual renewal	Exports: Coffee, tea, cotton, hides, etc.; Imports: Machinery, equipment, and manufactured goods;	..	Tass - Press Release, Moscow: April 29, 1964
Libya with:	Soviet Union	Trade Agreement	May 30, 1963 Automatic annual renewal	Exports: Groundnuts, wool, tobacco, hides, citrus fruits; Imports: Agricultural and construction machinery;	..	International Commerce, Washington, D.C.: June 24, 1963
Mali with:	Bulgaria	Trade and Payments Agreement	June, 1961. Renewed: January 26, 1963. Automatic annual renewal	Exports: Cotton fibers, hides, wool, citrus fruits, rice, industrial diamonds; Imports: Machinery and equipment, chemicals, cotton textiles, etc.;	..	Le Moniteur Africain, Paris: September 1, 1962
	Czechoslovakia	Trade Agreement	February 15, 1961. Validity: 2 years. Automatic renewal	See commodity exchange with Bulgaria;	..	Czechoslovak Foreign Trade, Prague: No. 4, 1961
	Eastern Germany	Trade and Payments Agreement	November 17, 1961 Automatic annual renewal	See commodity exchange with Bulgaria;	Settlement of balances via clearing accounts. Total turnover to amount to $10.1 million	Le Moniteur Africain, Paris: September 1, 1962
	Poland	Trade Agreement	November 2, 1962. Automatic annual renewal	See commodity exchange with Bulgaria;	..	Le Moniteur Africain, Paris: September 1, 1962

Morocco with:

			See commodity exchange with	Settlement of balances in U.S. Dollars	Vneshnyaya Torgovlya, Moscow: No. 5, 1961
Soviet Union	Trade and Payments Agreement	March 18, 1961 Automatic annual renewal	See commodity exchange with Bulgaria;	Settlement of balances in U.S. Dollars	Vneshnyaya Torgovlya, Moscow: No. 5, 1961
Bulgaria	Trade Agreement	August 2, 1957 Renewed: August 1, 1962 Automatic annual renewal	Exports: Vegetables, cereals, canned fish, superphosphates, linseed, etc.; Imports: Butter and cheese, tobacco and cigarettes, construction machinery;	Trade turnover to be doubled every year. Settlement of balances in local currencies	Board of Trade Journal, London: January 26, 1962
Czecho-slovakia	Trade and Payments Agreement	December 22, 1959. Renewed: February 2, 1963, and February 20, 1964. Automatic renewal	Exports: Fruits and vegetables, phosphates, cereals, etc.; Imports: Food products, agricultural machinery, transport equipment, electrical equipment, etc.;	Settlement of balances in U.S. Dollars	Czechoslovak Foreign Trade, Prague: No. 4, 1963, and No. 4, 1964
Eastern Germany	Trade and Payments Agreement	August 8, 1960 Renewed: August 8, 1963. Automatic annual renewal	Exports: Vegetables, olive oil, sardines, iron ore, phosphates, cement, etc.; Imports: Industrial machinery and equipment;	Compensation accounts. Trade to be increased by 10 per cent a year	..
Hungary	Trade Agreement	September 2, 1960. Renewed: July 17, 1962. Automatic annual renewal	Exports: Dried and fresh vegetables, fruit juices, phosphates; Imports: Food products, industrial equipment, chemicals, etc.;	Settlement of balances in Swiss francs	..
Poland	Trade Agreement	December 1, 1959 January, 1962 Automatic annual renewal	Exports: Vegetables, phosphates, chemicals; Imports: Machinery and electrical equipment, cotton and synthetic fibers, consumer goods;	Settlement of balances in U.S. Dollars	Board of Trade Journal, London: April 27, 1962

Continued

TABLE 4 (Continued)

Africa Trading Partner	Soviet or Eastern European Trading Partner	Nature of Agreement	Signatory Date and Validity[b]	Details of Commodity Composition	Payments Agreements and General Conditions	Source[d]
	Soviet Union	Trade and Payments Agreement	April 19, 1958 Renewed: January, 1962 Automatic annual renewal	Exports: Vegetables and fruits, phosphates, etc.; Imports: Crude oil, paper, chemicals, machinery, photographic equipment, etc.;	Compensation agreements	Board of Trade Journal, London: May 25, 1962
Niger with:	Czechoslovakia	Trade Agreement	January 1, 1962 Automatic annual renewal	Exports: Groundnuts and oil, gum, onions, and local handicrafts; Imports: Electrical machinery, steel industry products, compressors, insecticides;	Settlement of balances in U.S. Dollars	Africa South of the Sahara, Paris: January 18, 1962
	Poland	Trade Agreement	January 1, 1962 Automatic annual renewal	Exports: as to Czechoslovakia; Imports: Spirits, food products, cement, electrical equipment, etc.;	Settlement of balances in convertible currencies	Board of Trade Journal, London: June 22, 1962
	Soviet Union	Trade Agreement	April 25, 1962 Automatic annual renewal	Exports: as to Czechoslovakia; Imports: Machinery and equipment, petroleum products, cement, etc.;	Settlement of balances in convertible currencies	Pravda, Moscow: April 27, 1962
Nigeria with:	Czechoslovakia	Trade Agreement	September 19, 1961. Validity: 2 years. Automatic annual renewal	Exports: Rubber, groundnuts, cotton seeds, palm oils, copra, cocoa, fruits, etc.; Imports: Machinery (all categories), chemicals, canned foods, textiles, etc.;	Settlement of balances in Pound Sterling	West Africa, London: October 7, 1961

Country	Agreement	Date	Exports / Imports	Settlement	Source
Bulgaria	Trade Agreement	September, 1962 Automatic renewal	Exports: Cotton, coffee, and tobacco; Imports: Machinery, rolling stock, electrical equipment, etc.;	Settlement of balances in Pound Sterling	Africa South of the Sahara; Paris: October 1, 1962
Soviet Union	Trade Agreement	July 2, 1963 Automatic annual renewal	Exports: Cocoa beans, cotton, and rubber, etc.; Imports: Transport and agricultural equipment, cement, textiles, soap, etc.;	MFN clause on all trade and shipping matters. Settlement of balances in Pound Sterling	Pravda, Moscow: July 3, 1963
Senegal with:					
Soviet Union	Trade Agreement	June 14, 1963 Automatic renewal	Exports: Groundnuts and oil, fruits, fish, hides, and leather; Imports: Tool machinery, transport equipment, construction equipment;	..	Board of Trade Journal, London: November 1, 1963
Sierra-Leone with:					
Soviet Union	Trade and Friendship Agreement	September, 1961 Renewal clause	Exports: Palm oil, cocoa, ginger, coffee; Imports: Industrial manufactures;	..	Africa South of the Sahara, Paris: October 19, 1961
Somalia with:					
Czecho-slovakia	Trade Agreement	1961	..	..	Czechoslovak Foreign Trade, Prague: No. 7, 1961

Continued

47

TABLE 4 (Continued)

African Trading Partner	Soviet or Eastern European Trading Partner	Nature of Agreement	Signatory Date and Validity[b]	Details of Commodity Composition	Payments Agreements and General Conditions	Source[d]
	Soviet Union	Trade and Payments Agreement	June, 1961 Renewal clause	Exports: Textile fibers, fruits, oil-seeds, raw hides, ivory, sponges, etc.; Imports: Tool machinery, petro-chemical products, food products;	..	Vneshnyaya Torgovlya, Moscow: No. 7, 1961
The Sudan with:	Bulgaria	Trade Agreement	April 5, 1962 Automatic annual renewal	Exports: Cotton, arabic gum, sesame oil, groundnuts, hides, and skins, etc.; Imports: Machinery and transport equipment, rolling stock, radio and TV sets, refrigeration plants, etc.;	Settlement of balances in Pound Sterling or other convertible currencies	Africa South of the Sahara, Paris: October 22, 1962
	Czecho-slovakia	Trade and Payments Agreement	June 5, 1962 Automatic annual renewal	Exports: As to Bulgaria; Imports: Electrical and agricultural machinery, pharmaceuticals, etc.;	Clearing accounts. Settlement of balances in Pound Sterling	Czechoslovak Foreign Trade, Prague: No. 7, 1962
	Eastern Germany	Trade and Payments Agreements	June 9, 1955 Renewal clause	Commodity exchange not specified	..	..
	Hungary	Trade and Payments Agreement	May 29, 1955 Renewal clause	Exports: As to Bulgaria; Imports: Textiles, footwear, consumer goods;	..	..
	Poland	Trade and Payments Agreement	May 20, 1955, and March, 1963	Exports: Cotton, vegetable oils, etc.; Imports: Sugar, cement, footwear, etc.;	Settlement of balances in Pound Sterling	Africa South of the Sahara, Paris: March 21, 1963

Rumania	Trade Agreement	February 1, 1961 Automatic annual renewal	Exports: As to Bulgaria, plus hashab gum, spices, livestock, fodder; Imports: Industrial machinery, chinaware, food products, cereals, sugar, etc.;	Settlement of balances in convertible currencies. Trade to be conducted at world market price levels	..
Soviet Union	Trade Agreement	March 19, 1959 Validity: 3 years. Renewal clause	Exports: As to Bulgaria and Rumania: Imports: Machinery and equipment, wheat, sugar, carbon, and coke;	Settlement of balances in convertible currencies. Trade to be conducted at world market price levels. Provisions for establishment of U.S.S.R. trade fairs in the Sudan and other means of trade promotion	Vneshnyaya Torgovlya, Moscow: No. 5, 1959
Tanzania with:					
Soviet Union	Trade Agreement	August 14, 1963 Renewal clause	Exports: Sisal, coffee, tobacco, hides, and skins; Imports: Metals, tools, automobiles, aircrafts, photographic equipment;	..	West Africa, London: October 25, 1963
Bulgaria	Trade Agreement	October 5, 1963 Renewal clause	Commodity exchange not specified;	MFN clause on all trading matters	Board of Trade Journal, London: November 8, 1963

Continued

TABLE 4 (Continued)

African Trading Partner	Soviet or Eastern European Trading Partner	Nature of Agreement	Signatory Date and Validity[b]	Details of Commodity Composition	Payments Agreements and General Conditions	Sourced
Togo **with:**	Bulgaria	Trade Agreement	June, 1962 Renewal clause	Exports: Phosphates, coffee, cocoa, and copra; Imports: Agricultural machinery, cement, sugar, and watches;	..	Board of Trade Journal, London: June 25, 1962
	Soviet Union	Trade Agreement	June 12, 1961		..	Vneshnyaya Torgovlya, Moscow: No. 9, 1961
Tunisia **with:**	Bulgaria Czecho-slovakia Eastern Germany Hungary Poland	Trade and Payments Agreement	All agreements concluded be-tween 1960-62. Renewal clauses	Exports: Phosphates, olive oil, aluminum, cement, plastic articles, wool, etc.; Imports: Industrial and mechan-ical products, machinery for ex-tractive industries, automobiles, etc.;	Clearing and compensation accounts	United Nations; Eco-nomic Commission for Africa; Apercu du commerce exteri-eur (E/CN.14/STC/FTN/5-6), Nos. 5 and 6, 1963
	Soviet Union	Trade Agreement	March 14, 1962	Commodity exchange as above;	MFN clause on all trade	Tass - Press Release, Moscow: March 15, 1963
Uganda **with:**	Soviet Union	Trade Agreement	April, 1964	Exports: Coffee, cotton, tea, hides, skins, groundnuts, etc.; Imports: Transport equipment, watches, radio receivers, etc.;	..	Africa South of the Sahara, Paris: May 14, 1964

Sources: In addition to what is indicated in the table, the following material has been used: (1) U.N., ECA, Les accords bilatéraux de commerce et de paiements conclus en Afrique (E/CN.14/STC/24, November 14, 1963)(Addis Ababa, 1963), pp. 1-56. (Limited distribution); (2) République Arabe Unie, Annuaire du commerce extérieur et du change (Cairo: July,1962); (3) Dengi i Kredit, No. 6 (Moscow: June,1962); (4) United Nations, UNCTAD, Past Trade Flows and Future Prospects of Trade between the Centrally Planned Economies and Developing Countries (E/Conf.46/35, February 13, 1964)(Geneva, 1964); (5) V. Rymalov, Ekonomicheskoe Sotrudnichestvo SSSR so Slaborazvitymi Stranami (Economic Cooperation between the U.S.S.R. and Underdeveloped Countries) (Moscow: Gostorgizdat, 1960).

Notes:
aThe list may be incomplete. It should be noted that in most cases only basic and confirmed trade and payments agreements are listed. Protocols and routine renewals are not included.

bIf nothing else is mentioned, agreements have been signed for one year, with clause for automatic renewal.

cWhere no details are mentioned, it is assumed that trade is conducted on the basis of straight commodity exchange with settlement of balances in convertible currencies. Where "swing credits" are granted, they will be mentioned.

dWhere no source indication is given, information on agreements has been derived from compiled works mentioned above.

eEthiopia is known to have current trade agreements with Czechoslovakia, Eastern Germany, and Poland, although no sources nor any confirmation have been found for these.

However, the pattern here is spotty, and trade
participation is uneven on both sides. The leading
role is clearly that of Egypt, Ghana, Guinea, and
the Sudan, which together account for the majority
of African agreements with the Eastern trade area,
while the Soviet Union is responsible for more than
one third of the latter group's trade links with
Africa.

As will be seen from Table 4, the U.S.S.R. also
tends to pioneer agreements by being the first centrally planned economy on the spot.

Although these agreements should not be considered as anything but "shopping-lists" they do
point out a fact which will later be confirmed: the
overwhelming preponderance of primary products in
the structure of African exports to the centrally
planned economies. The import structure--at least
the one stipulated in the agreements--is more decep-
tive. As we shall see, in most cases the centrally
planned economies have exported far less technical
equipment than the impression the agreements appear
to give. Most products in this category are destined
for installation in Soviet Bloc-financed technical
assistance projects, and certainly in case of more
recent agreements, these products have not yet left
the Eastern trade area.

GROWTH OF TRADE

On this structure, the relatively recent trade
relations between Africa and the Soviet Bloc have
developed from their initial very low levels. True,
several centrally planned economies traded actively
with Africa in the inter-war period, but any meaningful postwar trade did not gain momentum until the
mid-1950's.[18] The turning point might be said to be
the signature of the Egyptian-Soviet trade and payments agreement of March, 1954,[19] for thereafter
volume of commodity exchange grew fast, so fast, in
fact, that trade between Africa and the centrally
planned economies has been the most rapidly expanding element of the external economic relations of

that continent over the past decade. From 1955,
when total turnover of trade with the Soviet Union
and Eastern Europe amounted to $215 million,[20] this
commerce expanded by about 400 per cent and by the
end of 1965 commodity exchange with the Eastern
trade area totalled $1.065 million.[21]

We can put this growth in a better perspective
by illustrating it in a comparative light: in the
same period African trade with developed market
economies increased from $10.250 million to $15.750
million--or by some 50 per cent, and with developing
countries in Asia and Latin America from $815 million
to $1.317 million--by about 60 per cent.[22]

Despite the increase in trade with the Soviet
Bloc, however, the former colonial powers continue
to play a predominant role in the foreign trade picture of Africa, and they accounted, as late as 1966,
for about three fourths of total turnover of African
trade.[23] Moreover, these trade flows have--on a
year-to-year basis--been maintained at a reasonably·
stable level, while African commodity exchange with
the centrally planned economies has not been marked
by any particular stability in growth. Behind the
average rate of increase over the period, trade in
both directions has fluctuated rather widely, with
African exports manifesting a relatively steep upward trend and imports from the Eastern trade area
increasing more slowly. From the following table it
will be seen that this commodity exchange reached
its climax in 1961, after which it declined somewhat.

In the country studies that follow in Chapters
4 to 7, this trade will be observed more closely,
but even at this point it is interesting to note
the marked difference between African trade with the
Soviet Union and such trade with the Eastern European countries separately.

Commodity exchange with the Soviet Union has
experienced wider fluctuations and has been more
unstable than similar exchanges with Eastern Europe.
Moreover, while African-Soviet trade admittedly has
been growing it has "increased on a declining trend."

TABLE 5

AFRICA

Growth of Trade with the Centrally Planned Economies

1955-65

(U.S.$ million and percentages)

African	Trade 1955	Per- centage Change	Trade 1958	Per- centage Change	Trade 1959	Per- centage Change	Trade 1960	Per- centage Change	Trade 1961	Per- centage Change
Exports to:										
Soviet Union	11.0		107.6		112.2		109.6		195.8	
Eastern Europe	96.8		143.1		134.7		147.3		178.9	
Total Trade	107.8		250.7		246.9		256.9		374.7	
Percentage Change		+243.0		-4.4		+4.0		+45.0		-8.5
Imports from:										
Soviet Union	26.9		143.4		174.8		208.8		152.6	
Eastern Europe	80.1		118.4		123.5		135.7		169.7	
Total Trade	107.0		261.8		298.3		344.5		322.3	
Percentage Change		+250.0		+13.5		-13.4		-6.8		-2.9

TABLE 5 (Continued)

African	Trade 1962	Per-centage Change	Trade 1963	Per-centage Change	Trade 1964	Per-centage Change	Trade 1965
Exports to:							
Soviet Union	169.1		146.0		. .		. .
Eastern Europe	185.0		200.0		. .		. .
Total Trade	354.1		346.0		360		455
Percentage Change		-2.3		+0.4		+38.0	
Imports from:							
Soviet Union	138.0		95.0		. .		. .
Eastern Europe	175.0		182.0		. .		. . .
Total Trade	313.0		277.0		440		610
Percentage Change		-11.5		+70.0		+32.0	

Sources: U.N., Monthly Bulletin of Statistics, Vol. 15, No. 3; Vol. 17, No. 3 and Vol. 21, No. 3, Special Table E-II.

An explanation, though not an interpretation of this
phenomenon, may lie in the fact that Soviet activities in Africa have mainly been centered on financial aid and technical assistance while the centrally planned economies in Eastern Europe have been
relatively more active in trade. This, but also
the much larger "absorption capacity" of the Eastern
European market for African primary products may explain why trade with these countries has enjoyed a
steady rise--which did not fall victim to the 1960-61
recession experienced in African commodity exchange
with the Soviet Union--but carried on through 1962,
1963, 1964, 1965, and, judging from incomplete statistical returns, through 1966 as well.

On the basis of year-to-year figures we can
also detect large discrepancies in the relative
shares of Soviet and Eastern European trade with
Africa. Of the two areas--until the late 1950's--
the latter was by far Africa's predominant trading
partner. This situation changed in 1959. From that
year until 1961 trade with the Soviet Union exceeded
that of Eastern Europe by an average of 15 per cent
annually. In 1961 African commodity exchange with
the two areas was about equal; in 1962, 1963, 1964,
and in 1965 trade with Eastern Europe again gained
in importance, and this trend continued into 1966.[24]

One reason for the irregularity in Soviet trade
with Africa is to be found in the fact that this is
closely linked to programs of financial and technical
assistance. On many grounds, not the least of which
the political, deliveries under such schemes are of
a more sporadic nature and may cause greater fluctuations in trade statistics than regular commodity exchange with which the Eastern European countries have
been more actively involved.[25]

However, the Soviet share of total Eastern group
trade with Africa will probably increase in the next
few years to come.[26] This assumption is based not
only on changes in consumption habits in the Soviet
Union, toward e.g., a more diversified diet consisting of food products the country may find more prof-
itable to import rather than produce locally; but

also the fact that current deliveries under Soviet
programs of financial and technical assistance to
Africa have not exceeded 30 per cent of commitments.[27]
The outstanding 70 per cent may come to account for
a large increase in imports of Soviet capital equipment to Africa, while Eastern Europe will probably
continue to remain an important market for African
exports.[28]

COMMODITY STRUCTURE

A typical feature--and a basic weakness--of
most African countries is a heavy dependence on raw
materials for exports. This can be illustrated
graphically by pointing to a recent year, 1965, when
the structure of African commodity sales presented
itself as follows:

TABLE 6

AFRICA

Global Commodity Structure of Exports
1965

(Percentage Shares)

Food, beverage crops and tobacco	33.6%	Primary Products: 81.8%
Textile fibers and vege- table oils	34.1%	
Fuels	14.1%	
Machinery and transport equipment	0.9%	Manufactures: 18.2%
Chemicals	1.8%	
Other (metals, minerals, etc.)	15.5%	

Source: U.N., Monthly Bulletin of Statistics, Vol.
         21, No. 3 (March, 1967), Special Table E-II,
         pp. xviii-xxxi.

This pattern also coincides with the commodity flow to Western Europe and North America where, in recent years, the proportion of primary products to manufactures has been 4:1.[29]

As latecomers to the African market, the centrally planned economies have had to contend with a larger share of the continent's traditional exports, and in 1965 more than nine tenths of African commodity sales to the Eastern trade area consisted of primary products. Within this category one product group has been by far the most predominant--raw cotton, cotton seeds and cotton fibers made up more than three fourths of all exports. This development can be seen in a better perspective from Table 7 (Page 60) where we have set out the value and commodity structure of African trade with the centrally planned economies in three selected years of the 1955-65 period.

On the import side we find--not unnaturally--that machinery and manufactured goods accounted for more than seven tenths of total commodity purchases from the centrally planned economies in 1965. These proportions have by no means, however, remained entirely stable throughout the period, and we can detect changes reflecting not only the intense efforts toward industrialization in Africa, but also the fact that, slowly, these are beginning to bear fruits. Foremost among these diversions is the shift that has taken place in African imports from the Eastern trade area.

At the beginning of the period--in 1955--light manufactures, mostly consumer goods, accounted for 40 per cent of total purchases from the Soviet Bloc; by 1965 the share of this commodity group had dropped to 25 per cent while that of machinery and transport equipment had risen from 22 to 46 per cent. There is nothing surprising in this. In 1955 few African countries had formulated any realistic development plans with clearly set investment priorities, nor had they any significantly developed industries. Following independence and the elaboration of investment targets for industry and infrastructure and the

development of some basic and lighter industries,
the Eastern group was able to channel--both relatively and totally--a larger part of its exports into machinery and equipment for projects. This shift
from "product to project exports" has also been reflected in the commodity composition of shipments of
light manufactures (SITC Sec's. 6 and 8). In the
early part of the period these consisted, to a large
degree, of nondurable consumer goods, while by 1965
the relative share of tools, instruments, and auxil-
iary technical equipment had become the predominant
in this product category.[30]

The increase in the rate of industrialization
in Africa is to a certain degree reflected in the
structure of the continent's exports to the centrally
planned economies. Relatively, the share of shipments
of manufactured goods (SITC Sec's. 6 and 8) have increased, from a very low level, by 110 per cent from
1955 to 1965 while at the same time we have seen a
10 per cent decline in exports of raw cotton products.

Shipments of food products in both directions
have throughout the period increased steadily, but
within this group as well we see a shift in the commodity composition. Particularly since 1959, Africa
has increased her exports of citrus fruits to Eastern
Europe, and in a smaller degree to the Soviet Union,[31]
which explains the 120 per cent increase in shipments
of products in this commodity group since 1959.

We do not, at this point, want to include too
much of what follows in the country studies, but some
mention might be made of the individual African country's position in this trade picture. From the trade
direction statistics of the Economic Commission for
Africa it is clear that Egypt is the predominant
African trader with the centrally planned economies.
In fact, over the 1954-65 period, this country alone
accounted for 61 per cent of total African turnover
of trade with the Eastern group. Of course, no other
country ever came close to this share. Ghana with
7.9 per cent, the Sudan with 5.7 per cent, Morocco
with 5.6 per cent, South Africa with 4 per cent and

TABLE 7

AFRICA

Value and Commodity Structure of Trade with the Centrally Planned Economies
1955, 1960, and 1965

A = U.S. $ million; B = Percentage shares
(SITC numbers at heads of columns)

	Year	Total Trade (0 - 9)		Food, Beverages, Tobacco (0,1)	
		A	B	A	B
I: Total exports					
	1955	5,310	100	1,920	100
	1960	5,820	100	2,000	100
	1965	7,670	100	2,430	100
of which to:					
Soviet Union	1955	130	2.4	22	1.1
and	1960	260	4.5	31	1.5
Eastern Europe	1965	455	5.9	74	3.0
II: Commodity structure of exports	1955	130	100	22	18.0
to the centrally planned	1960	260	100	31	11.4
economies:	1965	455	100	74	21.0
I: Total imports					
	1955	6,290	100	880	100
	1960	7,190	100	1,100	100
	1965	8,080	100	1,220	100
of which from:					
Soviet Union	1955	115	1.8	2	0.2
and	1960	346	4.8	21	1.9
Eastern Europe	1965	610	7.5	33	2.7
II: Commodity structure of imports	1955	115	100	2	1.9
from the centrally planned	1960	346	100	21	6.0
economies:	1965	610	100	33	5.4

| Raw Materials and Fuels | | | | | | Machinery, Transport Equipment (7) | |
| total (2 - 4) | | Materials (2,4) | | Fuels (3) | | | |
A	B	A	B	A	B	A	B
2,260	100	2,210	100	50	100	68	100
2,585	100	2,480	100	105	100	70	100
3,610	100	2,560	100	1,050	100	67	100
100	4.4	100	4.5	--	--	--	--
210	8.1	210	8.4	--	--	1	0.1
260	7.2	256	10.0	4	0.4	--	--
100		100	78.0	--	--	--	--
210		210	80.0	--	--	1	0.3
260		256	56.0	4	1.1	--	--
785	100	295	100	490	100	1,700	100
920	100	330	100	590	100	2,400	100
990	100	410	100	580	100	2,740	100
32	4.0	16	5.4	16	3.2	26	1.5
64	6.9	26	7.8	38	6.4	60	2.7
62	16.1	31	7.5	31	5.3	310	11.3
32		16	14.0	16	14.0	26	22.6
64		26	7.5	38	10.9	60	17.3
62		31	5.2	31	5.2	310	50.8

Continued

TABLE 7 (Continued)

	Year	Other Manufactured Goods					
		Total (5,6,8)		Chemicals (5)		Other (6,8)	
		A	B	A	B	A	B
I: Total exports							
	1955	1,047	100	77	100	970	100
	1960	1,145	100	95	100	1,050	100
	1965	1,360	100	100	100	1,250	100
of which to:							
Soviet Union	1955	6	0.5	--	--	6	0.7
and	1960	22	1.0	1	1.0	21	2.2
Eastern Europe	1965	73	5.4	--	--	73	5.8
II: Commodity structure of exports	1955	6		--	--	6	4.0
to the centrally planned	1960	22		1	0.3	21	8.0
economies:	1965	73		--	--	73	16.0
I: Total imports							
	1955	2,705	100	405	100	2,300	100
	1960	2,810	100	490	100	2,320	100
	1965	3,150	100	600	100	2,550	100
of which from:							
Soviet Union	1955	54	1.9	8	1.9	46	2.0
and	1960	79	2.7	22	4.5	57	2.4
Eastern Europe	1965	171	5.4	26	4.3	145	5.7
II: Commodity structure of imports	1955	54		8	6.5	46	40.0
from the centrally planned	1960	79		22	6.4	57	16.5
economies:	1965	171		26	4.3	145	23.8

Sources: U.N., Monthly Bulletin of Statistics, Vol. 15, No. 3 (March, 1961),
Special Table E-II, pp. xviii-xxxi; and Ibid., Vol. 21, No. 3
(March, 1967), Special Table E-II-III, pp. xviii-xxxi.

Guinea with 3.4 per cent of total turnover, all--in
a relative sense--contributed to making up the remainder of this trade flow, but for none of these
countries was trade with the Eastern group as important as it was for Egypt.[32]

However, in all discussions of changes in the
structure of African commodity exchange with the centrally planned economies, we should recall that this
has been growing from a very low base level. Thus,
we would be well advised to relate its relative value
to the total--in 1965, commodity exchange with the
Eastern group still did not account for more than 5.3
per cent of turnover of global African trade.

✓   FOREIGN TRADE PRICE POLICIES

It is not the object of this study to do a detailed analysis of Soviet and Eastern European foreign trade pricing.[33] However, a broad outline of
how prices are set in the external trade of the centrally planned economies may be useful.

Because of the complete divorce of internal
from external price calculation, a reliance of world
market prices is necessary for value determination
of imports and exports in the Eastern trade area.
The stated principle in foreign trade of the centrally planned economies is that "prices should be
established on the basis of average world market
prices on the principal market for the commodity in
a clearly defined period."[34] However, it is accepted that these prices should be adjusted to eliminate
short-term fluctuations, the influence of speculation,
"monopolistic practices" and "other undesirable factors." Transport costs are usually shared equally
between buyer and seller.[35]

Very little information is available on actual
unit prices in trade between Africa and the centrally
planned economies. The only major trade flow on
which we are fairly adequately informed--and is the
most important--is that between Egypt and the Soviet
Union. In the period 1955-59 terms of trade between
these countries moved as follows:

Export Prices in Terms of Import Prices
(1955 = 100)

Egyptian trade	1956	1957	1958	1959
with the world	108	107	..	..
with the Soviet Union	114	118	114	126

Source: U.N., ECA, African Trade with the Centrally
          Planned Economies, (E/CN.14/STC/5)(Addis
          Ababa: September, 1962), Section 4, p. 21
          of manuscript version.

During this period Egypt enjoyed more favorable terms
of trade in her commodity exchange with the Soviet
Union than with the rest of the world. In no sense,
however, should this example be considered typical,
it is too dated for that. What rather seems to be
the case is that, by and large, African trade with
the centrally planned economies is conducted at prices which generally correspond to accepted market
levels.

    There is, however, one important qualification
to this statement. In a later chapter we compare
Soviet prices with "world" prices received for major
African export commodities,[36] and find that, in order
to gain access to new supplies, the U.S.S.R. usually
starts off by paying bonus prices that, one to two
years after initiation of trade relations are brought
down to "world market" levels. The same phenomenon
seems to hold true for Soviet exports. These are
priced at bargain rates to gain footholds in new
markets, but once sales have attained the desired
volume, prices are raised to market levels.[37]

    However, these findings should not be accepted
at face value. As pointed out above, an increasingly
large element in African-Soviet Bloc trade is the
supply by the latter of machinery and equipment for

"packaged" agricultural, industrial, or infrastructural development projects in Africa. Prices of individual components are then probably estimated as
part of total project costs, but a "market price" for
the complete installation is difficult and hazardous
to determine. In the final analysis noneconomic factors such as the political relationship between buyer
and seller must play a large role in determining the
cost of a project, and consequently unit comparisons
of prices in African-Western world trade and African-
Soviet Bloc trade are not very valuable.

NOTES TO CHAPTER 2

1. U.N., Yearbook of International Trade Statistics, 1964, Table A, pp. 16-17.

2. In 1965 Western Europe and North America received 76 per cent of Africa's exports, and supplied
the continent with 74 per cent of its imports. Simi-
larly, the same two areas accounted in 1965 for more
than 80 per cent of all foreign investment in Africa.
Source: U.N., Monthly Bulletin of Statistics, Vol.
21, No. 3 (March, 1967), Special Table E-II.

3. P. A. Cherviakov, Organizatsia i Tekhnika
Vneshnei Torgovli SSSR (Moscow: Vneshtorgizdat, 1962),
Chapter 2.

4. However, assessment of the level of exports
likely to be achieved on acceptable terms may lead to
a revision of the original estimate of import needs.

5. Both Czechoslovakia and Poland have in 1965
and 1966 experimented with allowing individual enterprises (particularly in the capital equipment field)
to set up their own sales outlets abroad, thus circum-
venting the foreign trade corporation.

6. U.N., UNCTAD, The Participation of Czechoslovakia in International Economic Relations (Views
of Czechoslovak Economists)(E/CONF. 46/117, May 22,
1964)(Geneva, 1964), p. 7. This document also states
that the number of representatives of the foreign

trade corporations abroad is steadily growing. In
1963, the 18 Czech foreign trade corporations had altogether 3,971 trade agents abroad, of which 2,177
had been active in developing countries. In the same
year 26 foreign affiliations of the corporations
(consignment stores, parts depots, etc.) were active
in Western countries. At present the Soviet Union
has (in July, 1967) 31 foreign trade corporations,
Bulgaria - 20, Czechoslovakia - 18, Eastern Germany -
21, Hungary - 18, Poland - 24, and Rumania - 11.

7. For discussion of African foreign trade and
development planning, see U.N., UNCTAD, Foreign Trade
Plans in Selected Countries in Africa (E/CONF. 46/85,
March 16, 1964)(Geneva, 1964).

8. For a description of African commodity
marketing boards, see Peter T. Bauer, West African
Trade: A Study in Competition, Oligopoly and Monopoly
in a Changing Economy (Cambridge: Cambridge University
Press, 1954).

9. The Financial Times (London), November 15,
1963. This corporation was established mainly with
a view to balance bilateral trade flows between Ghana
and the U.S.S.R.

10. U.N., ECE, Committee on the Development of
Trade, A Review of Long-Term Trade and Payments
Agreements (res. Trade/104, September 20, 1960)
(Geneva, 1960), p. 21.

11. For a discussion of the trade-creating versus the trade-diverting effects of Soviet Bloc trade
with Africa, see Chapter 8, pp. 255-58.

12. Re-exports are unpopular in Africa, to the
point of being specifically prohibited in the agreements. See agreement between Egypt and the Soviet
Union of June 23, 1962, in Table 4, p. 40.

13. Robert L. Allen, Soviet Economic Warfare
(Washington, D.C.: Public Affairs Press, 1960),
p. 101.

14. U.N., ECE, <u>A Review of Long-Term Trade and Payments Agreements</u>, p. 22.

15. <u>Ibid</u>., p. 23.

16. We understand "basic" trade agreements to mean the initial agreements. Protocols and renewals of already existing agreements are not included. New agreements, only to the extent that they constitute departures from former arrangements, are included in Tables 3 and 4. Agreements on financial and technical aid are discussed in Chapter 3.

17. Between 39 independent African states (mid-1967) and 7 members of the Eastern trade area.

18. Useful reviews of the early phases of this trade include: (1) U.S.S.R., Ministry of Foreign Trade, <u>Vneshnyaya Torgovlya SSSR za 1918-40 gody</u> (Moscow: Gostorgizdat, 1960), pp. 1117-19; (2) A. Nove, "Soviet Trade and Aid," <u>Lloyds Bank Review</u> (January, 1959), No. 51, pp. 1-19; and (3) H. G. Aubrey, "Sino-Soviet Economic Activities in Less-Developed Countries," <u>Comparisons of the United States and Soviet Economies</u>, Joint Economic Committee, 86th Congress, 1st Session, Part II (Washington, D.C.: Government Printing Office, 1959), pp. 445-66.

19. <u>Bulletin of the National Bank of Egypt</u>, Vol. VII, No. 1 (Cairo, 1954), p. 34.

20. U.N., <u>Monthly Bulletin of Statistics</u>, Vol. 21, No. 3 (March, 1967), Special Table E-II, pp. xviii-xix.

21. <u>Ibid</u>.

22. <u>Ibid</u>.

23. Provisional figures based on 1965 trade volumes and estimated rates of growth.

24. U.S. Department of Commerce, <u>Value Series</u>, Report of March, 1965, and IMF, <u>Direction of Trade</u>, January, 1967.

25.   For a good account of Soviet political ac-
tivities in Africa, see Alexander Dallin, "The Soviet
Union: Political Activity," in Z. Brzezinski, ed.
Africa and the Communist World (Stanford, Cal.:
Stanford University Press for the Hoover Institution,
1963), pp. 7-48.

26.   Over the period 1954-64, African trade with
the Soviet Union accounted for about 40 per cent of
total commodity exchange with the centrally planned
economies.   See Chapter 8, Table 32.

27.   For a discussion of aid committed and aid
delivered, see Chapter 9, pp. 263-74.

28.   See Chapter 8, pp. 258-61; and FAO, Agricultural Commodities - the Outlook for 1970 in Eastern Europe (Rome, 1963), pp. 16-17.

29.   U.N., Monthly Bulletin of Statistics, loc.
cit.

30.   U.N., ECA, Foreign Trade Statistics of
Africa, Series B, Trade by Commodity, Nos. 1-10 (October, 1962 - July, 1966) (E/CN.14/STAT/Ser. B/10).

31.   The important citrus fruit exporters are
Egypt, Ghana, Guinea, and Morocco.   Foreign Trade
Statistics of Africa, loc. cit.

32.   U.N., ECA, Foreign Trade Statistics of
Africa, Series A, Direction of Trade, Nos. 1-7 (December, 1960 - January, 1966) (E/CN.14/STAT/Ser. A/1-7).

33.   For detailed discussion of domestic and for-
eign pricing practices in the Eastern trade area, see
M. Bornstein, "The Soviet Price System," The American
Economic Review, Vol. 52, No. 1 (March, 1962), pp.
64-103; M. Kaser, Comecon; Integration Problems of
the Planned Economies (London: Oxford University
Press for the Royal Institute of International Af-
fairs, 1965), pp. 140-57; and Frederick L. Pryor,
The Communist Foreign Trade System (London: George
Allen and Unwin, 1963).

34. Cited from Basic Principles of the International Division of Labour (Moscow, no page, no year).

35. V. Rymalov, Ekonomicheskoe Sotrudnichestvo SSSR co Slaborazvitymi Stranami (Moscow: Gostorgizdat, 1960), pp. 70-81. Clearly, for some exports such as "packaged turnkey projects," for which no world market price exists, prices will be a matter of negotiations between buyer and seller. Also there will be volume discounts on large purchases. It might here be mentioned that in many respects the term "world market price" is entirely meaningless. Robert L. Allen in his book: Soviet Economic Warfare, p. 168, states that:

> There is, in fact, no world market. Rather this is a euphemism that describes an incredibly complex network of trading, financial, and institutional arrangements by which goods move in international commerce. It becomes even more complex when goods themselves are subject to various classifications and degrees of complexity. Even raw materials are by no means homogeneous. Cotton, for example, has many different grades and qualities. The country of origin of even relatively homogeneous products makes a difference. There are markets in London, Liverpool, New York, New Orleans, Singapore, Alexandria, and other cities where prices differ beyond the customary transportation and insurance differences because of subtle variations in grade, origin, or other characteristics. The market in each city changes from day to day, has seasonal patterns, as well as secular trends. Thus any "world market price" at which the Soviet Bloc agrees to buy and sell is a very ephemeral standard and difficult to approximate in the practical realities of international trade.

36. See Chapter 8, pp. 249-55.

37. Ibid.

CHAPTER **3** FINANCIAL AID

AND TECHNICAL

ASSISTANCE

OVER-ALL SCOPE

Passing from trade to the other important element that constitutes economic relations between Africa and the centrally planned economies, we find that extending credits under programs of financial aid and deliveries of industrial components under schemes of technical cooperation are modes of development assistance that are not only beginning to loom as large as the trade flows between the two groups but, in relations with some African countries, are taking on an importance that supersedes that of trade.

The scale of these deliveries can best and most quickly be illustrated by pointing to the Soviet Union, where industrial components and equipment for technical assistance projects constituted over 10 per cent of total exports in 1966--about 18 per cent of total exports to less-developed areas,[1] and, what is particularly relevant, about one half of all exports to Africa.[2]

As is the case with trade, this aid has been unevenly distributed. For some African countries and their development programs it is playing a significant role. Other recipients have benefited less from CMEA financial and technical assistance, and it is more difficult to point to growth patterns in their economies, which have been speeded up by Soviet and Eastern

European economic aid. This difficulty notwithstanding, there can be no doubt that Africa has received
a very sizable share of financial and technical aid
directed from the CMEA group to all developing countries. Over the period 1954-62 the centrally planned
economies committed altogether $4.7 billion in eco-
nomic assistance to the so-called third world. Of
this total, $1.35 billion or about 28 per cent was
committed to Africa, and this share has increased to
about 35 per cent in the five years following.[3]

     Any figure of this size is meaningless if not
put in proper perspective. One would naturally like
to ascertain the meaning of the terms "financial"
and "technical assistance" as employed by economists
and politicians in the centrally planned economies,
how they distribute their aid, and how much aid has
been extended. In other words--to use a cliché often
employed in economic development terminology--what is
the "aid technique" of the Soviet Union and her Eastern European partners?[4]

     These questions certainly merit answers, as do
several others which we consider important. For in
any purely economic discussion of foreign aid the
ultimate question always concerns the nature of this
aid and its significance for the progress of economic
growth in the recipient country.

     Regarding many points that will be touched on in
this chapter source information is far too sparse to
allow for any hard and fast answers to these questions;
in some cases only estimates and assumptions can be
provided.

     Nevertheless, none of this affects a basic assump-
tion we shall make here: Soviet and Eastern European
financial and technical aid has, over the past decade,
been invariably significant for the development programs of most African recipients. While for some it
has been of major importance, for others it has been
even of vital importance.

     For a fuller understanding of this aid program,
however, one must start at the beginning: What is
Soviet and Eastern European foreign aid?

DEFINITION OF AID

From the outset it should be kept in mind that Soviet and Eastern European financial and technical aid are not separate approaches as such, but are intimately linked with the total concept of the group's economic relations with Africa.[5] Agreements for financial and technical assistance are often signed in connection with the conclusion of a trade agreement, and deliveries of materials and equipment for completion of technical assistance projects will normally be included in the commodity list attached to the protocol of a current trade agreement. This point is important because practice here differs much from that which is usual in the West. Soviet and Eastern European financial aid to Africa is almost always accorded for a technical assistance project of a predetermined nature. Such aid is usually in the form of credits granted for a specific purpose which is worked out with the recipient government.

As such, these agreements are always bilateral.[6]

The terms and conditions under which the credits are extended may vary. Soviet credits to Africa normally carry an amortization period of twelve years and a annual interest rate of 2.5 per cent, which is calculated exclusively on the outstanding balance of the utilized credit. Practice in the Eastern European countries differs somewhat. There is no specific principle either as to conditions or as to amortization periods, and interest rates usually depend on the size of the credit involved. Normally, it is safe to say that the larger the credit, the longer the amortization period and the lower the interest rate. Czechoslovakia seems to favor repayment periods of five-eight years at interest rates which are slightly higher than those charged by the U.S.S.R. The same is the case for Hungary and Poland.[7]

In all cases, however, the usual practice is that the loan will begin its amortization period one year after completion of the project for which the credit was extended, thus enabling the recipient

country to start repayment at a time the investment
has begun to produce income.

The centrally planned economies very rarely accord outright grants or gifts. On the other hand,
they turn over any project they have financed--lock,
stock, and barrel--to the recipient country. Thus,
after project completion, the CMEA creditor has
neither any say in its operation nor any part of its
profits.

The credits offered by the centrally planned
economies to Africa are, as a rule, earmarked to
cover the following expenditures: (a) geological
surveys and prospecting, preparation of projects,
research and studies prepared by the organizations
of the donor country; (b) delivery of machinery and
equipment for construction works, and of building
materials not available in the recipient country;
(c) delivery of machinery and equipment for the project constructed with the aid of the donor country;
(d) cost of travel both ways for experts from the
donor country, with the exception of certain preliminary missions, the services of which are, in some
cases, granted free of credit to the recipient country; (e) training and education of nationals of the
recipient African country in technical schools in
the CMEA donor country; (f) cost of preparation and
transmission of documents dealing with technical
processes and procedures necessary for the operation
of the project. No patent, license, or other fee is
charged to the credit of the recipient country for
this documentation.[8]

What this amounts to is, of course, that credits
extended by the Soviet Union and Eastern Europe cover,
as a rule, only goods and services which cannot be
produced by the recipient country itself. Experience
has shown that the centrally planned economies normally finance one third of total project costs.

Expenditures of agencies of the donor country
on wages and salaries of technical assistance personnel sent to the recipient country are normally
covered by the credit, and must be reimbursed by the

government of the recipient country in local currency
paid into the donor country's account in a local bank.
These deposits are then used by agencies of the donor
country for current expenses, while unspent parts may
be used by the creditor centrally planned economy to
pay for imports, or--if so agreed--may be reimbursed
in convertible currencies.[9] While little information
is available on the salary scale of technical assistance experts sent from the centrally planned economies
to Africa, it is of interest to note that several
credit and technical assistance agreements concluded
by the People's Republic of China stipulated that the
salaries of Chinese experts and qualified workers
should be equal to those paid to counterpart nationals
of the recipient country,[10] while Soviet and Eastern
European personnel are usually paid normal home-
country wages with occasional supplements for living
abroad.

Credits for construction of industrial installations are but one aspect of the economic program
directed by the centrally planned economies toward
Africa--though perhaps the most important part.
Another aspect is the provision of technical assistance, which is closely linked to the supply of capital goods. On this point, it is noteworthy that the
Soviet Bloc concept of technical assistance differs
much from that described by the Organization for
Economic Cooperation and Development some years ago
and which is understood to comprise mainly technical
advice and vocational training.[11]

Soviet and Eastern European activities certainly
include this and much more. According to a Soviet
writer, technical assistance, based on bilateral
agreements with African recipients, covers the following functions:

Research and planning work; delivery of
machinery, equipment, and other materials;
assignment of Soviet experts to assist in
the selection of construction sites; the
building of enterprises and other installations; the assembly and adjustment of

machinery and equipment, and putting them
into operation; as well as the training of
local personnel for running the enterprise.[12]

The latter activity probably points to one of
the most important features of Soviet and Eastern
European technical assistance--the achievement,
wherever possible, of the widest participation of
African skilled personnel in the technical preparation of projects. On-the-job training of engineers,
construction workers, and other qualified labor has
become a significant feature of technical assistance
of the centrally planned economies, facilitated, in
many cases, by the presence of a large number of
qualified construction workers and engineers from the
donor countries.[13] Thus, for instance, in the construction of the Aswan High Dam in Egypt, the work
was accompanied by continuous on-the-job training of
Arab engineers and qualified workers, so that Arab
specialists were able to take an active part in all
stages of the dam construction.[14]

Regarding financial and technical assistance,
therefore, a parallel cannot be drawn between Soviet
and Eastern European programs and corresponding Western programs, inasmuch as assistance from the former
is more akin to Western capital investment in developing countries. Indeed, if any parallel is to be
found, it must rather be sought in the activities of
Western private enterprise in the field of direct investments, particularly where these are of a "package"
or "turnkey" nature.

THE "AID TECHNIQUE" OF THE
CENTRALLY PLANNED ECONOMIES

It immediately becomes apparent that the framework of financial and technical assistance agreements
between the centrally planned economies and African
recipients is largely determined by the fact that,
with minor exceptions, agreements are made between
central or governmental authorities. Since credits
are extended by government to government, it is
generally true that they are intended for utilization

within the public sector of the recipient economy.
This has, of course, not precluded the use of sub-
contractors by the recipient government.[15] Thus, it
is fair to say that credits from the centrally
planned economies have contributed primarily to the
growth of the public sector in recipient countries,
although indirectly this growth will naturally have
implications for the private sector as well.

The procedure of bilateral loan agreements is
best illustrated by taking the case of the Soviet
Union, which has extended by far the largest credits
given to Africa by any centrally planned economy.
Although institutions and procedures in other countries of the Eastern trade area may differ to some
degree, the arrangements of the Soviet Union are
fairly representative of the broad pattern of activities related to foreign aid in the centrally
planned economies.

Negotiations for aid projects can be initiated
by either recipient or donor. Normally, the initial
request comes from the Ministry of Economic Affairs
or from the National Planning Commission in the recipient country, and is, in the first instance, directed to the economic division of the relevant
Soviet or Eastern European diplomatic representation
in that country.

There is, however, nothing to prevent a centrally
planned economy from suggesting projects to prospective recipients. Naturally, both requests and suggestions are surveyed locally by the donor. The more
realistic ones are then referred to its Ministry of
Foreign Trade, where preliminary discussions take
place. After these have been completed, the central
authorities call upon various government committees
and agencies for the general evaluation of the economic implications of the credits.[16] The findings
of these agencies provide the general basis for
government decisions with respect to granting loans,
preceding formal conclusion of the general agreement
with the recipient country.[17] Normally the agreement
specifies the amounts of credits to be awarded, and
enumerates the projects which will be built with aid

from the donor country, as well as conditions and
schedules of repayment. As a rule, this general
agreement provides the basis for more detailed "protocols" signed by representatives of the contracting
parties. These, in turn, lay down in greater detail
the sequence of construction and deliveries of goods,
cost of equipment, preparation of projects and surveys, as well as wages and salaries of technical
personnel to be sent to the recipient country.[18]

This is an interesting point which leads us to
another aspect of Soviet and Eastern European "aid
techniques." It has commonly been put forward as an
argument against technical assistance from the centrally planned economies that, when extending credits,
they apply no stringent criteria as to the necessity
of the project's future contribution to the recipient's economy or its impact on that economy. Frequently held up as proof of this argument is the construction of a 25,000-seat stadium in Conakry,
Guinea.[19]

The argument further holds that the planned
economy group dispenses with any preliminary study
and, regardless of economic circumstances, even tends
to favor only those projects which the West has re-
fused to finance. The classical example cited here
is, of course, the Aswan High Dam in Egypt.

It would be a mistake, however, to deduce from
this that the centrally planned economies do not
bother about investigating practical details in advance. In reality, the reverse has repeatedly been
the case, for authorities in the Eastern trade area
go into greater detail and operate probably as bureau-
cratically as do their opposite numbers in the West.
Before any project is executed, the whole scheme is
examined in minutest detail; for instance, careful
lists of every piece of equipment are drawn up as a
basis for negotiations with authorities of the developing country. The extreme detail and length of
the texts of these agreements are in themselves evidence that the centrally planned economies undertake
preliminary studies and planning with great thoroughness.

They do differ from Western countries, however,
in their practice of consenting in advance to provide necessary capital and plant by signing a broad
skeleton agreement, which may largely conform to the
wishes of the developing country, but which, in the
last analysis, contains no specific obligations concerning any individual projects. In fact, the general agreement leaves room for any of the separate
projects cited to be replaced at any time by different or more suitable projects, after preliminary in-
vestigations in the field and negotiations with the
developing country have been completed.

In the Soviet Union responsibility for supervision of the implementation of financial and technical assistance is entrusted to the State Committee
for External Economic Relations attached to the
Council of Ministers. This committee carries out
its obligations through four specialized agencies
responsible for aid activities in specific fields.[20]
Each specialized agency either deals directly with
various enterprises, agencies, or institutions in or-
dering goods and services required for any given
project, or assigns this responsibility to a single
large enterprise or institution.[21]

In commenting generally on aid methodology employed by centrally planned economies, it might be
added that, normally the donor will undertake an
evaluation of the over-all economic effectiveness of
various projects, the availability of raw materials,
the level of contribution to the recipient's economy,
as well as other factors, in order to determine the
choice of projects to be constructed. Here it must
be pointed out, however, that the evaluation of investment efficiency undertaken by agencies of the
donor country are not aimed at achievement of maximum profitability of a given project. Since almost
all projects built with Soviet Bloc assistance are
state undertakings, there is, of course, ample scope
for application of investment criteria similar in
many respects to those in use in the centrally planned
economies. The hallmark of these is that the choice
of a project is determined by its possible contribution to the acceleration of the growth rate of the

entire economy of the recipient country--whenever
this is possible. Frequently this is tantamount to
selection of projects facilitating future increase
in the rate of capital accumulation and the lessen-
ing of dependence on imports of machinery, equipment,
and other capital goods from abroad.

Granting of credits, however, has not been made
dependent on acceptance by the recipient country of
these investment choices. The final decision with
respect to selection of projects to be financed rests
in all cases with the government of the recipient
country.

CREDITS FOR DEVELOPMENT

Having given a general description of the
Soviet and Eastern European programs of financial
and technical aid, we now pass on to a discussion of
specific economic data.

Table 8 presents the results of efforts to establish the approximate value of credits which African countries received from the Eastern trade area
in the period 1957-66. The total amounts to $2,335.0
billion. To put this figure in perspective, also included is the total area distribution of financial aid to
other developing areas, in a representative period: 1957-62.

The figures in Table 8 must, however, be taken
with reservations. Some totals may have been over-
estimated, and others underestimated. The latter
pertains certainly to Latin America where Cuba and
Brazil must have received larger amounts of financial
assistance than indicated.

Nonetheless, this does not change the basic conclusion: that Africa accounts for close to one third
of total Soviet and Eastern European aid commitments
to the developing world.

What has been the purpose of this assistance,
and on what terms and conditions has it been granted?
Table 9 that follows, has established a breakdown,
both as to country distribution of individual grants
and as to the major purpose of the allocations.

TABLE 8

AFRICA

Credits Received from the Centrally Planned Economies, in Proportion
to Total Soviet Bloc Credits to All Developing Areas, 1957-66
(U.S.$ billion)

Recipient Country or Area	Credit Commitments 1957-66	Percentage Share of Total	Rank as Recipient
Algeria	346.5	14.8	2
Congo-Brazzaville	9.0	0.4	14
Egypt (U.A.R.)	1,404.0	60.1	1
Ethiopia	114.0	4.9	3
Ghana	89.0	3.8	4
Guinea	49.0	2.1	9
Kenya	56.4	2.4	7
Mali	75.5	3.2	5
Morocco	12.0	0.5	13
Somalia	74.0	3.2	6
Sudan	22.0	0.9	10
Tanzania	20.0	0.8	11
Tunisia	50.0	2.2	8
Uganda	15.4	0.7	12

	Credit Commitments 1957-66	Percentage Share of Total		Credit Commitments 1957-62	Percentage Share of Total
Total Africa 1957-66	2,336.8	100.0			
Africa 1957-62				1,351	28
Latin America				576	12
Western Asia				500	11
Far East				2,335	49
Total 1957-62				4,762	100

Sources: Table 9, "Africa - Country Distribution and Major Allocation Breakdowns
of Soviet and Eastern European Credits, 1957-66," pp. 81-89, and UNCTAD,
Financing for an Expansion of International Trade, Table 26, pp. 112-13;
and current press releases.

TABLE 9

AFRICA

Country Distribution and Major Allocation Breakdowns of Soviet and Eastern European Credits

1957-66[a]

(U.S. $ million)

Recipient Country	Credits	Date of Agreement or Announcement	Amount	Terms and Conditions	Chief Purpose of Credit Allocations	Source[b]
Algeria	Eastern Germany	December 21, 1966	120	..	Loan for purchase of agricultural and industrial equipment	Middle East Economic Digest, January 12, 1967
	Soviet Union	October 4, 1963	100	2.5 per cent interest over a 12-year amortization period	Construction of schools, technical institutes, dams, irrigation network, and industrial installations	Pravda, October 10, 1963
	Soviet Union	May 3, 1964	126.5	2.5 per cent interest, amortization over 12 years	Construction of completely integrated metallurgical complex	Pravda, May 5, 1964
Algeria	Total assistance from the centrally planned economies		346.5			
Congo-Brazzaville	Soviet Union	December 14, 1964	9	2.5 per cent interest, amortization over 12 years	Irrigation of Koukaya plateau, construction of hydro-electric power station, building of 120-room hotel in Brazzaville, and mineral prospecting	Tass, Press Release, December 16, 1964

Continued

TABLE 9 (Continued)

Recipient Country	Credits	Date of Agreement or Announcement	Amount	Terms and Conditions	Chief Purpose of Credit Allocations	Source[b]
Congo-Brazzaville	Total assistance from the centrally planned economies		9			
Egypt (U.A.R.)	Czechoslovakia	.. 1957	56[c]	..	These two loans have financed the construction of 35 complete industrial installations in Egypt since 1956. They include: 2 power plants, cement mills, equipment for 1 nonferrous metallurgical rolling plant, and various consumer goods industries	Czechoslovak Foreign Trade, Prague: No. 8 (August), 1962
	Czechoslovakia	June, 1960	23	Repayment period: 2 years		
	Czechoslovakia	.. 1962	172	..	Construction of power plants, several drinking-water filtering stations, and a technical institute	Loan is not confirmed but mentioned in Czechoslovak Foreign Trade, Prague: No. 10 (October), 1962
	Eastern Germany	March 1, 1965	100	..	Credit granted in two parts: (1) $70 million in long-term industrial credits for Egypt's second development plan, and (2) $30.8 million for short-term industrial credits	The New York Times, Int. Ed., March 2, 1965
	Hungary	.. 1960	14	..	..	
	Poland	.. 1960	15	..	..	

82

Country	Date	Amount (millions)	Terms	Purpose	Source
Poland	..1962	20	3 per cent interest, repayment over 8 years	General economic development work	..
Soviet Union	January 29, 1958	175	2.5 per cent interest, 4 years utilization period, amortization over 12 years	Construction and expansion of enterprises in metallurgical, machinebuilding, oil, electric power, food and other industries. Mineral prospecting, and economic development work	Pravda, January 30, 1958
Soviet Union	December 27, 1958	100	2.5 per cent interest, repayment over 12 years	Construction of first stage of Aswan High Dam (first allocation)	Vedomosti Verkhovnogo Soveta SSSR (Gazette of the Supreme Soviet of the U.S.S.R.) No. 8 (940), 1959
Soviet Union	August 27, 1960	225	Same as above	Credit allocated for construction of second stage of Aswan High Dam	Vedomosti Verkhovnogo Soveta SSSR, No. 11 (1046), 1961
Soviet Union	Summer, 1962	170	Same as above	Construction of first stage of Aswan High Dam and for supporting installation (second allocation)	Credit not confirmed, but reported in Izvestiva, July 21, 1962
Soviet Union	June 18, 1963	57[d]	Same as above	For purchase of Russian hydro-electric power transfer equipment for transfer of power from Aswan to Cairo, Alexandria, and to the Red Sea	The Financial Times; London; November 19, 1963

Continued

TABLE 9 (Continued)

Recipient Country	Credits	Date of Agreement or Announcement	Amount	Terms and Conditions	Chief Purpose of Credit Allocations	Source[b]
	Soviet Union	May 24, 1964	277	Same as above	To finance Egypt's second development plan, 1965-70. Land reclamation, industrial development, and technical assistance	Pravda, May 28, 1964
Egypt (U.A.R.)	Total assistance from the centrally planned economies		1,404[e]			
Ethiopia	Czechoslovakia	May 11, 1960	14	..	Construction of shoe factory, delivery of hospital equipment, and staffing of medical establishments	Czechoslovak Foreign Trade, Prague: No. 4, (April), 1961
	Soviet Union	July 11, 1959	100	2.5 per cent interest, amortization over 12 years	Construction of oil refinery, mineral prospecting, and steel mill studies	Vneshnyaya Torgovlya, No. 8 and No. 9, 1959
Ethiopia	Total assistance from the centrally planned economies		114			
Ghana	Czechoslovakia	May 22, 1961	14	Long-term	Construction of complete industrial installations, rubber and bicycle factories	West Africa, London: September 8, 1962
	Hungary	April, 1961	7	Long-term	Construction of complete factories and industrial installations	West Africa, July 14, 1961

	Date	Amount	Terms	Purpose	Source
Poland	April 20, 1961	14	Repayment over 8 years	Complete factories and industrial installations (shoe, tire, and ceramic plants)	West Africa, March 24, 1962
Poland	December, 1961	14	Same as above	Construction of sugar refinery, and vocational training	Board of Trade Journal, London: May 25, 1962
Soviet Union	August 4, 1960	40	2.5 per cent interest, amortization over 12 years	Construction of industrial enterprises, power stations, mineral prospecting, and vocational training	Vedomosti Verkhovnogo Soveta SSSR, No. 51 (1035), December 30, 1960
Soviet Union	October, 1963	81	Gift	Purpose unclear, and not confirmed. This amount is not included in total.	..
Ghana Total assistance from the centrally planned economies		89			
Guinea Czechoslovakia	May 25, 1961	10	..	Complete industrial installations, and technical assistance	Czechoslovak Foreign Trade, Vol. II, No. 10 (October), 1962
Poland	.. 1960	4	Low interest rate, repayment over 5 years	Formation of joint fishing company, and technical assistance	Marchés tropicaux, No. 810, Paris: May 28, 1961, p. 1317
Soviet Union	August 24, 1959	35	2.5 per cent interest, amortization over 12 years	Construction of several factories, a polytechnic institute, development of agriculture, and mineral prospecting	Sovremennyy Vostok, No. 5 (May) 1960, and Pravda, March 1, 1962

Continued

TABLE 9 (Continued)

Recipient Country	Credits	Date of Agreement or Announcement	Amount	Terms and Conditions	Chief Purpose of Credit Allocations	Source[b]
Guinea	Total assistance from the centrally planned economies		49			
Kenya	Soviet Union	November 20, 1964	45	Same as above	Irrigation work, and hydro-electric installations, constructions of textile mills, a radio station, and food processing plants	Tass, Press Release, October 27, 29, and November 20, 1964
Kenya	Soviet Union	February, 1966	11.4	Same as above	Site construction	East African Standard, February 11, 1966
Kenya	Total assistance from the centrally planned economies		56.4			
Morocco	Poland	October, 1962	12[e]	Low interest rate, repayment over 8 years	General economic development work	Izvestiva, October 17, 1962
Morocco	Total assistance from the centrally planned economies		12			

Mali	Bulgaria	12.5[c]	.. 1961	Low interest rate, repayment over 5-10 years	Industrial installations	Africa South of the Sahara, Paris: May 28, 1962
	Czechoslovakia	10	June 13, 1951	Low interest rate, repayable over 5 years	Construction of textile mill, and installations for hospitals and laboratories	Africa Economic News Letter, July 22, 1961
	Poland	8	.. 1962	Low interest rate, repayable over 8 years	General economic development work	West Africa, September 8, 1962
	Soviet Union	45	March 18, 1961	2.5 per cent interest, amortization over 12 years	Construction of cement factory, power station, railroad construction, and geological prospecting	Pravda, March 22, 1961
Mali	Total assistance from the centrally planned economies	75.5				
Somalia	Czechoslovakia	30	.. 1961	Low interest loan, repayable over 3-8 years	Economic development work, and vocational training	Africa South of the Sahara, April 2, 1962
	Soviet Union	44	June 2, 1961	2.5 per cent interest, amortization over 12 years	General economic development work	Pravda, June 6, 1961
	Soviet Union	5.6	September, 1966		Development loan for equipment supply	Somali News, September 8, 1966

Continued

TABLE 9 (Continued)

Recipient Country / Credits	Date of Agreement or Announcement	Amount	Terms and Conditions	Chief Purpose of Credit Allocations	Source[b]
Somalia					
Total assistance from the centrally planned economies		74			
Sudan					
Bulgaria	January 2, 1967	..		Construction of textile factory and tomato processing plant	R. Omdurman, January 2, 1967
Soviet Union	November 21, 1961	22	Same as above	Construction of grain elevators, food processing plants, scientific research laboratories, and an experimental station for cotton selection	Pravda, November 23, 1961
Sudan					
Total assistance from the centrally planned economies		22			
Tanzania					
Soviet Union	May 27, 1966	20	Same as above	Construction of industrial installations	Tanzania Standard, May 28, 1966
Tunisia					
Czechoslovakia	.. 1961	10	..	General economic development work	Czechoslovak Foreign Trade, No. 11 (November), 1961
Poland	November 7, 1960	10	Low interest rates, repayable over 8 years	General economic development work	West Africa, February 25, 1961

88

Tunisia	Soviet Union	February 9, 1962	30	3 per cent interest, re-payable over 12 years	Construction of three hydro-electric stations, and a national technical institute for the University of Tunisia	Vedomosti Verkhovnogo Soveta SSSR, No. 11 (1098), March 15, 1962
	Total assist-ance from the centrally planned economies		50			
Uganda	Soviet Union	February 9, 1965	15.4	2.5 per cent interest, amortization over 12 years	Construction of textile factory, meat refrigeration installations, dairy products plant, and a training center for mechanized agriculture	Uganda Argus; Kampala: February 10, 1965

Source: In addition to sources mentioned above, the following material has been utilized in the preparation of this table: V. Rymalov, Ekonomicheskoe Sotrudnichestvo SSSR so Slaborazvitymi Stranami (Moscow: Gostorgizdat, 1960, pp. 44-45); Dengi i Kredit, Moscow: No. 6 (June, 1962); H. Kralova, "Prospects of Development of Czechoslovak Trade Relations with Cambodia, Indonesia, and U.A.R.," Czechoslovak Foreign Trade, Vol. I, No. 7 (July, 1961), p. 18; La documentation française, Notes et Etudes Documentaires, Série Economique et Financière (Paris: Secrétariat Général du Gouvernement, Direction de la Documentation) - The following reports: No. 2760: "L'Aide soviétique aux Pays sous-développés; Les Accords de Coopération industrielle et technique entre l'U.R.S.S. et les Pays sous-développés d'Afrique et d'Asie" (March 13, 1961); No. 2833: "L'Evolution de l'Economie tchécoslovaque en 1960" (November 1, 1961); No. 2972: "L'Evolution de l'Economie tchécoslovaque" (March 13, 1963); OECD, The Flow of Financial Resources to Developing Countries in 1961 (Paris: OECD, July, 1963), p. 17; UNCTAD, Financing for an Expansion of International Trade. Report prepared by the U.N. Bureau of General Economic Research and Policies, (E/Conf. 46/9, March 10, 1964)(Geneva, 1964); GATT, International Trade News Bulletin (1954-59); and Developments in Commercial Policy (1960-64).

Notes: [a]Smaller, unconfirmed credits may have been omitted; and all ruble amounts have been converted to dollars at rate in effect when the credit was extended;

[b]Where no special source indication is given - See general sources above;

[c]This loan was not used in the period under review, and was revived in late 1964 (New York Times, Int. Ed., January 5, 1965);

[d]These are loans that may equally well be classified as "commercial credits." They are included here, mainly due to the "technical assistance" purpose for which they are intended;

[e]In addition to this, there are unconfirmed reports of following credit commitments made in 1963 and 1964: Rumania - $70 million; Eastern Germany - $35 million; and Poland - $25 million (New York Times, Int. Ed., January 5, 1965).

From these tables we can now draw several conclusions as to the over-all scope and structure of
financial and technical assistance which Africa received from the Eastern trade area.

The most striking feature is the heavy concentration of aid on both sides--recipient and donor.
In Africa, Egypt emergès as not only the largest
debtor to the Eastern trade area--she has received
close to two thirds of all Soviet and Eastern European aid to the continent--but with total receipts
of $1.4 billion she is also the largest recipient of
such aid in the entire developing world.

This finding holds true, also when considering
committed aid on a per capita basis.

TABLE 10

AFRICA

Per Capita Distribution of Aid From the Centrally
Planned Economies, 1958-66

Recipient	Population (Millions, mid-1964)	Committed Aid Per Capita U.S. $
Algeria	11.3	30.6
Congo (B)	0.8	10.9
Egypt (U.A.R.)	27.8	50.3
Ethiopia	21.0	5.4
Ghana	7.1	12.4
Guinea	3.2	14.8
Kenya	8.6	6.3
Mali	4.3	17.5
Morocco	12.3	0.9
Somalia	2.2	32.8
Sudan	12.5	1.7
Tunisia	4.3	11.6
Uganda	7.1	2.1

Sources: Table 8; and U.N. Statistical Yearbook,
           1965, Table 19, pp. 80-84.

It might in this regard be noted that more recent recipients, e.g., Algeria, Mali, and Somalia
have--on a relative basis--received more economic
aid than countries that initially benefited from
Soviet and Eastern European financial assistance
to Africa.

The allocation picture of this aid shows us
that, while it is not exactly a one-country show,
the paramount role of the Soviet Union as the chief
source of credits is clear. In fact, the high degree of concentration in the credit flow has been
duplicated by the donor side:

TABLE 11

AFRICA

Soviet and Eastern European Credits
Breakdown by Donor Country

1954-66
(U.S. $ million)

Donor Country	Credits Committed	Percentage Distribution	
U.S.S.R.	2,336.8		70.4
Bulgaria	13.0	0.5	
Czechoslovakia	339.0	14.5	
Eastern Germany	220.0	9.5	
Hungary	21.0	0.9	
Poland	97.0	4.2	29.6
Total	2,336.8		100.0

Source: Table 9.

These proportions are, of course, far different
from those pertaining to African trade with the Eastern trade area. In Chapter 8, we shall see that over
the ten-year period 1954-64, the U.S.S.R. accounted
for 44.0 per cent of all Soviet Bloc exports to
Africa, and for 36.0 per cent of all imports. During
the same period, corresponding figures for the six
Eastern European countries were 56.0 and 64.0 per
cent.[22]

We also find that, apart from Egypt, where close
to 80 per cent of all aid from the Eastern trade area
originates in the Soviet Union, aid from other centrally planned donor countries is more evenly distributed among African recipients. In fact, in no
other African country does the proportionate share of
Soviet aid alone come close to that of Egypt's. This
ranges between 30 and 50 per cent in most other recipient countries and the Eastern European contribution is correspondingly more significant.

The structure of financial and technical aid from
the centrally planned economies is more difficult to
ascertain. There are several reasons for this. Not
all credits are disclosed as to amounts and utilization, and the purpose for which the credit originally
was given may change after "on-site" investigation
has taken place. A stated principle of Soviet and
Eastern European foreign aid, however, has been to
give a predominance of financial assistance to projects
of an industrial nature. Within this limitation credits are destined for development of projects that will
have a stimulating effect on the mobilization of internal resources for economic growth.

As such, we find that more than half the resources placed at the disposal of developing countries by members of the Council of Mutual Economic
Assistance was used for construction of enterprises
in heavy industry and power generation. About 35 per
cent of credits was used for power stations, metallurgical plants, and the coal industry, and 25 per cent
was allocated to the chemical industry, oil refineries,
engineering, and building materials industries. The remainder was utilized to finance the construction of

transport and communication facilities, geological
surveys, prospecting, construction of enterprises in
light and food industries, as well as scientific,
medical, educational institutions, and housing.[23]

Obviously, this distribution pattern must be
adapted to local circumstances, and considering
total Soviet and Eastern European aid to Africa over
the past ten years, proportionately more was devoted
to building dams for power generation and irrigation
purposes than was the case with the rest of the developing world. It is difficult to make any exact
assessment here, but it might be estimated that
closer to 35-40 per cent of aid delivered by the
centrally planned economies to Africa has been utilized for irrigation and hydro-electric power plant
construction. The balance has been divided among
disbursements for the construction of public facilities (airports, roads, radio communication stations,
etc.), vocational training and construction of light
manufacturing industries--mainly those producing
consumer goods.[24] Relatively little aid has been
extended to African agriculture. The only reported
cases have been the establishment of model farms in
Ghana, Guinea, and Egypt,[25] but work on these projects
has not met with much success and has been virtually
abandoned.

Here one might ask to what extent the centrally
planned economies cooperate in their efforts to develop the African economies. The answer, it appears,
would be largely negative, for in our findings, we
have not encountered any significant case of such
cooperation in providing development assistance. Nor
is there any formal coordinating body within the
structure of the Council for Mutual Economic Assistance for this purpose, although we must assume that
informal exchange of information on planned or projected undertakings are being circulated within the
Eastern trade area so that overlapping of projects
can be avoided.[26]

What all this adds up to is that, as yet, there
is no distinctive pattern of Soviet and Eastern European aid to Africa. The generalization might perhaps

be made that the Eastern European countries tend to sponsor comparatively small undertakings and to supply plants for a variety of light or secondary industries, whereas the Soviet Union is more concerned with basic industrial development of the recipient country, and has also been more involved in projects of a purely infrastructural nature.

But an absolute impression of these relations cannot be had from any over-all, perspective glance. To uncover the true nature of Africa's economic relations with the Eastern trade area it will be necessary to examine how trade and aid have been applied to each recipient, and what effects this has had on their economies.

An attempt to answer the first part of the question will be made in the following chapters, which are a country-by-country examination of the operation of Africa's economic relations with the centrally planned economies.

NOTES TO CHAPTER 3

1. Vneshnyaya Torgovlya, No. 12, 1966.

2. U.N., ECA, African Trade with the Centrally Planned Economies (E/CN.14/STC/5), Section 1, p. 5.

3. UNCTAD, Financing for an Expansion of International Trade, U.N. Bureau of General Economic Research and Policies (E/CONF. 46/9, March 10, 1964) (Geneva, 1964), Table 26, p. 112, and OECD, The Flow of Financial Resources to Less-Developed Countries, 1956-63 (Paris: OECD, 1964), pp. 54-57.

4. The term "Soviet and Eastern European Programs of Foreign Aid" may lead to some misunderstanding as to the extent of cooperation among the centrally planned economies where financial and technical assistance to developing countries is concerned. The term is used here merely as an all-inclusive phrase to indicate which donor countries are involved. As will be explained on Page 93, there is very little

cooperation between any individual member country of
the Council of Mutual Economic Assistance and only
insignificant coordination of policy as regards trade
with developing countries.

5. For general descriptions of Soviet and Eastern European financial and technical aid, see Joseph
S. Berliner, Soviet Economic Aid (New York: Frederick
A. Praeger, Inc. for the Council on Foreign Relations,
1958), pp. 30-47; I. Kapranov, "U.S.S.R. Technical
Assistance to Foreign Countries," (in Russian), Vneshnyaya Torgovlya, No. 6, 1961; Basile Kerblay, "L'aide
économique de l'U.R.S.S. au Tiers-Monde," Développement et civilisations, No. 10 (April-June, 1962), pp.
37-50; and Klaus Billerbeck, Die Auslandshilfe des
Ostblocks für die Entwicklungsländer (Hamburg: Verlag
Weltarchiv G.m.b.H., 1960), pp. 40-54.

6. The shortcomings of strictly bilateral credit
agreements providing for shipments of goods rather than
for a supply of convertible currency are clearly recognized by the centrally planned economies. The possibility of introducing a certain form of multilateral arrangement has been envisaged in connection with the creation of the "International Bank for Economic Cooperation" of the CMEA countries, and the introduction of the
transferable ruble and multilateral composition of payments balances between the CMEA countries. These are
intended to operate within the framework of bilateral
agreements.

Although these measures are, at present, to be applied only to the CMEA countries, they may possibly be
extended to other countries. Recent official and semiofficial statements indicate that the new bank of the
CMEA group may--in the future--extend to developing
countries credits in rubles convertible within the CMEA
area. This would, of course, enable the recipient countries to use these credits for financing deliveries of
goods from any CMEA country, on the basis of triangular
or multilateral agreements. These facilities need not
be limited to credits offered by the bank, and may ideally
also be extended to credits offered by individual CMEA
countries to developing countries within the framework of
special agreements. At the same time, the repayment of

credits to one centrally planned economy could also
be affected by the use of transferable rubles earned
from exports to another CMEA country, rather than by
direct exports of commodities to the donor country.

7. Josef Jonás, "Czechoslovak Socialist Republic; An Exporter of Complete Industrial Plants,"
Czechoslovak Foreign Trade, Vol. 1, No. 10 (October,
1961), pp. 3-5. See also Table 9, pp. 81-89.

8. UNCTAD, Financing for an Expansion of International Trade, op. cit., p. 125.

9. Ibid., p. 126.

10. Ceylon: Ministry of Finance, Foreign Economic Aid, A Review from 1950-62 (Colombo, 1963), p. 33.

11. Maurice Domergue for OECD, Technical Assist-
ance--Definitions and Aims, Ways and Means, Conditions
and Limits (Paris: OECD, 1961).

12. V. Rymalov, Ekonomicheskoe Sotrudnichestvo
SSSR co Slaborazvitymi Stranami (Moscow: Gostorgizdat,
1960), p. 61.

13. La documentation française, Notes et Etudes
Documentaires, "L'Aide soviétique aux Pays sous-
développés. Les Accords de Coopération industrielle
et technique entre l'U.R.S.S. et les Pays sous-
développés d'Afrique et d'Asie," Report No. 2760
(Paris: March 13, 1961).

14. Sovetskaya Kirgiziya, March 22, 1963, reported
that two large training centers had been set up in Egypt
with Soviet aid. The one at Aswan would train skilled
workers for the Aswan hydroelectric works. The other,
in Alexandria, would train workers for the big shipyard
built with Soviet aid.

15. The Aswan High Dam project is being constructed
by an Egyptian contracting concern, Industrial and
General Enterprises Engineering Co., S.A.A. (Osman Ahmed
Osman and Co.).

16. Among the purely economic considerations en-
couraging the expansion of foreign credits may be the
desire to promote increasing foreign trade and to ensure higher imports from primary-producing countries
in the future. The granting of long-term credits cre-
ates a favorable climate for the expansion of trade.
Not only do the construction of enterprises and the
delivery of machinery and equipment on credit create
a market for spare parts and possibly stimulate cash
purchases of investment goods, but the repayment of
credits also finances a return flow of imports in the
future. The development of such bilateral trade movements could increase the possibility of expanding imports without the commensurate increase in convertible
currency expenditures. (See also pp. 258-61.)

Owing to the need of the developing countries for
complete installations or large individual purchases
of equipment, it might, from the Soviet and Eastern
European point of view be argued that it would be quite
impracticable to achieve the same effect on trade without credits, that is, by balancing current exports of
investment goods to each country against current imports.

While the importance of these economic factors cannot be assessed, there is probably no doubt that they do--
to some extent--reduce the high opportunity cost of foreign aid extended by the centrally planned economies to
Africa.

17. Of course, numerous political considerations
also enter into the decision, but such considerations
are not always as thoroughly evaluated as described
above. It has been claimed, although this cannot be
substantiated, that the $277 million credit to Egypt
(U.A.R.) announced by former Premier Khrushchev was a
result of his personal initiative and was not discussed
with the U.S.S.R. Government prior to its announcement.
(New York Times, Int. Ed., May 24, 1964). Among the
possible political reasons for this credit may have been
the desire of Mr. Khrushchev to secure for the U.S.S.R.
a seat at the "Nonaligned Nations" Conference in Cairo,
September, 1964.

18.   Rymalov, op. cit., pp. 43-70.

19.   Agreement of August 24, 1959, between the
U.S.S.R. and Guinea. See also Table 9, pp. 81-89.

20.   These four foreign trade corporations are:
Tekhnoexport, Tekhnopromexport, Tyazpromexport, and
Prommashexport. They are solely export organizations
but also responsible for implementing technical assistance projects. Source: P. A. Cherviakov, Organizatsia
i Tekhnika Vneshnei Torgovli SSSR (Moscow: Vneshtorgizdat, 1962), p. 61.

21.   Ibid., and UNCTAD, Financing for an Expansion
of International Trade, p. 129.

22.   See Chapter 8, Table 32, pp. 236-41.

23.   UNCTAD, Financing for an Expansion of International Trade, p. 122.

24.   See sources to Table 9, p. 89.

25.   La documentation française, Notes et Etudes
Documentaires, No. 2760, "L'Aide soviétique aux Pays
sous-développés," loc. cit.

26.   An interesting development, which may change
this conclusion, is cooperation among several centrally
planned economies in the supply of medical equipment to
developing countries. Medicor (Hungary), Kovo (Czechoslovakia), Varimex (Poland), Medoexport (U.S.S.R.), and
Feinmechanik-Optik (Eastern Germany) have cooperated in
establishing the first cooperative trading enterprise
in the Soviet Bloc specializing in the supply of medical
equipment (mobile hospital units, mobile operating rooms
as well as mobile water and food control laboratories).
To avoid duplication, each contract is negotiated by one
of the firms acting as main contractor. This firm or-
ganizes credit facilities and subcontracts to its partners as required. Terms will probably be amortization
over eight to ten years with a 4 per cent interest.
(Source: The Economist, June 3, 1967, p. 1019.)

PART II

TRADE AND AID IN OPERATION

II

Having discussed the general structure of economic relations between Africa and the centrally planned economies, we can now begin to examine these in greater detail, particularly as they apply to each of the African partners of the exchange.

We recall that by mid-1967 upward of twenty-nine African countries maintained economic relations with the Soviet Bloc. As objects of the country studies we have chosen a group of twelve of these countries, all of which have two things in common: Not only do they trade with the centrally planned economies—in fact, they are the largest trade partners of the Eastern group in Africa—but up to the middle of 1967 this group of twelve countries included the most significant African recipients of Soviet and Eastern European financial and technical aid.

The question might be asked at this point: Why did members of the Soviet Bloc decide to single out certain countries for attention, while ignoring others? Part of the answer may surely be found in the fact that regardless of national wealth, no single donor—or even group of donors—can afford to cover effectively the needs of the entire developing world. Pure limitations on economic capacity alone would forbid this, and therefore a selection must be made. By and large it is difficult, if not well-nigh impossible to make objective selections on the basis of needs alone—all developing countries today are in need of external aid. So the choice of recipient might with equal reason be made on political grounds. This is a criterion that all donors of foreign aid apply and, of course, the centrally planned economies are no exception here.

The Western philosophy of aid to newly independent countries rests on the assumption that nationalist

régimes, preferably with a strong emphasis on economic and cultural development, offer to developing
nations the best and probably the only workable
alternative to Communism. The aid policy of the
Soviet Bloc countries (to the extent it can be said
they have one) rests on not very different assumptions, but, of course, the objective is directly the
opposite. Support, the centrally planned economies
feel, can profitably be given to nationalist régimes,
provided this strengthens them against capitalism,
and provided this also brings these régimes into
closer alignment with major Soviet policies. Or to
put it more succinctly, as did former Premier Khrushchev during his visit in Egypt in May, 1964:

> It has been correctly said here that the
> Soviet Union renders assistance without
> any political conditions. But I shall
> say frankly that we take great satisfac-
> tion in giving aid to countries that are
> embarking on the path of socialist con-
> struction.[1]

In Africa, the countries that have been considered prepared to "embark on the path of socialist
construction" represented by mid-1967 all parts of
the continent but the South. They included countries in North, West-Central, and East Africa, and
for the convenience of the reader we shall group
our country studies according to the above areas.

In general, a uniform pattern will be followed
during the ensuing discussion. After a brief outline of the economic structure of the area and its
constituent countries, relations with the centrally
planned economies will be outlined under the following three headings: (1) trade, (2) financial and
technical aid, and (3) cultural and educational relations wherever these have strong economic overtones.

Since Egypt is by far the most important trade
partner and the largest recipient of Soviet and Eastern European development assistance, it is only natural to start the review with this country.

---

1. <u>Pravda</u>, May 20, 1964.

CHAPTER **4** EGYPT (U.A.R.)

Nowhere else in the developing world has the Soviet Bloc been more active than in Egypt. This country stands today as the by far most important trade partner of the centrally planned economies, and had, by mid-1967 received about 20 per cent of all Soviet and Eastern European development aid committed to the "third world." In fact, since 1958, the Soviet Bloc has contributed about 30 per cent of all external aid (excluding U.S. food aid) to Egypt.[1]

Seen in an African perspective these proportions take on an even greater significance. In the ten-year period 1955-65, Egyptian trade accounted for close to two thirds of total African turnover of trade with the centrally planned economies, and she received the same proportion of Soviet Bloc development aid to Africa.[2]

There are many reasons why Egypt has been selected for such singular attention from the Eastern group. Historically, she is the oldest trade partner of the centrally planned economies in Africa. While Czechoslovakia was the first of the Eastern European countries to trade with Egypt, Soviet foreign trade corporations—such as Arcos and Textilimport—began operating in Egypt as far back as in 1923.

But political reasons are no less pertinent. Egypt is the cornerstone in the Arab world, Cairo the headquarters of the Arab League, and by virtue of her foreign policy, the country is a major political force both in the Middle East and in Africa. On the domestic scene, the increasingly communal organization of the Egyptian state also seems to find favor with the Soviet Bloc:[3]

> The nationalization of banks and big in-
> dustrial enterprises, the monopoly created
> in foreign trade, the creation of a state
> sector in the economy, the agrarian reform
> and the development of cooperation in agri-
> culture speak more than any words of the way
> in which the people of the U.A.R. has re-
> jected the capitalist system of oppression
> and exploitation and has risen to struggle
> for social emancipation.[4]

Moreover, from an economic point of view, Egypt
is a relatively "easy" country to aid. She possesses
a good infrastructure, a well trained cadre of technicians and some of the largest construction firms
in the Middle East are headquartered in Cairo--a fact
which facilitates subcontracting of development projects. Nor should it be forgotten that with large
segments of economic activity in the hands of the
State--Egypt faces a relatively easier task in commercial dealings with the centrally planned economies
than do countries where negotiations have to pass
through a multitude of levels before any decisions
can be made.

Partly due to the rapid changes the country has
undergone in the past few years, its economic structure is today very uneven. Egypt is faced with a
population increase so explosive that it threatens
to obliterate in two decades any gains from development investments made today,[5] and despite very real
efforts toward industrialization, Egypt remains
basically a one-crop economy based on cotton, a commodity for which she has, over the past years, received steadily declining prices. This, and other
factors have had unfortunate effects on her holdings
of foreign exchange which fell from $1,353 million
in 1948 to $57 million by late 1965.[6] Equally, the
Egyptian balance of payments is in serious difficulties with large arrears both on the goods and
services, and trade balance accounts.[7] These difficulties have only been compounded after the failure
of the armed conflict with Israel in June, 1967.

To alleviate the heavy dependence on cotton,
Egypt has, during President Nasser's administration,

pursued a conscious policy of channeling all available investment funds into industry and infrastructure.
For the plan period 1960-65, 23 per cent of Egyptian
capital expenditure was assigned to industry, and
figures for agricultural development, infrastructure,
and other projects were 23, 24, and 30 per cent respectively.[8] As many of these investment targets
were based on steady earnings from export sales and
increasing allocations of economic aid, this was the
point where Egypt's economic relations with the centrally planned economies became important.

TRADE

Commodity exchange with the Eastern trade area
was all but broken off by the Second World War, and
reciprocal trade did not gain momentum until after
the conclusion of a large-scale barter agreement with
the Soviet Union in 1953 (wheat and petroleum in exchange for cotton). This was followed by the signature of a virtually permanent trade and payments
agreement in early 1954. The turning point in relations came in 1956 when a Soviet trade delegation
was established in Cairo. In the course of that year
turnover of commodity exchange between the two countries almost tripled. During the five years that
followed, Egypt concluded trade and payments agreements with every centrally planned economy, with the
result that there has been a shift in the direction
of Egyptian foreign trade away from the West to the
Soviet Bloc. The latter now accounts for more than
one fifth of Egypt's foreign trade turnover.

The growth pattern of trade, however, has been
very uneven; on the average through the 1958-64
period, the centrally planned economies accounted
for 20 per cent of Egyptian imports and for 38 per
cent of her exports. However, on a year-to-year
basis we find that imports from the Soviet Bloc have
registered a steady decline from a high of 27.5 per
cent in 1958 to a low of 14.5 per cent in 1963. The
growth pattern of exports has not been more even; an
examination of the period reveals large annual fluctuations which culminated in 1961, but leveled off
toward the middle of this decade.

TABLE 12

EGYPT (U.A.R.)

Value of Trade with the Centrally Planned Economies, 1958-64[a]
(Egyptian Pounds and U.S. $ million, imports c.i.f., exports f.o.b.)

| | 1958 | | | | 1959 | | | | 1960 | | | |
| | Imports | | Exports | | Imports | | Exports | | Imports | | Exports | |
	E.₤ million	%	E.₤ million	%	E.₤ million	%	E.₤ million	%	E.₤ million	%	E.₤ million	%
Total trade	238.2	100.0	162.6	100.0	214.4	100.0	153.0	100.0	225.0	100.0	190.6	100.0
of which:												
Soviet Union	31.7	13.3	28.6	17.6	26.9	12.5	28.3	18.5	23.0	10.0	30.9	16.2
Eastern Europe	35.9	15.2	38.1	22.3	28.8	13.4	39.3	25.7	26.4	11.9	38.4	20.2
Bulgaria	1.5	0.7	1.3	0.8	1.3	0.6	1.4	0.9	1.4	0.6	1.9	1.0
Czechoslovakia	10.1	4.3	15.0	9.2	8.0	3.8	16.2	10.6	8.0	3.7	12.9	6.8
Eastern Germany	9.1	3.8	7.8	4.8	8.9	4.1	10.5	6.9	8.8	3.9	10.0	5.3
Hungary	4.7	2.0	5.5	2.2	3.4	1.6	2.5	1.6	2.4	1.1	2.1	1.1
Poland	4.3	1.8	4.8	3.0	2.7	1.2	5.8	3.8	2.9	1.3	7.7	4.0
Rumania	6.2	2.6	3.7	2.3	4.5	2.1	2.9	1.9	2.9	1.3	3.8	2.0
Soviet Union	31.7	13.3	28.6	17.6	26.9	12.5	28.3	18.5	23.0	10.0	30.9	16.2

| | Jan.-Sept. 1961 | | | | 1962 | | | | 1963 | | | | Jan.-June 1964 | | | |
| | Imports | | Exports | | Imports | | Exports | | Imports | | Exports | | Imports | | Exports | |
	E.₤ million	%	E.₤ million	%	E.₤ million	%	E.₤ million	%	U.S. $ million	%	U.S. $ million	%	U.S. $ million	%	U.S. $ million	%
	163.3	100.0	133.0	100.0	300.9	100.0	157.4	100.0	916.3	100.0	521.6	100.0	428.4	100.0	319.3	100.0
	18.1	11.1	25.4	19.1	24.6	8.1	24.0	15.2	49.1	5.3	101.7	19.6	20.7	4.9	57.9	18.0
	18.7	11.6	38.3	28.8	35.1	11.7	30.2	19.3	84.3	9.0	105.3	19.9	32.4	7.4	64.2	20.0
	0.9	0.6	1.0	0.8	2.3	0.8	1.0	0.7	3.7	0.4	4.0	0.8	--	--	--	--
	4.8	3.0	21.8	16.4	10.2	3.4	12.6	8.0	25.2	2.7	50.7	9.7	14.3	3.3	32.7	10.2
	6.5	4.0	5.7	4.3	7.9	2.6	5.9	3.8	17.1	1.9	15.0	2.8	6.7	1.5	10.6	3.3
	1.9	1.2	2.8	2.1	4.4	1.5	2.7	1.7	15.2	1.6	12.2	2.3	--	--	--	--
	2.2	1.3	2.6	1.9	5.8	1.9	3.3	2.1	13.3	1.4	10.9	2.0	7.3	1.7	11.2	3.5
	2.4	1.5	4.4	3.3	4.5	1.5	4.7	3.0	9.8	1.0	12.5	2.3	4.1	0.9	9.7	3.0
	18.1	11.1	25.4	19.1	24.6	8.1	24.0	15.2	49.1	5.3	101.7	19.6	20.7	4.9	57.9	18.0

Sources: Figures for 1958 to 1963 from Egypt (U.A.R.), Department of Statistics and Census, Monthly Summary of Foreign Trade, December, 1958; December, 1959; December, 1960; September, 1961; December, 1962--in all issues, Table IV, pp. 16-23. Figures for 1963 and 1964 from IMF, Direction of Trade, July, 1964, p. 50 and July, 1965, p. 79.

Note: aCurrencies are denominated in Egyptian pound up to 1963, thereafter in U.S. dollars. (1 E.₤ = $2.30)

The decline in Egyptian trade with the centrally
planned economies has been more pronounced in her
commodity exchange with the Soviet Union than with
Eastern Europe, and in relative terms the former has
fallen off rapidly since 1961. This can very well be
seen in a yearly comparison of absolute values as
well. The reason is not hard to find; it is related
to the wholesale decline in Soviet cotton purchases
which set in in 1962 and continued thereafter.

The Soviet Union and Eastern Europe account for
about equal proportions of Egyptian trade with the
centrally planned economies. Actually, these are
4:6 in favor of Eastern Europe. For each year of
the period under review, the Soviet Union supplied
Egypt with an average of 10 per cent of her imports
and purchased 18 per cent of her exports. The corresponding figures for Eastern Europe are 12 and 23
per cent. Among the countries of the latter group,
Czechoslovakia has been the most active trade partner, followed by Eastern Germany and Poland.

The commodity structure of Egyptian exports to
the Eastern trade area naturally centered on cotton
products. Throughout the 1958-64 period this commodity accounted for about 73 per cent of all Egyptian sales to the Soviet Union and close to 70 per
cent of her sales to the Eastern European countries.[9]
The remainder of exports to the Eastern group was
made up of shipments of rice and citrus fruits. Of
the latter, the centrally planned economies in Eastern
Europe, both relatively and absolutely, purchased more
than the Soviet Union.

Since cotton figures so prominently in Egyptian
exports to the Soviet Bloc, it might be interesting
to consider the significance of shipments to this
area of total Egyptian cotton exports.

On an average throughout the five-year period
the centrally planned economies purchased more than
50 per cent of all Egyptian cotton exports. Of these
50 per cent the six Eastern European countries purchased about two thirds. The significance of this
figure becomes even greater when we mention that

EGYPT (U.A.R.)

Share of Exports to the Centrally Planned Economies of Total Egyptian Cotton Exports

(Metric cantars thousands[a] and percentages)

	1958/59		1959/60		1960/61		1961/62		1962/63		1963/64	
	Quantity	%	Quantity	%	Quantity	%	Quantity	%	Quantity	%	Quantity	%
Total Egyptian cotton sales	5,368	100	7,191	100	5,967	100	4,588	100	6,061	100	5,835	100
of which to:												
Bulgaria	68	1.3	97	1.3	74	1.3	43	0.9	57	0.9	39	0.7
Czechoslovakia	220	3.6	261	3.6	168	2.8	198	4.3	186	3.1	614	10.5
Eastern Germany	695	13.5	834	11.6	1,036	17.4	464	10.1	701	11.6	165	2.8
Hungary	102	1.9	173	2.4	178	3.0	101	2.2	139	2.3	114	2.0
Poland	282	5.3	384	5.3	367	6.1	156	3.4	209	3.4	220	3.8
Rumania	84	1.6	168	2.3	188	3.1	234	5.1	224	3.7	184	3.1
Total Eastern Europe	1,451	27.2	1,917	26.5	2,011	33.7	1,196	26.0	1,516	25.0	1,336	22.9
Soviet Union	1,458	27.1	1,259	17.5	1,429	23.9	895	19.5	1,744	28.8	1,307	22.4
Soviet Union and Eastern Europe	2,909	54.3	3,176	44.0	3,440	57.6	2,091	45.5	3,260	53.8	2,643	45.3

Sources: Egypt (U.A.R.), Ministry of Economy, Fortnightly Cotton Bulletin, 1958–61; and Egypt (U.A.R.) Central Organization of Public Mobilization and Statistics, Weekly Cotton Statistics, 1961–64.

Note: [a] 1 cantar = 44.928 kg.

TABLE 14

EGYPT (U.A.R.)

Share of the Centrally Planned Economies in Imports of Capital Equipment

(Imports c.i.f., E. Ł thousand and percentages)

	1958		1959		1960		1961	
	Imports	%	Imports	%	Imports	%	Imports	%
Metals and Manufactures								
of which:								
Pig iron, hematite, etc.	472.4		332.8		512.7		798.9	
Soviet Union	443.5		231.5		382.1		615.8	
		87		69		73		76
Ferro alloys	191.2		359.4		137.0		95.9	
Czechoslovakia--Poland	5.8		--		10.1		4.0	
Soviet Union	81.6		275.1		47.0		75.2	
		45		79		41		83
Iron and steel profiles	2,033.3		2,332.4		2,967.0		2,456.4	
Czechoslovakia	456.1		210.2		290.7		66.0	
Hungary--Poland--Rumania	203.0		133.8		305.1		9.6	
Soviet Union	94.4		441.7		532.0		434.6	
		37		34		38		25
Railway rails	294.5		588.5		234.8		1,259.6	
Czechoslovakia--Soviet Union	18.7		287.2		15.1		42.0	
		6		48		6		3
Iron or steel rods	56.7		..		355.3		310.1	
Soviet Union	--		--		248.4		230.4	
						69		74
Wire	276.9		194.9		176.7		152.7	
Czechoslovakia	33.3		29.0		122.8		20.3	
Soviet Union	--		--		14.9		13.0	
		12		14		77		20
Sheet steel and iron	1,202.8		1,041.9		1,384.3		1,149.8	
Czechoslovakia--Hungary--								
Poland	248.3		248.9		291.8		283.1	
Soviet Union	346.7		155.6		387.8		200.3	
		49		38		48		32
Galvanized iron, steel	345.2		188.1		258.1		194.2	
Soviet Union	--		31.7		143.1		102.8	
				15		55		51
Tinplate	943.8		857.9		1,367.7		713.3	
Eastern Germany--Soviet								
Union	348.1		19.2		199.0		144.7	
		37		2		14		26

	1958		1959		1960		1961	
	Imports	%	Imports	%	Imports	%	Imports	%
Special steels and ingots	272.7		250.9		430.9		391.3	
Czechoslovakia	57.4		47.3		85.2		41.1	
Soviet Union	12.0		40.9		60.4		22.0	
		26		35		33		16
Tubes and pipes	1,044.9		1,894.0		3,418.4		1,129.1	
Czechoslovakia	76.9		18.0		--		56.0	
Hungary	--		264.5		112.4		215.3	
Poland	44.0		53.1		--		10.1	
Soviet Union	95.4		151.8		214.3		176.2	
		20		25		9		30
Coated tubes, pipes, joints	367.9		352.6		744.5		587.9	
Czechoslovakia	73.4		60.4		106.8		67.4	
Hungary	--		11.5		20.3		67.4	
Soviet Union	105.8		111.0		112.8		236.1	
		38		36		32		61
Iron or steel structures	1,578.6		1,116.0		1,226.8		928.9	
Czechoslovakia	246.0		451.3		101.4		84.3	
Eastern Germany	219.1		5.8		44.3		3.9	
Hungary	179.7		51.2		33.2		--	
Poland	6.0		--		177.4		12.8	
Rumania	--		62.9		--		--	
Soviet Union	--		--		--		397.7	
		36		51		28		53
Cast iron, steel tools	131.5		205.9		190.5		122.4	
Czechoslovakia	..		..		42.1		22.5	
Eastern Germany	..		..		23.0		15.7	
Poland	..		..		38.7		22.8	
Soviet Union	..		..		2.2		--	
						55		49
Machine tools (hand)	149.7		140.3		123.3		103.0	
Czechoslovakia	..		..		27.5		16.6	
Eastern Germany	..		..		23.8		11.4	
Hungary	..		..		9.3		4.8	
Poland	..		..		9.2		1.9	
Soviet Union	..		..		--		--	
						56		33
Other tools	161.6		179.1		156.8		113.3	
Czechoslovakia	..		34.7		32.5		25.5	
Eastern Germany	29.6		37.6		25.1		12.1	
Poland	..		--		--		6.4	
Soviet Union	..		--		--		--	
		18		40		33		38

Continued

111

TABLE 14 (Continued)

	1958		1959		1960		1961	
	Imports	%	Imports	%	Imports	%	Imports	%
Cable and wire rope	119.0		76.9		127.4		90.4	
Czechoslovakia--Eastern Germany--Soviet Union	--		7.4		20.0		26.5	
				9		15		29
Roller bearings	236.5		195.8		363.5		231.0	
Czechoslovakia	--		10.7		41.9		20.7	
Eastern Germany	--		--		4.4		2.7	
Soviet Union	--		17.1		41.2		39.3	
				14		24		28
Other steel manufactures	498.4		305.4		316.5		341.3	
Czechoslovakia	80.3		30.5		58.2		25.3	
Eastern Germany	5.7		6.4		25.0		8.5	
Hungary	22.2		4.9		8.9		6.5	
Poland	--		16.3		24.6		27.3	
Soviet Union	--		--		29.9		58.3	
		23		18		46		37
Aluminum sheets	167.0		203.2		326.5		203.9	
Hungary	--		46.3		63.4		5.0	
Soviet Union	55.0		24.2		58.6		59.8	
		32		34		37		32
Tin-crude	765.5		517.3		285.0		578.9	
Soviet Union	301.8		294.7		187.0		123.5	
		38		57		65		21
Machinery, Apparatus, and Electrical Material of which:								
Boilers and steam generators	363.2		194.6		197.0		59.4	
Czechoslovakia	--		--		--		--	
Eastern Germany	--		--		11.6		19.2	
						6		32
Pumps-irrigation	220.9		184.8		184.0		131.9	
Czechoslovakia	34.2		18.3		8.6		4.5	
Eastern Germany	--		29.4		25.9		26.4	
Hungary	5.5		11.2		12.8		8.8	
		18		30		25		30
Mechanical pumps	221.5		383.0		366.1		349.4	
Czechoslovakia	--		--		29.2		16.1	
						8		5

	1958 Imports	1958 %	1959 Imports	1959 %	1960 Imports	1960 %	1961 Imports	1961 %
Stationary engines	1,631.2		1,715.1		2,029.1		1,531.9	
Czechoslovakia	302.3		252.0		281.4		64.9	
Eastern Germany	162.8		191.6		284.3		216.1	
Hungary	45.1		11.0		12.7		324.9	
Poland	--		11.4		12.3		18.7	
Soviet Union	. 31.9		55.8		40.9		99.7	
		33		30		39		51
Tractors	443.6		754.2		1,142.3		606.7	
Czechoslovakia	75.0		145.8		211.4		191.8	
Eastern Germany--Rumania	42.5		57.0		56.7		19.0	
Soviet Union	201.7		352.0		446.3		219.3	
		71		73		62		70
Caterpillar tractors	294.6		493.4		1,480.5		783.2	
Eastern Germany--Soviet Union	191.5		246.1		1,057.9		599.0	
		65		48		71		75
Locomotives and tenders	763.7		433.6					
Czechoslovakia--Soviet Union	--		20.5		--		--	
				4				
Spare parts for engines	448.1		634.0		798.0		696.3	
Czechoslovakia--Hungary	--		0.3		11.8		10.2	
Eastern Germany--Soviet Union	17.6		126.5		170.7		78.1	
		4		20		22		11
Lifting apparatus	851.0		523.5		632.4		509.5	
Czechoslovakia	31.6		51.8		26.9		13.0	
Eastern Germany	--		22.0		55.7		19.1	
Hungary--Poland	10.6		32.3		--		14.3	
Soviet Union	91.9		64.0		21.0		109.2	
		16		32		16		30
Machine tools-bench	1,582.9		1,193.5		1,003.6		650.2	
Czechoslovakia	357.9		152.0		144.7		102.4	
Eastern Germany	11.0		211.0		189.9		124.3	
Bulgaria--Hungary	262.7		43.5		40.9		34.6	
Poland	114.5		53.0		44.9		17.3	
Soviet Union	268.0		124.9		195.6		55.7	
		68		49		61		51
Machines, looms-weaving	373.7		486.1		227.0		355.9	
Czechoslovakia	--		102.0		40.7		71.7	
				20		18		19

Continued

TABLE 14 (Continued)

	1958		1959		1960		1961	
	Imports	%	Imports	%	Imports	%	Imports	%
Other weaving machinery	2,031.7		3,903.0		3,915.6		2,311.9	
Czechoslovakia	62.0		27.6		35.9		146.9	
Eastern Germany	--		--		1,404.7		104.4	
Poland--Soviet Union	150.3		59.7		5.3		22.4	
		11		3		47		10
Type-setting machines	203.0		234.8		400.1		214.3	
Eastern Germany	72.3		11.4		30.6		68.9	
Soviet Union	44.4		12.4		9.8		20.5	
		55		11		10		41
Machinery and apparatus for agriculture	5,873.8		9,535.5		9,042.9		2,655.5	
Czechoslovakia	667.8		285.5		242.5		23.0	
Eastern Germany	66.4		105.7		198.2		95.8	
Bulgaria--Hungary	206.7		36.7		8.6		0.7	
Poland	--		--		64.9		4.0	
Soviet Union	66.5		81.4		337.7		179.6	
		19		3		9		11
Electric generators	1,405.4		1,244.1		1,141.9		1,052.3	
Czechoslovakia	--		86.0		123.9		106.5	
Eastern Germany	140.5		96.6		150.8		85.0	
Hungary	35.7		18.6		44.7		16.5	
Poland--Rumania	--		--		43.6		57.4	
Soviet Union	21.0		40.3		53.4		21.5	
		14		18		27		27
Accumulator parts	174.5		149.6		180.2		156.4	
Eastern Germany	21.0		44.1		40.0		22.2	
Czechoslovakia--Soviet Union	7.3		3.2		4.2		26.1	
		15		31		24		31
Lighting equipment	266.2		239.7		185.5		176.3	
Czechoslovakia	--		7.7		7.3		8.0	
Eastern Germany	--		4.2		14.1		9.0	
Hungary	77.7		125.3		49.0		120.2	
Poland	--		--		2.4		3.9	
Soviet Union	--		--		8.1		5.4	
		29		57		43		84
Electric apparatus and parts	1,634.9		2,409.5		2,697.0		1,861.9	
Czechoslovakia	--		123.4		120.7		77.0	
Eastern Germany	154.1		159.3		60.8		133.0	
Hungary	97.7		32.3		58.1		53.3	
Poland--Rumania	--		45.3		22.4		14.6	
Soviet Union	--		32.0		14.4		36.1	
		15		17		11		16

	1958		1959		1960		1961	
	Imports	%	Imports	%	Imports	%	Imports	%
Transport Equipment **of which:**								
Motor cars, trucks, buses, and chassis	4,609.9		6,216.7		4,782.3		3,772.8	
Czechoslovakia	221.2		219.7		154.6		261.5	
Eastern Germany	463.7		158.3		161.3		98.7	
Hungary	115.7		107.6		18.3		1.0	
Soviet Union	381.1		810.4		537.1		581.2	
		25		14		18		29
Spare parts	1,951.8		2,213.7		1,625.2		819.3	
Czechoslovakia	--		46.3		58.8		52.7	
Eastern Germany	--		59.2		47.0		62.5	
Hungary	--		16.8		34.9		7.7	
Soviet Union	--		526.7		175.6		79.2	
				29		18		25

Sources: U.A.R., Department of Statistics and Census, <u>Monthly Summary of Foreign</u>
<u>Trade</u>, December, 1958, 1959, and 1960 and September 1961. In each issue--
Table I, general section: "Imports by Articles of Principal Countries
whence consigned."

cotton normally accounts for 70-75 per cent of global
Egyptian exports.[10] Consequently, where her most important export product and foreign exchange earner is
concerned Egypt is quite dependent on markets in the
centrally planned economies.

The commodity structure of Egyptian imports from
the Eastern trade area is more variegated, but again,
certain product groups stand out in importance.

We have analyzed in Table 14--over the 1958-61
period--the share of the centrally planned economies
in Egyptian imports of three commodity groups: (1)
metals and manufactures, (2) machinery, apparatus, and
electrical material, and (3) transport equipment.

In this period products in the three groups accounted for about 45 per cent of total Egyptian imports.[11] Of this the Eastern trade area provided 32
per cent in 1958, 31 per cent in 1959, 34 per cent in
1960, and 35 per cent in 1961. In other words--of
capital goods which constitute close to one half of
global Egyptian imports--the centrally planned economies annually provided for more than one third, moreover, this share has been slowly increasing.

There is, of course, a very natural explanation
for this. Most deliveries of a "capital goods nature"
are intended for use in Soviet and Eastern European-
financed development projects, and indeed, in product
categories that can be directly connected with financial and technical assistance activities (i.e., tractors, earthmovers, dambuilding-equipment, etc.), imports from the centrally planned economies are predominant. The Eastern trade area, by the end of 1961,
accounted for more than two thirds of global Egyptian
imports of tractors and earthmoving equipment, machine
tools, stationary engines, power aggregates, and iron
and steel structures. Furthermore, in all these product groups, the share of the centrally planned economies increased over the period.

By and large, the Soviet Union has provided 60
per cent of Egyptian capital goods imports from the

TABLE 15

EGYPT (U.A.R.)

Commodity Structure of Trade with the Soviet Union

Aggregate Figures, 1960-63

(U.S.$ thousand imports and exports f.o.b. unless otherwise indicated)

Commodity Group	Unit	Imports 1960-63 Quantity	Value
Total Imports	$ Mill.	-	133.8
Machinery and Equipment--Total of which:	$ Mill.		83.0
Machine tools and spare parts	Units	133	435.0
Forging and pressing equipment	-	-	14.5
Power equipment	-	-	952.0
Mobile electric stations	Units	105	265.0
Stationary Diesels	Units	1,729	333.0
Stationary Diesel generators	Sets	2	22.0
Spare parts for power equipment	-	-	133.0
Electro-technical equipment	-	-	116.0
Small-capacity electric motors	Units	350	8.0
Electric motors, 1-100 kw.	Units	19	17.0
Synchronized generators	Units	52	26.0
Alkaline accumulators	Units	1,302	18.0
Oil drilling equipment	-	-	178.5
Cranes	Units	17	234.5
Hoisting machines	Units	33	124.5
Equipment for light industry	-	-	16.5
Equipment for chemical, cellulose, building, and other industries	-	-	5,476.0
Excavators, road-building equipment	-	-	5,370.0
Mobile graders	Units	62	737.0
Bulldozers	Units	87	1,200.0
Scrapers	Units	189	2,681.0
Road rollers	Units	18	113.5
Asphalt layers	Units	12	149.0
Spare parts for excavators	-	-	6.6
Spare parts for road building machines	-	-	421.5
Pump and compressor equipment	-	-	36.5
Pumps	Units	31	4.5
Compressors	Units	4	19.0
Spare parts for compressor equipment	-	-	13.5
Printing equipment	-	-	5.5
Cinema apparatus	-	-	2.2
Equipment and materials for projects	-	-	43,909.0
Appliances	-	-	218.0
Medical equipment	-	-	70.0

Continued

117

TABLE 15 (Continued)

Commodity Group	Imports 1960-63		
	Unit	Quantity	Value
Rolling friction bearings	1,000 units	248	352.0
Instruments	-	-	172.0
Tractors and agricultural machinery	-	-	2,087.0
Tractors	Units	502	1,000.0
Spare parts for tractors	-	-	998.0
Silo cutters	Units	15	5.5
Transport and garage equipment	-	-	22,278.0
Heavy motor vehicles	Units	4,463	16,135.0
Light motor vehicles	Units	731	1,163.0
Buses	Units	98	268.6
Trailers	Units	339	700.0
Spare parts for vehicles	-	-	1,895.5
Special vehicles	Units	330	2,392.0
Aircraft, etc.	-	-	2,162.0
Tires	1,000 units	1.1	100.0
Crude Materials--Inedible			
of which:			
Coal	1,000 tons	15	195.0
Coke	1,000 tons	18	298.5
Crude oil	1,000 tons	926.8	11,338.0
Petroleum products	1,000 tons	47.7	1,695.0
Gasoline	1,000 tons	37.7	1,990.0
Diesel fuel	1,000 tons	4.7	129.0
Mazut	1,000 tons	3.1	4.6
Paraffin	1,000 tons	0	7.7
Cellulose	1,000 tons	4.5	627.0
Manufactured Goods			
of which:			
Ferrous metals	-	-	3,945.0
Cast iron	1,000 tons	21	1,111.0
Iron castings	1,000 tons	1.4	183.0
Rolled ferrous metals	1,000 tons	13.7	1,593.0
Tin plate	1,000 tons	0.9	207.0
Gas pipes	1,000 tons	1.6	293.0
Metal products	-	-	105.0
Wire	tons	597	67.0
Nonferrous metals	-	-	2,397.0
Chemicals--Total	-	-	537.0
of which:			
Caustic soda	1,000 tons	1.5	67.1
Soda ash	1,000 tons	1	25.3
Sodium bichromate	tons	62	13.5
Naphthalene	tons	21	2.2
Resin	tons	530	108.0
Aniline salt	tons	137	36.5

Commodity Group	Imports 1960-63		
	Unit	Quantity	Value
Chemicals (Cont'd)			
Hydrogen peroxide	tons	139	33.5
Dyes, varnishes, and tanning agents	-	-	186.0
Coal and dyes	tons	116	127.0
Stains and varnishes	-	-	45.1
Dry bleaches	tons	46	10.0
Other dry dyes	tons	19	4.5
Miscellaneous Manufactured Articles			
of which:			
Cutlery	-	-	27.5
Medical supplies	-	-	166.0
Cultural and household goods	-	-	259.0
Household machines and appliances	-	-	123.2
Household sewing machines	Units	5	..
Household clocks	1,000 units	16.4	76.0
Cameras	1,000 units	2.4	31.0
Radio receivers	Units	503	10.5
Incandescent electric lamps	1,000 units	49	16.5
Printed matter	-	-	39.0
Motion pictures	-	-	715
Office equipment and drawing machines	-	-	1.5

Commodity Group	Exports 1960-63		
	Unit	Quantity	Value
Total Exports	million		123
of which:	rubles		
Gasoline for vehicles	1,000 tons	69.9	1,215.0
Raw cotton	1,000 tons	99.5	89,970.0
Cotton thread	1,000 tons	10.6	17,893.0
Groundnuts	1,000 tons	0.4	80.0
Rice	1,000 tons	84.2	9,508.0
Fresh vegetables	1,000 tons	8.2	752.4
Oranges	tons	8,200	1,483.0
Cotton fibers	1,000 metric	662	240.0
Printed matter	-	-	5.5
Motion pictures	-	-	35.0

Sources: Section on Egypt (U.A.R.) in Vneshnyaya Torgovlya Soyuza SSSR za 1963 god. (Moscow: Vneshtorgizdat, 1964).

planned economies. This hangs together with the much
larger development effort the U.S.S.R. is making in
Egypt, and in examining imports from this country
separately, the extent of Soviet aid becomes clear
(as shown in Table 15).

    In the period 1960-63, the Soviet Union exported
a total of $133.8 million worth of commodities of all
categories to Egypt. Of this, $83 million, or about
two thirds, consisted of machinery and equipment.
If we isolate from this the following items: excavators and road-building equipment--$5.37 million;
equipment for cellulose, chemical, building, and other
industries--$5.47 million; and equipment for materials
and projects--$48.29 million, we arrive at a total of
$59.13 million. This amounts to 44 per cent of total
Egyptian imports from the Soviet Union. In other
words, close to one half of all Soviet exports to
Egypt were, in the 1960-63 period, destined for use
in Soviet-financed development projects in the Arab
Republic.

    The importance of the Eastern trade area to the
future development of Egyptian trade is somewhat difficult to foresee. Surely, its significance as a
supplier of capital goods can be expected to be maintained at present levels, and even increase. On a
conservative basis it can be estimated that by mid-
1967, about 35 per cent of all committed Soviet Bloc
development aid to Egypt had been delivered.[12] Utilization of the remaining credits will certainly cause
further increases in imports of capital equipment from
the centrally planned economies.

    Egyptian deliveries to the Eastern group appear
more uncertain, in particular it is questionable
whether the Soviet Union is willing to maintain her
presently high--but declining--rate of cotton purchases. The U.S.S.R. recently announced large planned
increases in her own production of this commodity, as
well as the development of synthetic fibers. While
she may desire, for political reasons, to continue to
purchase some Egyptian long-staple cotton, from a
commercial point of view this trade flow does not appear entirely justified, particularly as the Soviet
Union at present is exporting more cotton than she is
importing.

Commodity exchange with the Eastern European
countries is another matter. This area is not a
large indigenous producer of cotton, and may--for
reasons of comparative costs and a desire for economic independence from the Soviet Union--want to
shift some cotton imports from this source to larger
purchases from the developing world. Coupled with
this is the fact that the last three years have seen
commitments of new, substantial credits from Eastern
Europe to Egypt, and the far more complementary trade
flows between the two areas should indicate a maintenance, if not an increase in the commodity exchange
both ways. Moreover, Eastern Europe's imports of
Egyptian citrus fruits can be expected to increase
much above present levels, particularly as dietary
standards in the planned economies are rising. If
the principle of autofinancing is applied when planning Soviet Bloc development projects in the Arab Republic, we may see a proportionately larger share of
Egyptian exports of nontextile crops, semi-manufac-
tures, and possibly some consumer goods as well.

FINANCIAL AND TECHNICAL ASSISTANCE

By mid-1967, Egypt had received a total of
$1.404 million worth of development aid from the
centrally planned economies, of which 80 per cent
were credits extended by the Soviet Union. If we
compare value of committed credits to commodity exchange, the former has, in fact, amounted to 50 to
60 per cent of volume of turnover of trade between
Egypt and the Soviet Bloc in the period 1958-66. An
even better idea of the magnitude of the credits committed may be had by relating these to estimates of
Egyptian national income.

On the basis of IMF figures we have calculated
the aggregate national income of Egypt, in the 1958-
64 period, at $26.9 billion, or an average of $3.8
billion per year.[13] In the same period commitments
of Soviet and Eastern European financial and technical assistance amounted to $1.2 billion--or an
average of $175 million annually. In other words--
committed credits from the Soviet Bloc accounted for
4.5 per cent of the Egyptian national income for each
year of the period mentioned.

Although some minor loans were accorded in the
mid-1950's, the massive "program" of financial and
technical aid to Egypt first got under way with the
signature of the January, 1958, agreement with the
Soviet Union on general economic and technical cooperation. This, the first accord of a technical
assistance nature between any country in Africa and
the Eastern trade area, was comprehensive and all-
embracing in its form, for it included all three conventional forms of aid: (1) deliveries of equipment,
(2) training of professionally skilled workers, and
(3) provision for a large credit.

Specifically, the Soviet Union was to give Egypt
economic and technical assistance in the fields of
mining and oil prospecting, and in the construction
of metallurgical, machine tools, and electrical industries. She would also erect factories for the
processing of food and for the production of pharmaceutical products. Skilled workers would undergo
training both in the Soviet Union, and locally. For
the realization of all these undertakings Egypt was
granted a credit of $175 million, repayable over
twelve years at the usual 2.5 per cent rate of interest.[14] Under this agreement a protocol was signed
in April, 1958, providing for the construction of
seventeen industrial undertakings, and for the establishment of ten educational centers for industry.

As this was the first Soviet loan project to
Egypt, some time was required for planning and preparation, and actual execution did not get under way
until late 1960. By 1963, however, the Soviet Union
had completed, and turned over to Egypt: six metallurgical and six machine-building plants, eight oil
and chemical plants, seven food processing centers
and textile mills, and several other enterprises in
the light industry sector.[15] In spite of this activity, however, it was estimated that by the end of
1962, Egypt had drawn only $56 million of the $175
million credit.[16]

Earlier, in 1957, the Soviet Union had started
the construction of Egypt's first atomic reactor.
This was erected at Inshas near Cairo, and was put

into trial operation on July 27, 1961.[17] It was
later reported that the reactor had begun full-
capacity operation and was ready for the development
of radio-active isotopes.[18]

New contracts under the 1958 agreement were
signed in Cairo in March, 1962. These provided for
Soviet aid in the construction and commissioning of
three rolled-steel mills at the Helwan metallurgical
works. Each of these three mills was scheduled to be
highly automated in all processes, and to produce
200,000 tons of rolled metal a year--more than the
then total annual production of the U.A.R.[19] The
first mill was in operation in late 1964, while work
on the remaining two is in progress. Among other
projects financed by the 1958 credit, we might mention the opening near Cairo on July 3, 1963, of a
factory to produce electrodes for welding purposes.[20]

On a different tangent, an agreement on Egyptian-
Soviet cooperation in the fishing industry was signed
in Cairo, February 29, 1964.[21] This provides for an
exchange of experience in fishing techniques and for
joint research into the fishery resources of the Red
Sea and the North Indian Ocean. To complement this,
the Soviet Union would provide technical assistance
for the operation of a modern fishing industry and
help in the training of the U.A.R. personnel. For
this purpose the Soviet Union would send research
and depot vessels to the Red Sea.[22]

These projects, however, all part of the earlier
phase of Soviet financial and technical assistance to
Egypt, pale under the shadow of the most impressive
of them all: the construction of the High Dam at
Aswan. This is not only the most ambitious undertaking of any centrally planned economy in the developing world, but it is also the only time the
Soviet Union has involved itself in financing and in
taking the responsibility for completing a work which
will make its impact felt, not only on one sector,
but on the entire economy of the recipient country.
Because of the nature and magnitude of the construction of the High Dam complex at Aswan, it probably
warrants a closer description here.

We are not exaggerating in stating that the life
or death of Egypt depends on the waters of the Nile.
Of the nearly 40 million people who live in its basin,
27 million live within the frontiers of Egypt. Over
90 per cent of these 27 million Egyptians have their
homes along the banks of the river.

At the end of the 18th century the population
of Egypt numbered between 2-1/2 and 3 million. By
the middle of the 19th century it had risen to 3-3/4
million. Since then it has grown rapidly and is now
increasing at an alarming rate. In the 50 years end-
ing in 1952 Egypt's population had actually doubled,
while the national income increased by only 17 per
cent. In order to arrest this relatively declining
national income, one would have to maintain balanced
growth between population and production.[23]

The greatest deterrent to productive growth,
however, has been the lack of agricultural expansion
in the Nile Valley--based on a critical shortage of
water. For many centuries, the Egyptian Government,
using basin irrigation techniques, was able to trap
sufficient flood waters for the fellaheen to culti-
vate their single crops annually. But in the 19th
century, the rapid increase in population made further utilization of the Nile waters necessary. During
the rule of Mohammed Ali, the first of several major
barrages was constructed, and extensive irrigation
canals permitted parts of Egypt's arable land to be
placed under cultivation. Later--under British super-
vision--the system of perennial cultivation was advanced further, but little new land was reclaimed because minimum water requirements could not be guaran-
teed.[24]

While barrages and a dam constructed at Aswan
in 1902 permitted some additional cultivation during
spring and summer months, the fundamental problem of
Nile water control remained unsolved. There are great
seasonal and annual fluctuations in the river's discharge. On occasion, the total annual discharge has
been three times the river volume during an abnormally
low year, while the daily discharge during the spring
months averages about one fifteenth of the discharge

at flood peak. Although the annual mean flow of the
Nile would yield enough irrigation water to support
substantial agricultural expansion, the irregularity
of the Nile's discharge and the absence of adequate
storage facilities have--to date--made this a theo-
retical calculation. Instead, during years of a low
Nile, land under cultivation must be severely restricted, while in years of high flood great quantities of silt-laden water flow into the Mediterranean.[25]

Egypt has long considered the question of Nile
water to be of vital political and economic importance.
The construction of the High Dam (Sadd el Aali)--as
proposed in 1954--was seen as a broad approach to
solving the problem of supplying a fast-growing population with sufficient food, and industry with abundant
power. It was also conceived as a bold, direct method
for controlling Nile water resources for agricultural
expansion, protection against floods, improvement of
irrigation and draining conditions, as well as for the
development of fishery resources and recreational facilities.

The proposed dam was to be constructed five miles
south of the present dam, and its dimensions call for
the use of superlatives. As the Egyptians conceived
it, the barrage was to be a huge edifice; it was claimed
that the volume of materials required for its completion
would be seventeen times that of the Great Pyramid.[26]
It was to reach 110 meters (364 feet) above the river
bed and extend about 5,000 meters (2.6 miles) in length.
Seven diversion tunnels in the east bank were to carry
the river's normal flow. Another four tunnels, drilled
through the west bank were to lead to an extensive
hydroelectric station. Without doubt, however, the
most impressive feature of the High Dam was the size
of its proposed reservoir. According to tentative estimates, upwards of 130 billion cubic meters could be
stored, with the revervoir extending 150 kilometers
inside the Sudanese border. In comparison, the capacity
of the existing Aswan Dam is little more than 5 billion
cubic meters.[27]

That this project was going to be costly was beyond doubt. In 1956, total outlays were estimated at

$1.3 billion, of which Egypt would require $400 million in external financing. The early plans called for the country to put up $900 million of its own.[28]

The history of how this financing became a major foreign policy issue has been dealt with elsewhere, and only the main lines need to be recapitulated here. The loans necessary for the project were originally to be extended by a United States-World Bank consortium. This offer was, upon the instigation of Secretary Dulles, withdrawn in 1956, as he felt Egypt's commitments to purchase arms from Czechoslovakia, precluded its covering the loan. Angered by this withdrawal, Egypt nationalized the Suez Canal for the ostensible reason of having the canal dues pay for the external financing of the dam project. This, in turn, led to the abortive United Kingdom-French-Israeli invasion of Egypt in October-November, 1956.[29]

At this point, the Soviet Union entered the picture with a tentative offer of financial assistance for the construction costs. This was later presented to Egypt as a firm commitment, and on January 29, 1958, an agreement was signed between Egypt and the Soviet Union on the construction of the first stage of the Aswan High Dam. On December 27 of the same year, the Soviet Union extended a $100 million loan to cover part of the costs.[30] One and a half years later, in August, 1960, a new agreement was signed in Moscow, stating the U.S.S.R.'s intention to carry out the second and final stage of the dam construction as well.[3] For this purpose, Egypt was accorded a new loan of $225 million. These two loans were to be repaid in accordance with current trade and payments agreements, i.e., by deliveries of Egyptian traditional export commodities.

Shortly after the conclusion of the first Aswan agreement, the Russians sent down a technical mission, mainly composed of experts who had been responsible for the giant dam-building projects on the Volga, and new plans for construction were drawn up. These were of a relatively simpler nature than those proposed to the United States-World Bank consortium, and promised to reduce the time of construction as well as to cut

building costs by nearly 20 per cent. These reduc-
tions were to be achieved by following a Soviet pro-
posal to consolidate the seven originally proposed
diversion tunnels into one open-air canal, instead
of building underground constructions.[32]

The present dam design follows the conventional
practice outlined above. Water will be passed from
the reservoirs through an open diversion canal 1,835
meters long, 60 to 110 meters wide, and 100 meters
deep, cut through solid rock forming the East Nile
bank. In the part of the canal where it crosses the
main dam, a virgin plug will be left, in which six
control tunnels with iron service gates will be provided.[33]

After some initial delays, this work--which comprises the first stage of the Aswan High Dam project--
got under way in 1960. Almost immediately the Soviet
engineers were faced with equipment problems, mainly
due to faulty planning. Their plans called for the
use of Soviet-built earthmovers and excavators,
powered by electric motors with current generated by
the old Aswan Dam. The underlying principle here was
to save on Diesel fuel and use the cheaper local electricity for power generating purposes. There was, however, one essential flaw in the Soviet projections.
They neglected to supply their machinery with proper
intercoolers to make up for the extreme heat at Aswan,
which can reach 40 to 45° centigrade (ca. 110° F.) in
the shade on really hot days, and which seldom drops
below 30° centigrade (ca. 90° F.). This soon caused
the Soviet equipment to collapse. Thus, for several
months the work came to a complete standstill. At
this point the Egyptians called in a team of Swedish
consultant engineers. Plans were redrawn, new heavy
equipment provided, and substantial Soviet apparatus
was modified. Revised cost estimates necessitated
a further loan of $170 million for the completion of
the first stage; this was granted in the summer of
1962.[34]

In spite of pessimistic prognostics to the contrary, work progressed satisfactorily after this. This
is not to say that relations between Egyptians and

Soviet engineers have been frictionless. The former
repeatedly remarked on the apparent inelasticity of
Soviet construction planning, whereas the Soviets, on
their side, bitterly complained about Egyptian lazi-
ness and lack of motivation. A Russian journalist,
Kondrashov, in an article in Sovremennyy Vostok, made
some interesting observations in this context when he note

> . . . their (the Egyptians) refusal to attend
> building-instruction courses arranged for them,
> their indecent haste to lay down tools at the
> end of the shift, and the inconsistency and
> confusion which followed when an Arab subcon-
> tractor suddenly left to take up more lucra-
> tive work elsewhere.[35]

Additionally, the Russians on repeated occasions,
complained about Egypt's insufficient appreciation for
the Soviet contribution and about the inadequate publicity given to it in the Egyptian press.[36]

However, bickerings of this nature are perhaps
unavoidable on any project of such magnitude, and they
did not prevent the Soviet engineers,[37] and the Arab
contractors from finishing the first stage on schedule,
and in time for Mr. Khrushchev to push the button on
May 14, 1964, and cause the explosion that opened the
diversionary canal.[38]

The second stage of the Aswan project will mainly
comprise the construction of the main dam and the power
plant. This is designed for the ultimate installation
of twelve main generating units, with an output of 10
billion kilowatts.[39]

Any project of this scope will necessarily have
repercussions on all aspects of the national economy.
It is difficult, at this point, to foresee the end result, but it has been estimated that, when fully completed, the High Dam at Aswan will: (1) supply enough
irrigation water to develop 1.9 million acres, thereby
increasing the present area of crop-growing land by
about 25 per cent; (2) meet the full irrigation needs
of existing land and new development areas even in
years when the river is at its lowest; (3) increase

rice-growing areas to one million acres per year. In
past years the sizes of these areas have varied from
373,000 acres (1953) to 875,000 acres (1947); (4) create improved water drainage conditions as the result
of a lower and more stable water table, and a more even
distribution of water in the river and the irrigation
canals throughout the year; (5) put an end to fluctuations in the flow and level of water in the river and
canals which today interfere with navigation. Once
water levels become more or less stabilized as a result of the High Dam, tonnage carried by inland water-
ways is expected to increase by 20 to 30 per cent; (6)
be a major step toward full utilization of the vast potential energy in the waters of the Nile. When completed in 1971, the power station at Aswan will generate
a potential 9 billion kilowatts. By 1972, when more
water has been accumulated in the reservoir, power production should reach a maximum capacity of 10 billion
kilowatts per year.[40] This is an increase of five times
the present level of hydroelectric power production, an
increase which will facilitate the creation of numerous
new plants and the expansion of present industries.

It has been estimated that by the early 1970's--
when the dam will be fully operative--the sum of benefits from the project will annually increase Egypt's
national income by 45 per cent. If this estimate becomes a reality, the dam will pay for itself in two
years.[41]

The dam does have certain disadvantages, however.
There is no absolute certainty, for example, that it
will prevent the highest floods from wrecking havoc;
and strategically, of course, it presents an ideal tar-
get to potential enemies who, by aerial bombing, could
wash away the country. Other disadvantages would include: the possible flooding of some inhabited areas,
particularly in the Sudan; the high loss through evap-
oration in this mid-desert area, perhaps 10 billion
cubic meters a year, or almost double the capacity of
the present Aswan Dam; the fact that the huge lake will
act as a desilting basin, depriving the country of its
annual supply of enriching silt and gradually filling
the reservoir; and the possible erosional effects the
clarified water may come to have.[42]

In spite of these factors there can be no doubt
that the benefits the High Dam will bring to the
Egyptian people will by far outweigh the few disadvantages above. Moreover, these may be eliminated by
new discoveries and the passage of time. Not surprisingly, the huge edifice--judging from the effort expended in its construction--has become a symbol of
Egypt's progress along the road to economic development. The High Dam, however, is no absolute solution
to Egypt's growth problems; as such, it can only be
considered a stop-gap measure. True, the dam will increase radically the country's acreage under cultivation, but if the population continues to grow at its
present rate of 2.8 per cent per year, only 15 to 20
years will be needed to obliterate the gains made from
the dam. So, for all its impressive size, the Aswan
High Dam will rank with the Bonneville and Hoover Dams
in the United States and the Kariba Dam across the
Zambesi, among the world's largest, for all its dimensions; the scheme must be seen in the context of Egypt's
most complicated development problem--its inexorable
population pressure.

Although Soviet-financed projects continue to
dominate Egyptian development aid received from the
centrally planned economies, it is by no means the only
member of the Eastern trade area to be active in Egypt.
Indeed, the United Arab Republic has financial and technical assistance agreements with every Eastern European
country but Rumania. Of this latter group, development
aid from Czechoslovakia has--so far--played the largest
role, with her share of credits amounting to 17 per cent
of total financial assistance to Egypt from the centrall
planned economies.[43] These $241 million have been uti-
lized for a multitude of purposes. By 1962, Czechoslovakia claimed she had put at least thirty-five complete
industrial installations in operation.[44] During 1959
and 1960 alone, she turned over to the Egyptians power
plants, sugar refineries, cement works, refrigerating
equipment,and trolley buses.[45] Of the thirty-five plant
mentioned above, we find ceramics, clay, footwear, rubbe
bicycle, and radio factories; and in the capital goods
field--a rolling mill for nonferrous metals and a petroleum refinery.[46] This list is by no means exhaustive,
but mention must be made at least to three of the most

important Czechoslovak projects in Egypt, all scheduled for completion in 1966: two crude petroleum refineries, at Alexandria and Suez, each of which has
an annual capacity of one million tons; and a water
purification system for the city of Cairo, which is
to have a capacity of 300,000 cubic meters of puri-
fied water per day.[47] Added to this, Czechoslovakia's
contribution becomes manifest when we mention that in
1963 she imported some 40 per cent of Egyptian cotton
exports to European spinning mills, and has, for the
past eight years, been Egypt's most significant Eastern European customer, accounting for--on the average--
8 to 11 per cent of Egypt's turnover of foreign trade.[48]

     Relatively little aid has been extended by Hungary
and Poland, and total credits committed by these two
countries do not amount to more than $49 million, or a
mere 3.5 per cent of total development assistance to
Egypt from the centrally planned economies. Information
on the utilization of these credits is very scarce, but
presumably they have financed a few purely commercial undertakings in the small industry field.

     Of greater significance are the two most recent
credit commitments from the Eastern trade area: $277
million from the Soviet Union in May, 1964,[49] and $100
million from Eastern Germany in March, 1965.[50] These
loans are important not only because of their size, but
more so because of the stated intentions of the donors
to allow the credits to be utilized within the framework
of Egypt's emergency plan which is to run from 1967 to
the end of this decade. This indicates a change in Soviet Bloc foreign aid policy--turning away from the
sporadic granting of individual credits--to a coordination of these with the national economic planning in
the recipient country. For a country like Egypt, which
is pursuing its economic and social development by means
of long-range industrialization plans this kind of assurance is very valuable, since it is made before the period
of plan-execution and can thus be a consideration in the
financial planning which must precede any practical undertaking.

CULTURAL AND EDUCATIONAL RELATIONS

To complement advances made in trade and financial and technical aid, the U.A.R. has for several years had a program of cultural exchange with most countries in the Eastern trade area. This has perhaps not been as meaningful to Egypt as it has to many other African countries--mainly because she possesses locally a very adequate educational system that well provides for her needs. Nevertheless, some exchange has taken place, and the Egyptian Minister of Education is quoted as saying that, in the academic year 1963-64, sixty-two Soviet professors worked in Egyptian universities, and that the U.A.R. each year will send more than 200 students and postgraduates for specialist training in the U.S.S.R.[51] This program has been supplemented by technical training at the Aswan High Dam, at the Helwan steel plants and at shipyards in Alexandria.[52] Other centrally planned economies participate in cultural and educational exchange programs as well. In recent years about 150 Egyptian students have attended universities and other institutions of higher learning in Eastern Europe, mostly in Czechoslovakia and in Eastern Germany.[53] An interesting feature here is the program which the Státní Banka Československa has been conducting for Egyptian bank officers in the field of banking organization and techniques. Higher officials of this bank have visited Egypt where they have assisted in solving fundamental issues regarding the organization of financial and credit systems, and carrying out analyses of capital investments and financial planning.[54]

After more than a decade of experience, it is time to ask the question: What has been the impact of relations with the Soviet Bloc on Egyptian economic development? This cannot, of course, be answered concretely. What we must confine ourselves to are educated calculations and presumptions, but even on this basis it should be possible to outline some effects of development efforts the centrally planned economies, and particularly the Soviet Union, have devoted to the Egyptian economy.

It was mentioned that the major part of Soviet
Bloc financial and technical assistance to the Arab
Republic was contributed from 1958 to the present.
In this period, Egypt completed one development program and started on a second. It is necessary that
we briefly outline these, for only in this perspective can the Soviet Bloc contribution be clearly evaluated.

By the time of the military takeover in 1952,
Egypt had a limited industrial capacity. In fact,
investments in this sector, in 1952, did not exceed
12 per cent of total national investments and the
contribution of industry to national income accounted
for merely 10 per cent.[55] The country did, however,
have an industrial capacity for exceeding these levels,
and compared to other African countries, she possessed
an excellent infrastructure and an adequate cadre of
trained technicians and managers. To utilize this
capacity an industrialization program was drawn up in
1958, which was later absorbed into the First Egyptian
Development Plan, 1960-65.

For this plan period, total investments of $2.4
billion were envisaged. This would finance altogether
1,440 projects in mining, chemical, engineering, food,
and textile industries.[56] To provide for the foreign
exchange component of this program the U.A.R. Government received inter alia the $175 million loan from the
Soviet Union and $105 million from other centrally
planned economies.[57] Together, these loans financed
12 per cent of total costs of the first development
program (Aswan project excluded).

The sectoral allocations of these loans are more
difficult to establish in terms of totals and percentages. We have already mentioned some results. The
Soviet-built rolled-steel mills at Helwan will just
about double the Egyptian strip and sheet-steel output and raise this to a comparable level of steel production in the smaller European countries. The construction of a coking battery of chemicals works, also
at Helwan, will substantially increase Egypt's production of much-needed chemical fertilizers and the

country will, by the end of this decade, fully satisfy all local needs for nitrogenous and phosphatic
fertilizers,[58] about 50 per cent of which will be produced in Soviet Bloc-financed plants.

Apart from these larger projects the centrally
planned economies have participated in the construction of a number of smaller ones. Egyptian authorities planned 115 projects in the food industry. We
estimate that countries of the Eastern trade area
financed and developed at least 20 of these. In
the chemical industry sector 80 projects were planned,
of which the U.S.S.R. alone built 5 plants. In the
textile industry 70 projects were planned, the centrally planned economies executed no less than 10.
In the building material industry 5 enterprises were
projected, one of which--a cement plant--was put up
by the Soviet Union. The Soviet Bloc countries develope
7 of the 40 training centers which were foreseen.[59]
By 1970, almost all Egyptian television sets and one
half of the country's output of transistor radios will
be produced in Soviet-financed and -built factories.[60]
Additionally, the Soviet Union has erected transformer
stations throughout the country, planned model farms,
land reclamation works, and hydroelectric power trans-
fer lines.[61]

Partly as a result of this activity the value of
Egyptian industrial production more than doubled from
1958 to 1964, increasing from $722 million to $3.2
billion, and the share of the industrial sector of
Egyptian national income increased by about 50 per
cent. We can illustrate this growth even better by
pointing to some selected figures for 1958 and for
1964 (as shown on Tables 16 and 17).

What is interesting here is that pronounced
growth has been experienced in all sectors where the
centrally planned economies have been active. General
manufacturing has gone up by more than 250 per cent
and electric power output by some 350 per cent. Moreover, in this section we can expect a further wholesale growth with the completion of the Aswan project.

TABLE 16

EGYPT (U.A.R.)

Growth of Employment and of Industrial Output, 1958 and 1964

Index numbers: 1958 = 100

Industrial Sections	Employment		Industrial Output	
	1958	1964	1958	1964
General growth (excluding agriculture)	100	103	100	259
Mining	..	..	100	145
Manufacturing (total)	100	122	100	261
Food industries	..	..	100	160
Textile industries (mainly cotton)	..	..	100	170
Chemical and petroleum products industries	..	..	100	270
Basic metals and engineering industries	..	..	100	445
Electric power output	..	..	100	363

Sources: U.N., Statistical Yearbook, 1964, U.N., ECA, Industrial Development in the United Arab Republic (E/CN.14/AS/I/1/1) September 22, 1965, Idem., Engineering Products in the U.A.R. (E/CN.14/AS/II/2/h/1) (Addis Ababa: October 6, 1965).

TABLE 17

EGYPT (U.A.R.)

Growth in Number of New Plants, and
of Capital Investment in Industry
1958 and 1964

Industrial Sections	Number of New Projects		New Capital Investment U.S.$ million	
	1958	1964	1958	1964
Petroleum projects	3	22	21.2	224.9
Mining industry	9	95	0.9	242.5
Manufacturing industries:				
Food industry	24	339	5.7	362.5
Chemical industry	16	214	20.7	532.7
Metallurgical industry	1	32	80.1	242.0
Engineering industry	30	319	0.9	348.9
Textile industry	17	187	62.2	241.3
Training centers for industry	5	40	0.7	17.0
Total	105	1,248	192.4	2,211.8

Sources: See Table 16.

The increase in the number of new plants has
been equally noticeable, and pronounced growth can
be seen in food, chemical, engineering, and diverse
textile industries as well.

It is, of course, impossible to pinpoint the
precise Soviet Bloc contribution to this development,
but it is notable that accelerated economic growth in
Egypt first started in 1958, i.e., the year after the
centrally planned economies began in earnest to direct
their financial and technical assistance efforts to
the United Arab Republic.

It might well be asked at this point: What is
to be the future course of economic relations between
Egypt and the Eastern trade area? From agreements
already entered into it seems clear that ties fastened
are likely to be further solidified in the years to
come. Egypt did not fall victim to the general cessation of Soviet Bloc foreign aid commitments in late
1961, although trade flows between the two groups have
shown a slightly declining trend. True, the centrally
planned economies may here have been caught up in what
has been termed as a "quicksand" effect,[62] i.e., once
a program of trade and aid has begun, it is not easy
to withdraw. The experience of the past two years
has shown that Egypt has had severe balance of payments problems, has been unable to repay existing
debts, and has been in dire need of additional funds.[63]
In order not to jeopardize the positive economic and
political effects of development aid already committed,
the Soviet Union may have been forced by circumstances
to grant the May, 1964, credit.

All these factors notwithstanding, commodity repayments on the Aswan High Dam credits alone should
ensure that the Soviet Union will continue to remain
Egypt's most important foreign trade partner well into the next decade. The position of the Eastern European centrally planned economies is more unclear.
Surely--Czechoslovakia--by virtue of credits already
extended will continue to receive Egyptian export commodities, probably at the present rate; but significant new credits from that country or, for that matter,
from Hungary and Poland as well, are unlikely. What

remains then is Eastern Germany with which Egypt will
probably greatly expand her trade relations in the
coming five-year period. This seems likely, not only
because the credits will be repaid in commodity exports, but also because Eastern Germany--perhaps more
so than many other countries in the Soviet Bloc--is
eminently suited to absorb Egyptian exports of cotton,
textiles and, above all, of citrus fruits. It is perhaps significant here that in the period under review
Eastern Germany has clearly been Egypt's second largest
customer in Eastern Europe, accounting for an average
of 6-7 per cent of Egypt's turnover of foreign trade.
The recent $100 million credit promises to stabilize
and increase these relations.

We are here entering the field of conjecture, but
a reasonable assumption might be that the era of large
credits to Egypt from the centrally planned economies
is over. An indication of this may be taken from recent Soviet comments on the economic difficulties of
the "third world," and a study by Yu. M. Osipov em-
phasizes some of the Soviet Bloc reservations here.[64]
It appears that, particularly the Soviet Union, is
growing increasingly aware of the problems Egypt has
encountered in servicing her foreign debt and that the
centrally planned economies in general are becoming
sceptical about the Egyptian "foreign aid absorption
capacity."

The significance of these reservations--and where
they have portent for the future of Egyptian-Soviet
Bloc relations--lies in the acknowledgment of the reality of these problems.

NOTES TO CHAPTER 4

1. See for example OECD, <u>The Flow of Financial
Resources to Less-Developed Countries, 1956-63</u>, p. 56,
and Table V-3, p. 172.

2. U.S. Department of Commerce, <u>Value Series, 1954-65</u>,
and see also above, Chapter 3, Table 8, p. 80.

3. Speech by former Premier Khrushchev, reported in _Pravda_, May 11, 1964.

4. _Ibid_.

5. Egypt's population grows at the rate of 2.81 per cent per year.

6. IMF, _International Financial Statistics Supplement to 1964/65 Totals_, pp. 240-41.

7. _Ibid_., September, 1965, pp. 288-91.

8. U.N., ECA, _Industrial Growth in Africa_, Table 11, p. 22.

9. U.A.R. Department of Statistics and Census, _Monthly Summary of Foreign Trade_, December, 1958, 1959, 1960, and September, 1961, December, 1962, 1963, and 1964. In each issue, Table II--General Section: "Exports of Produce and Manufactures by Articles and Principal Countries."

10. U.A.R., _Monthly Summary of Foreign Trade_, _op. cit_., and U.N., _Yearbook of International Trade Statistics, 1961_ and _1964_.

11. Up to early 1962 Egypt did not classify her foreign trade statistics according to SITC. The three groups mentioned would correspond to SITC Sections 6 and 7. From January, 1962, onward, Egypt discontinued any effective classification of trade by destination or origin.

12. See Chapter 9, pp. 263-74.

13. IMF, _International Financial Statistics_, Vol. 18, No. 9 (September, 1965), pp. 290-91.

14. _Pravda_, January 30, 1958.

15. _Pravda_, April 28, 1963, and _Trud_, March 1, 1964.

16. IMF, Balance of Payments Yearbook, 1964, Section on U.A.R., p. 4.

17. Trud, July 29, 1961.

18. Izvestiya, October 10, 1961.

19. Egyptian Gazette, January 4, 1967.

20. Pravda, July 3, 1963.

21. Trud, March 1, 1964.

22. Although a stated intention of this study is not to discuss military aid, one can--at times-- not help reflecting upon Soviet technical assistance and some of the subsidiary purposes this may serve. This would, of course, be drawing the altruistic motives of the Soviet Union into doubt, but on a purely conjectural basis one might hypothetically connect this research into the fishery resources of the Red Sea with the location of the British naval base at Aden, and with British naval movements in the West Indian Ocean.

23. Taher Abu Wafa, "The Aswan Dam--Key to a Nation's Future," The UNESCO Courier (December, 1964), pp. 40-41.

24. Keith Wheelock, Nasser's New Egypt. A Critical Analysis (London: Stevens, 1960), p. 173.

25. Ibid., p. 174.

26. Egypt National Production Council, Permanent Council for the Development of National Production (Cairo, 1955), p. 148.

27. Ibid., p. 133.

28. U.S. Congress, Senate, Committee on Appropriations, Hearings, Financing the Aswan High Dam In Egypt, 84th Congress, 2nd Session (Washington, D.C.: G.P.O., January 26, 1956), p. 4.

29. For a detailed account of these events, see Wheelock, op. cit., pp. 173-205.

30. Vedomosti Verkhovnogo Soveta SSSR, No. 8, 1959.

31. Ibid.

32. Report of the main contractor on the Aswan project: The Industrial and General Enterprises Engineering Co., S.A.A. (Osman Ahmed Osman and Co.) (Cairo: Les Editions Universitaires d'Egypte, 1963).

33. Ibid.

34. Izvestiya, July 21, 1962.

35. Kondrashov, "Two Days in Asyut," Sovremennyy Vostok (Contemporary East) now Aziya i Afrika Segodnya (Asia and Africa Today), No. 6 (June, 1960), p. 21. This is the journal of the Russian Africa Institute in Moscow.

36. Izvestiya, September 14, 1961.

37. There are presently 600 Russian engineers, and about 26,000 Arab workers on the Aswan project.

38. Pravda, May 16, 1964.

39. Report of the General and Industrial Enterprises Engineering Co., S.A.A., op. cit.

40. Taher Abu Wafa, loc. cit.

41. V. Rymalov, Ekonomicheskoe Sotrudnichestvo SSSR co Slaborazvitymi Stranami, p. 45.

42. William A. Hance, The Geography of Modern Africa (New York: Columbia University Press, 1964), p. 125.

43. See Chapter 3, Table 9, "Africa--Country Distribution of Credits," pp. 81-89.

44. "Czechoslovakia in the U.A.R.," Czechoslovak Foreign Trade, Vol. 2, No. 9 (September, 1962), p. 9.

45. Communiqué of the Czechoslovak Press Bureau, (Prague: January 2, 1961).

46. Rude Pravo, November 19, 1962.

47. La documentation française, Notes et Etudes Documentaires, No. 2833: "L'Evolution de l'Economie tchéchoslovaque en 1960," (November 1, 1961).

48. See Table 12: "Egypt--Value of Trade with the Centrally Planned Economies," pp. 106-07.

49. Pravda, May 28, 1964.

50. The New York Times, March 2, 1965.

51. Pravda, April 27, 1963.

52. Izvestiya, July 6, 1960.

53. "Die Unterrichtshilfe des Ostblocks und die Entwicklungsländer--Kritisch Betrachtede," Handbuch der Entwicklungshilfe (Berlin: no publisher, 1961), pp. 8-9.

54. Mirko Svoboda, "Experience of Czechoslovak Banking Passed on to Developing Countries," Czechoslovak Foreign Trade, Vol. 4, No. 7 (July, 1964), pp. 3-5.

55. U.N., ECA, Industrial Development in the United Arab Republic (E/CN.14/AS/I/1/1, September 22, 1965) (Addis Ababa, 1965), p. 2.

56. Ibid., p. 11.

57. See Chapter 3, Table 9: "Africa--Country Distribution of Credits," pp. 81-89.

58. U.N., ECA, Industrial Development in the United Arab Republic, p. 17.

59. Pravda Vostoka, March 3, 1962.

60.   Krasnyaya Zvezda, September 10, 1963.

61.   Mirovaya Ekonomika i Mezhdunarodnye Otnosheniya
May 8, 1965.

62.   Marshall I. Goldman, "A Balance Sheet of Soviet Foreign Aid," Foreign Affairs, Vol. 43, No. 2
(January, 1965), p. 360.

63.   The New York Times, February 3, 1965, which
states that in the fiscal year 1964, which ended in
June, the foreign trade deficit of Egypt was nearly
$370 million, only slightly below the record deficit
figure of $400 million for fiscal 1963. Furthermore,
by the end of 1964 Egypt's short-term debt to the West
was $200 million, nearly half of which is overdue.
The U.A.R. was equally far behind in commodity repayments with other countries, mostly in the Eastern trade
area. A recent Soviet account states that the "U.A.R.
foreign currency reserves toward the end of 1965 are
estimated at a mere $8.4 million," Mirovaya Ekonomika
i Mezhdunarodnye Otnosheniya, No. 8, 1965, p. 145.

64.   "Problems of Financing the U.A.R.'s Economy,"
Kratkiya Soobshcheniya Instituta Narodov Azii, No. 79
(Moscow, 1964), pp. 87-108.

CHAPTER **5** NORTH AFRICA

A L G E R I A

After having occupied a primary position among French overseas territories as regards investment and general cultural attachment, Algeria obtained her independence on July 3, 1962, following seven years of war.

The French followed two courses in trying to postpone the advent of that day: firstly, military repression and, secondly, a heavy increase of extensive expenditures toward the economic and social development of that country. It is estimated that the Algerian war cost France some $10 billion; more than 200,000 persons were killed, of which 14,000 were members of the French forces and 18,500 were European civilians; moreover approximately one million Muslims were displaced and the country suffered considerable material damage.

Following the cessation of hostilities, most Europeans left for France and three million acres were left fallow, of which a large proportion were those situated in the more productive areas of the country; hundreds of small businesses and industrial enterprises were abandoned, representing an estimated 70 per cent of the total of such establishments and construction came almost to a standstill. Due to these chaotic conditions, most of the population was deprived of resources and depended almost entirely on food shipments from abroad, mainly from the United States.

Thus, in 1962 Algeria found itself in dire economic straits. Although it possessed a reasonably well developed infrastructure, it had neither the necessary means nor the capital to exploit it. French aid, while still quite substantial, was reduced to some $200 million a year;[1] aid from other countries, including an important loan granted by the U.S.S.R. was insufficient[2] and the main source of income, i.e., tax revenues, was greatly reduced after the exodus of the Europeans. Although Government authorities attempted to introduce austerity measures, emergency loans became necessary to cover expenses. Since 1958 exports have not amounted to more than 30 to 40 per cent of total imports.[3] Yields from the recently discovered Sahara oilfields totalled merely $39.7 million in 1962, which was far from adequate to fill the gap.

TRADE

Agriculture normally supports about two thirds of the Algerian population and accounts for about one third of the national income. In foreign trade, however, land products constitute almost 70 per cent of total exports,[4] with minerals, oil, and miscellaneous manufactured articles making up the remainder.[5] On the import side, there is a heavy predominance of industrial products.

It should come as no surprise that France is Algeria's most important trading partner. Close to 80 per cent of this North African country's trade is conducted with its former mother country.[6] Other important trade partners in the Western world include the United States,[7] Italy, the United Kingdom, and Western Germany. In the period 1958-65 these five countries accounted for nine tenths of Algeria's turnover of foreign trade.[8]

Compared to this, her share of trade with the centrally planned economies is insignificant. Algeria has current trade agreements with Bulgaria, Poland, and the Soviet Union, all concluded in 1963,[9] but this does not imply that commodity exchange did not exist before that time. Since prior to independence Algeria was

TABLE 18

ALGERIA

Value of Trade with the Centrally Planned Economies

Totals and Country Breakdowns

(U.S.$ million, imports c.i.f.; exports f.o.b.)

Country Distribution	1958		1959		1960		1961		January-June, 1962	
	Imports	Exports	Imports	Exports	Imports	Exports	Imports	Exports	Imports	Exports
Total Trade	957.7	410	1,123	360	1,228	588	1,010	364	387	188
of which:										
Soviet Union and Eastern Europe	5.24	2.6	8.21	3.72	8.15	1.94	7.16	1.56	6.58	0.8
Individual Country Breakdown										
Czechoslovakia	0.56	--	0.61	--	0.25	--	0.76	--	0.32	--
Poland	0.64	0.36	2.2	0.32	2.2	--	0.70	--	0.26	--
Rumania	1.8	0.04	1.6	0.4	3.8	0.34	5.1	0.66	1.3	--
Soviet Union	2.3	2.2	3.8	3.0	1.9	1.6	0.6	0.9	4.7	0.8

Source: U.N., Yearbook of International Trade Statistics, 1964, Table 4, p. 49.

considered as being an integral part of France, trade
with the centrally planned economies was conducted on
the basis of trade agreements these countries had concluded with the French Republic. But all these commodity flows were of a very modest nature.

Since the Algerian war of independence very
little information has been published on the direction
and commodity structure of trade with the centrally
planned economies. In the only trade flow of some importance, i.e., that between Algeria and the Soviet
Union, we find that in the 1961-63 period--wheat, sugar,
and oil-seeds constituted approximately 80 per cent of
the country's imports from the U.S.S.R., while machinery and equipment totalled merely 11 per cent. Algerian exports to the Soviet Union consisted mainly of
cork, and some wine, but in very small quantities.

In all respects it is probably far too early to
comment on and evaluate the commodity exchange between
Algeria and the centrally planned economies. These relations are too recent and their inception occurred
under such abnormal conditions that developments up to
the mid-1960's cannot be taken as indications of what
is to happen in the future. More promising, however,
are relations that have been initiated in the field of
financial and technical aid.

FINANCIAL AND TECHNICAL ASSISTANCE

The basis for this was an agreement signed with
the Soviet Union in Moscow on October 4, 1963.[10] The
U.S.S.R. undertook to grant Algeria a loan of 90 million rubles for the reconstruction of the mining industry, and for building a fertilizer plant, a sugar
refinery, a tannery, a cotton-ginning plant,and a
weaving mill. Included in the agreement was a provision for Soviet aid in constructing an irrigation
network and for the mechanization of agriculture. In
addition it was agreed that Algerians would be trained
to carry out the management of these enterprises.[11]

Work on some of these projects started fairly
soon after the agreement was signed, and already before

the end of the Algerian War Soviet mine disposal
squads were at work. By late 1964 these had neu-
tralized more than two million land mines along the
Tunisian and Moroccan frontiers and in this manner
cleared valuable land for agricultural use.[12]

Work was also started on schools and technical
institutes provided for under the agreement, and by
December, 1964, the Soviets reported the opening near
Algiers of a school for the training of industrial
and agricultural technicians.[13] In addition the
Soviet Union has undertaken to: (1) provide Algeria
with a textile college for industry specialists from
which 500 technicians and 50 textile engineers would
graduate yearly, (2) build two further educational
centers for 500 trainees in industry and agriculture,[14] and perhaps most significantly, (3) present
as a gift to Algeria an Oil and Gas Institute as well
as a special technical college providing for the
training of 2,800 students intended for work in the
Algerian oil industry.[15] Although these projects are
already under way, experience has shown that five to
seven years are required for the completion of Soviet-
financed projects in developing areas,[16] while educational undertakings like the construction of schools,
institutes, etc., are normally completed within one
to two years after commitment. It seems reasonable,
therefore, to expect that most of the projects mentioned above will be completed and handed over to the
Algerian Government by the 1970's--at the earliest.

Under the terms of the 1963 agreement, the Soviet
Union has also commenced work on the construction of
twenty-eight small and medium-sized dams for the irrigation of arid regions in Northern Algeria. Six of
these, all of them located in the Greater Kabylia dis-
trict, were completed in 1966.[17] Also completed that
year was the Soviet constructed iron works at Annaba
which will use local ore. In this connection it is
interesting to note that a group of Leningrad experts
estimated the Sahara deposits sufficient to last the
country for forty years.[18]

It is normal for the Soviet Union to create air-
links between Moscow and the major transportation

centers in the developing countries with which it has
economic relations. Algeria is no exception here and
in the 1963 agreement was a provision to supply Algeria with two IL-18 aircraft. These were delivered
in early 1964 and on February 18 the same year a bi-
weekly air-service between Algiers and Moscow was in-
augurated. Since only Soviet-built aircraft will be
used, the U.S.S.R. is training Algerians to operate
and maintain these planes.[19]

There is little reason to doubt economic ties between Algeria and the Soviet Union will remain close
in the years to come. A good proof of this is a second
agreement on economic assistance to the North African
republic. This was signed in Moscow in early 1964, and
involves a credit of 115 million rubles ($126.5 mil-
lion).[20] This loan will finance the most ambitious
Soviet undertaking in Algeria up to the present: a
complex of metallurgical works with an annual capacity of 350,000-400,000 tons of metals, with a complete
production cycle of agglomerate coke, pig iron, steel,
and rolled specialty steels, as well as chemical prod-
ucts--including sulphate of ammonia--on the basis of
the coke production. For this vast undertaking the
U.S.S.R. will prepare designs, supply complete equipment for the works, and provide all necessary technical assistance in assembling, commissioning, and running the complex. This project is due to be completed in the early 1970's.

CULTURAL AND EDUCATIONAL RELATIONS

The 1963 agreement included a provision for the
training of 65 Algerian students in institutions of
higher learning in the Soviet Union. But the U.S.S.R.
is not the only centrally planned economy to provide
Algeria with scholarships. In the academic year
1960-61--the latest for which we have reliable infor-
mation--30 Algerian students were pursuing their
studies in Czechoslovakia, 120 in Eastern Germany,
35 in the Soviet Union, and 40 in Hungary, Poland, and
Rumania.[21] This makes a total of 225 Algerian students in higher educational centers in the centrally
planned economies, and this figure has increased in
the years since.

We have already discussed the intense Soviet
school-building activity in Algeria.   The educational
assistance does not, however, end here.   Late in 1964
the Soviet Government presented the Algerian National
Navy with a naval research unit for oceanographic
studies.[22]   Moreover, the Soviet Union extended large-
scale medical aid to Algeria, and by the year-end
1965-66 more than 300 Soviet medical workers were
practicing and teaching in the North African country.
This includes general medical practitioners, as well
as training of samaritans and nurses.

Looking back at Algeria's economic relations
with the centrally planned economies, two factors are
apparent: (1) the very small, if not insignificant,
scale of commodity exchange between the two areas, and
(2) the large-scale and relatively important nature
of Soviet financial and technical assistance commitments.   It is clear that as funds under these are expended, amortization of the loans will have to be effectuated with return deliveries of Algeria's traditional export commodities.   Thus, one can expect a
gradual increase in the flow of trade, particularly
with the Soviet Union.

At this point it is too early to offer any more
than interim comments on the effects of Algeria's relations with the Eastern group.   By far the largest
part of the credits remains to be expended and the
speed with which Soviet-planned development projects
are implemented may to some degree be determined by
the foreign policy the Algerian Government decides to
follow.   To date, the possibly most valuable contribution of the centrally planned economies has been in
offering Algeria a possibility to diversify her very
strong economic ties with the former metropolitan
country.[23]   However, Soviet commentators do not promise Algeria an easy way out of her difficulties.
Mass poverty, unemployment, industrial stagnation, and
overstaffing of administration and services are de-
plored; the facile remedy offered being "speedy and
extensive industrialization with a simultaneous development of agriculture."   Even the self-management
system in agriculture (acclaimed by Soviet ideologists
as a specific Algerian contribution to "noncapitalist"

development) is considered by one Soviet observer on
the spot to have made only a very small contribution
to solving the over-all agricultural problem.[24]

T U N I S I A

Tunisia, the smallest of the North African
countries, has much in common with the rest of the
Maghreb; its Western Arab culture, its experience of
French rule, its Mediterranean and Saharan climates,
and its basic land use patterns. But there are also
profound differences which, in many respects, set the
country apart from its neighbors. Culturally, it is
more advanced with markedly bourgeois and secular
tendencies; also it is solidly unified under a strongly
centralized government which has placed great emphasis
upon cultural as well as economic modernization. President Bourguiba has instituted various programs to al-
ter traditional Islamic customs--insisting, for example,
on work requirements to take precedence over the Ramadan
rites.[25]

Tunisia's major economic problems today are the expansion of production and opportunities for employment
with a view to absorb the large number of unemployed or
underemployed and to improve general standards of living
which are particularly low in the southern regions.

Contrary to the inclination of many former colonies
to channel their major international economic relations
almost exclusively through the past metropolitan power,
Tunisia has managed to diversify her foreign trade outlets to a remarkable extent.[26]

TRADE

Commodity exchange with the centrally planned economies took firm shape when trade agreements were signed
during the 1960-61 period. Today Tunisia maintains commercial relations with every centrally planned economy
but Rumania.[27] All these agreements are strictly bilateral in character, with balances settled through
clearing or compensation accounts.

This commodity exchange has not constituted any
major trade flow for Tunisia, but has, from a very
low level, grown rapidly and by 1965 it constituted
about 6 per cent of Tunisia's total turnover of foreign trade.[28]

In its relative proportion to total Tunisian
trade, commodity exchange with the centrally planned
economies has been remarkably stable with relatively
little variation between imports and exports.

Throughout the period the most important partners in the Eastern trade area have been the Soviet
Union, Poland, and Czechoslovakia--in that order.

The commodity structure of Tunisia's trade with
the Soviet Bloc is also more variegated than what we,
so far, have been accustomed to observe.

Furthermore, this commodity structure is complementary to all partners of the exchange. Tunisia's
export products are easily marketable in the centrally planned economies--particularly in Eastern Europe--
and this area is well equipped to continue meeting
Tunisia's capital goods requirements. Particularly
imports in the latter commodity group can be expected
to increase over the next few years assuming that deliveries of Soviet and Eastern European equipment for
completion of projects under their financial and technical aid programs will increase.

FINANCIAL AND TECHNICAL ASSISTANCE

From the past four-year experience there is little
doubt that activities in this category are bound to increase. This statement may seem ambiguous because
Tunisia is not among the major recipients of Soviet
Bloc economic aid to Africa. With a total of $50 mil-
lion by mid-1967, she accounts for merely 2.2 per cent
of all Soviet and Eastern European aid to the continent
and this amount in itself would certainly not be enough
to substantiate any optimistic forecasts on trade increases.[29]

TABLE 19

TUNISIA

Value of Trade with the Centrally Planned Economies

Totals and Country Breakdowns

(U.S.$ thousand, imports c.i.f.; exports f.o.b.)

Country Distribution	1955-59		1960		1961	
	Imports	Exports	Imports	Exports	Imports	Exports
Total Trade	..	..	190,698	119,685	210,592	110,373
of which: Soviet Union and Eastern Europe	11,500	10,100	5,833	3,944	8,761	7,234
Individual Country Breakdown						
Czechoslovakia	3,400	3,200	1,532	1,060	2,202	2,275
Eastern Germany	200	100	19	-	200	278
Poland	1,800	3,300	958	1,129	2,039	1,302
Soviet Union	6,100	3,500	2,879	1,605	2,668	2,538

1962		1963		1964		Jan.-April, 1965	
Imports	Exports	Imports	Exports	Imports	Exports	Imports	Exports
216,319	115,876	221,783	126,005	247,675[a]	129,177[a]	82,903	39,895
6,097	6,041	12,553	7,613	16,661	8,921	3,433	2,567
1,227	1,060	3,058	1,578	4,118	2,622	717	507
242	166	447	126	1,860	426	454	125
1,607	1,493	3,386	2,044	5,693	2,206	910	743
2,232	2,310	4,375	2,615	3,825	1,152	940	401

Sources: Figures for 1955-59; U.N. Statistical Office, Direction of International Trade, Statistical Papers, Series T, Vol. X, No. 8 and Vol. XI, No. 9; U.N., ECA, Foreign Trade Statistics of Africa, Series A, Direction of Trade (E/CN.14/STAT/ Ser.A./2, 5, 7): 1960, No. 2 (November, 1962), pp. 8-9; 1961, 1962, and 1963: No. 5 (February, 1965), pp. 8-9; 1964 and January-April, 1965: No. 7 (January, 1966), pp. 4-5.

Note: [a]Due to the introduction of a new exchange rate in October, 1964, figures for January-December are calculated on a percentage basis.

TABLE 20

TUNISIA

Commodity Structure of Trade with the Centrally Planned Economies

(U.S.$ thousand, imports c.i.f.; exports f.o.b.)

| Commodity Group | 1960 | | | |
| | Imports | | Exports | |
	Total	Soviet Union and Eastern Europe	Total	Soviet Union and Eastern Europe
Total Trade	198,804	5,863	120,638	3,975
Major Product Categories				
Food products	34,934	1,244	39,004	310
Crude materials--inedible	6,983	541	32,922	2,513
Mineral fuels, lubes, etc.	17,578	648		
Manufactured goods	55,136	2,341		
Machinery, transport equipment	43,989	568		
Individual Product Breakdown				
Cereals and preparations (mainly wheat)	13,157	983		
Sugar and preparations	7,981	140		
Wood, lumber, cork	3,919	486		
Coal, coke, briquettes	853	580		
Textile yarn fabrics	25,066	1,430		
Iron and steel	10,576	494		
Glass and glassware	1,066	108		
Household equipment	1,417	136		
Agricultural machinery	5,368	150		
Road motor vehicles	14,274	242		
Sanitary, plumbing and heating equipment	803	53		
Footwear	265	50		
Petroleum and products	16,622	-		
Textile, leather machinery	1,297	-		
Clothing	7,455	-		
Citrus fruits			544	176
Raw cork			764	113
Natural phosphates			15,180	1,573
Iron ore			7,981	493
Olive oil			14,429	1,113
Fresh fruits and nuts				

| | 1961 | | | | 1962 | | | |
| | Imports | | Exports | | Imports | | Exports | |
Total	Soviet Union and Eastern Europe	Total	Soviet Union and Eastern Europe	Total	Soviet Union and Eastern Europe	Total	Soviet Union and Eastern Europe
211,119	8,857	111,241	7,292	215,706	6,089	115,930	6,054
56,438	2,502	21,270	551	49,568	-	24,137	490
8,493	618	30,689	3,847	8,747	664	29,955	3,265
17,525	1,270			17,134	838		
51,235	2,725			56,069	2,959		
46,944	762			48,913	776		
33,302	281			19,303	-		
7,129	1,872			6,652	-		
4,516	554			5,531	561		
978	714					680	489
19,883	1,940			18,565	1,998		
11,306	257			10,006	348		
891	110			1,478	57		
1,328	95			1,292	-		
3,029	-			950	-		
10,671	195			12,263	261		
885	83			1,036	78		
541	211			165	-		
16,547	556			15,882	349		
1,699	279			1,803	-		
6,474	117			7,419	-		
		520	204				
		902	362			790	591
		15,546	2,301			16,406	1,953
		7,252	985			5,662	628
		22,590	2,844			30,617	2,285
						7,334	472

Continued

TABLE 20 (Continued)

| | 1963 | | | |
| Commodity Group | Imports | | Exports | |
	Total	Soviet Union and Eastern Europe	Total	Soviet Union and Eastern Europe
Total Trade	221,810	12,502	125,996	7,611
Major Product Categories				
Food products	35,788	2,698	31,534	1,163
Crude materials--inedible	8,301	611	31,898	3,592
Mineral fuels, lubes, etc.	18,779	1,371	35	
Manufactured goods	62,586	5,109	4,343	
Machinery, transport equipment	54,963	1,223	459	
Individual Product Breakdown				
Cereals and preparations (mainly wheat)	12,088			
Sugar and preparations	7,860	2,689		
Wood, lumber, cork	3,567	594		
Coal, coke, briquettes			-	-
Textile yarn fabrics	10,365	1,022		
Iron and steel	-	-		
Glass and glassware	1,570	222		
Household equipment	1,596	127		
Agricultural machinery	2,787	-		
Road motor vehicles	11,607	123		
Sanitary, plumbing and heating equipment	448	-		
Footwear	101	23		
Petroleum and products	1,949	-		
Textile, leather machinery	1,773	164		
Clothing	4,452	102		
Citrus fruits			4,313	144
Raw cork			1,264	633
Natural phosphates			18,129	1,701
Iron ore			5,715	1,114
Olive oil			23,643	2,852
Fresh fruits and nuts			1,630	51

	January-June, 1964		
	Imports		Exports
Total	Soviet Union and Eastern Europe	Total	Soviet Union and Eastern Europe
129,007	7,829	67,296	4,273
20,633	2,783	19,248	1,356
5,612	461	16,810	1,417
8,348	324	169	-
38,908	2,197	2,855	-
36,597	1,575	152	-
2,634	-		
8,517	2,741		
2,392	410		
481	244		
6,183	372		
-	-		
820	80		
1,099	48		
1,593	12		
2,421	21		
155	6		
74	9		
2,950	-		
959	336		
2,376	93		
		4,283	96
		308	71
		10,467	1,083
		2,613	215
		10,257	1,429
		977	23

Sources: U.N., ECA, Foreign Trade Statistics of Africa, Series B, Trade by Commodity (E/CN.14/STATS/Ser.B/1, 3, 6, 7, and 8): Figures for 1960: No. 1 (October, 1962), pp. 21-33; 1961: No. 3 (February, 1963), pp. 17-29; 1962: No. 6 (November, 1964), pp. 3-18; 1963: No. 7 (May, 1965), pp. 3-32; January-June, 1964: No. 8 (March, 1966) pp. 3-29.

However, when examining the projects planned, it is apparent that either these are of such a nature that they do not require Soviet Bloc equipment until local installations have been completed, or project preparation has been executed and equipment is to be installed in the near future.

The major part of Soviet Bloc financial assistance--$30 million--was granted by the Soviet Union in February, 1962.[30] This loan will mainly finance a system of hydroelectric power stations with five dams.[31] By the end of 1965 Soviet specialists had completed work on the Rezala River Dam which, 31 meters high and 450 meters long, will hold back a lake of 10.5 million cubic meters of water with a gravity flow for irrigation. This dam was designed to be an integral part of the larger hydroelectric irrigation scheme in the Lake Ishkal region of Northern Tunisia.

The Soviet loan is also financing work to straighten out the beds of the Tin and Tindja rivers. This scheme, which is being carried out by Tunisians under Soviet supervision, will be completed by 1970 when the total irrigated area will have reached 20,000 hectares.[32] In conjunction with this project, a further contract was signed in Tunis whereby the Soviet Union agreed to build a dam and a power station on the Oassdo River. The agreement provides for assembling, installing, and commissioning the necessary machinery, and for training of local personnel.[33]

Czechoslovakia's aid to Tunisia is still only in the planning stage, but will be concentrated on the building of a textile mill at Monastir. This factory will use Vienna wool, and all processing work, such as unraveling, spinning, weaving, and dyeing will be done on the spot. Total costs are estimated at $5 million (or one half of the Czechoslovak loan). Tunisian operating teams will be training in Czechoslovakia.[34] This project is interesting, for here we see for the first time that two centrally planned economies cooperate in its execution--Poland will work with Czechoslovakia in material supply and personnel training.

In addition to the textile mill, Czechoslovakia will also provide Tunisia with a pharmaceutical products plant and train Tunisian public health personnel.[35]

Eastern Germany has no formal program of financial or technical aid to Tunisia, but will deliver, as part of its current trade agreement, ten fishing boats at a value of $0.6 million, a clothing factory, and a dry cleaning plant at Menzel-Bourguiba, estimated at $1.5 million. The East German Government has also undertaken to build a factory which will supply polyvinyl for the manufacture of plastic goods, and to provide equipment for an increase in the production of Tunisian lead, iron, and zinc.[36]

The most significant project of a cultural and educational aid nature is the construction of a Soviet-financed National Institute of Technology at Tunis. This will have a capacity of 700 students, and the curriculum will include courses in surveying, hydraulics, rural construction, civil engineering, and public works.[37]

There is no doubt that, seen in an African perspective, Tunisia's economic relations with the Eastern trade area are on the modest side. Probably not more than 10 to 20 per cent of all aid committed has been disbursed. This is not more than a fraction of the $245.5 million worth of official grants, loans, and private export credits Tunisia has received from member countries of the OECD group over the 1960-63 period.[38]

However, in spite of its relatively modest size, Soviet and Eastern European development aid to Tunisia appears to have been well planned and executed in a fashion that is well within the plan requirements of the country.

It is too early to make any valid assessment of the impact of this aid on the Tunisian economy. At best, Soviet Bloc projects will not be completed until the end of this decade, and even then no more than their primary effects will be difficult to estimate. However, with a caution on future noneconomic developments, we can say that economic relations between

Tunisia and the centrally planned economies are in
for a period of reasonable growth. On the other hand,
one should not expect these trade and aid flows to become a major determinant of the future course of the
Tunisian economy.

NOTES TO CHAPTER 5

1. U.N., ECA, International Economic Assistance
to Africa, 1962 (E/CN.14/280, February 11, 1964)
(Addis Ababa, 1964), Table 8, p. 22. French aid in
1960 amounted to $290 million and in 1961 to $348
million.

2. This loan amounted to 90 million rubles
($100 million), Pravda, October 5, 1963.

3. U.N., Yearbook of International Trade Statistics, 1964 (New York, 1966), Table 2, p. 47.

4. Ibid., Table 2, p. 48.

5. Iron ore and some transport equipment.

6. Ibid., Table 2, p. 47.

7. The United States figure almost exclusively
in Algerian import statistics, and accounts for only
an insignificant part of the country's exports. This
is due to large-scale food aid.

8. Ibid., Table 2, p. 47, and unofficial Algerian
statistics.

9. See Chapter 2, Table 4, "Africa--Trade and
Payments Agreements Concluded with the Soviet Union
and the Eastern European Centrally Planned Economies,
1953-64," (hereafter referred to as "Africa--Trade and
Payments Agreements"), pp. 37-51.

10. Pravda, October 10, 1963.

11. Ibid.

12. Pravda, December 20, 1964.

13. Ibid., December 5, 1964.

14. Ibid., May 7, 1964.

15. Ibid.

16. See pp. 265 and 272-73.

17. Pravda, August 28, 1964.

18. Tass Press Release, Moscow: January 22, 1965.

19. Ibid., February 21, 1965.

20. Pravda, May 5, 1964.

21. Anon., Die Unterrichtshilfe des Ostblocks und die Entwicklungsländer--Kritisch Betrachtet (Berlin, 1961, no publisher), pp. 8-9.

22. Mirovaya Ekonomika i Mezhdunarodnye Otnosheniya, No. 1 (January, 1965).

23. By the end of 1963 Algeria had received $1,488 million in grants and loans from the OECD group. (OECD, The Flow of Financial Resources to Less-Developed Countries, 1956-63, Table V-3, pp. 172-73). The Soviet loan of $100 million of 1963 amounts to 6 per cent of total Algerian aid receipts by the end of 1963, but even less if we include the $50 million received as a long-term, interest-free loan from China on October 11, 1963, (NCNA, October 12, 1963). In addition to this we estimate from NCNA press releases that China in the 1957-63 period presented Algeria with at least $10 million worth of gifts. Moreover, in spite of the additional $126.5 million Soviet loan in May, 1964, the U.S.S.R. contribution of total financial aid to Algeria has declined due to important new French loan allocations in 1964 and in 1965.

24. Pravda, September 19, 1966.

25. William A. Hance, The Geography of Modern Africa (New York: Columbia University Press, 1964), p. 99.

26. See U.N., Yearbook of International Trade Statistics, 1964, pp. 744-45.

27. See Chapter 2, Table 4, "Africa--Trade and Payments Agreements," pp. 37-51.

28. Figures for 1964 from U.S. Department of Commerce, Value Series, Report of March, 1965. In the period January-October, 1964, trade between Tunisia and the Soviet Bloc took this form:

	Exports	%	Imports	%
Total	115,194	100.0	203,173	100.0
Soviet Union and Eastern Europe	6,211	5.4	13,703	6.8

29. See Chapter 3, Table 9, "Africa--Country Distribution of Credits," pp. 81-89.

30. Vedomosti Verkhovnogo Soveta, No. 11, p. 1098 (March 15, 1962).

31. Ibid.

32. Tass Press Release, December 23, 1963.

33. Ibid., December 26, 1964.

34. L'Action (Tunis) January 3, 1964 (A.R.L. Vol. 1, p. 84).

35. Ibid., May 30, 1964 (A.R.L. Vol. 1, p. 84).

36. Ibid., March 16, 1965 (A.R.L. Vol. 2, p. 276).

37. Le Peuple (Algiers), September 25, 1964 (A.R.L. Vol. 1, p. 156).

38. OECD, The Flow of Financial Resources to Less-Developed Countries, 1956-63, Table V-3, p. 172.

CHAPTER **6** WEST AND CENTRAL

AFRICA

In the headlong scare of "Soviet Bloc economic penetration in Africa" in the late 1950's, no countries appeared at that time more vulnerable to "Communist takeover" than Ghana and Guinea. Not only did these two nations have a conspicuous entry into the state of independence, but almost overnight they became subjects of intense attention from the centrally planned economies. The almost "indecent" haste in which aid agreements were signed and trade flows initiated is, of course, something one has since gotten used to, and is now treated more as a matter of fact, whereas at the end of the last decade this represented, in the eyes of the West, something new and frightening in African politics.

Be this as it may, Ghana and Guinea became the first countries in West Africa to enter into economic relations with the Soviet Bloc. On a commercial basis these were placed on solid foundations. Trade was to be conducted in complementary commodities and the centrally planned economies appeared to the West African countries to be offering development projects almost indiscriminately.

Relations with Mali and the Sudan, on the other hand, got off to a more modest start and this region has so far received relatively little attention from the Soviet Bloc. True, the centrally planned economies represent in the case of both countries fairly significant trade partners, but the commodity exchange—at least in the direction of the Eastern group—is not

only competitive with local production, but it also
consists of commodities these countries already import in abundant quantities from other sources. Only
modest amounts of financial and technical assistance
have been granted.

G H A N A

As the first British colony in tropical Africa
to achieve independence--having become a member of
the Commonwealth in March, 1957--Ghana replaced the
Gold Coast and the British Trust Territory of Togo-
land.[1] On July 1, 1960--with a population of some
seven million people--the country became a republic.

The few short years since independence have
brought striking changes to this West African country.
Its political history, at best, has been turbulent,
passing through, perhaps, more than its share of the
growing pains of a newly independent nation. In its
search for identity Ghana has run through the gamut
of two-party and one-party systems, virtual one-man
rule under Nkrumah, to end up--by mid-1966--as a
country governed by its military forces with promise
of later constitutional rule.

With a per capita gross domestic product of
$232 in 1964,[2] Ghana may be considered among the po-
tentially richest countries in tropical Africa and,
indeed, after the Republic of South Africa and Liberia
the third wealthiest on the continent.

An arbitrary figure as this should not, however,
be taken as indication that Ghana's economy is devoid
of problems. Like that of many developing countries,
hers is essentially a one-crop economy with cocoa accounting for 60 per cent of total exports, and this
crop has seen a declining price trend on world markets
over the past few years. Coupled with this has been
a wholesale program of capital investments in industry
and infrastructure which has radically reduced Ghana's
foreign exchange reserves. Some of the losses here,
however, have been kept in check by exports of Ghana's

other major products--gold, manganese, diamonds
(Ghana is Africa's second largest producer), and
bauxite.

In 1963 the country started an ambitious seven-
year development plan which, among other things, calls
for:

. . . full employment; liquidation of the
colonial economic legacy; designing of a
new economic structure dovetailed to meet
the demands of economic integration of the
sub-region of Africa as a whole; and massive
expansion of the public section of the economy to ensure a shift toward a socialist
structure.[3]

During the plan period, Ghana estimates an
annual increase in her gross national product by 5.5
per cent, in total consumption by 5.9 per cent, and
in capital formation by 8.0 per cent.[4]

To finance these accomplishments Ghana has proved
rather adept at eliciting aid from both East and West.
The country has concluded six agreements on financial
and technical aid with the centrally planned economies,[5] but the contribution of the latter group has
been more pronounced in the field of trade than in aid.

TRADE

Here Ghana has entered into trade agreements with
every country in the Eastern trade area, all in the
two-year period 1960-62.[6] This, however, is not to
say that commodity exchange between the two areas did
not exist prior to that time. The Soviet Union and
several Eastern European countries alike were important customers of Ghana's main export commodities,
albeit indirectly through the London commodity markets. Direct dealings did not start until Ghana became independent, but from there onward relations
have expanded rapidly. Since 1960, trade between the
two areas has become active to the point where, in

TABLE 21

GHANA

Value of Trade with the Centrally Planned Economies

Totals and Country Breakdowns

(U.S.$ thousand, imports c.i.f.; exports f.o.b.)

Country Distribution	1955-59		1960		1961	
	Imports	Exports	Imports	Exports	Imports	Exports
Total Trade	..	..	362,099	342,752	399,925	322,37
of which:						
Soviet Union and Eastern Europe	..	..	12,044	21,171	18,668	10,22
Individual Country Breakdown						
Czechoslovakia	)	..	4,858	–	4,250	20
Eastern Germany	) 2,690	..	3,154	759	3,807	..
Poland	)	8,400	1,820	42	3,419	1,54
Soviet Union	5,600	63,000	1,576	20,370	6,166	8,57

| 1962 | | 1963 | | 1964 | | January-May, 1965 | |
Imports	Exports	Imports	Exports	Imports	Exports	Imports	Exports
333,485	312,697	365,161	299,195	340,458	317,660	154,455	158,973
18,320	19,054	31,827	33,526	47,671	27,663	32,218	29,306

3,997	852	8,580	1,809	10,981	52	4,708	3,853
2,431	1,750	4,419	6,054	4,015	2,209	2,398	1,916
4,794	3,600	5,811	4,372	8,123	6,093	8,017	3,154
5,120	11,104	9,126	20,001	16,758	17,224	10,365	17,052

Sources: Figures for 1955-59: U.N., Direction of International Trade, Statistical Papers, Series T, Vol. X, No. 8, Vol. XI, No. 9; U.N., ECA, Foreign Trade Statistics of Africa, Series A, Direction of Trade (E/CN.14/STAT/Ser.A/2, 4, 5,and 7); 1960: No. 2 (November, 1962), pp. 28-29; 1961 and 1962: No. 4 (February, 1964), pp. 36-38; 1963: No. 5 (February, 1965), pp. 36-38; 1964 and January-May, 1965: No. 7 (January, 1966), pp. 28-30.

TABLE 22

GHANA

Commodity Structure of Trade with the Centrally Planned Economies

(U.S.$ thousand, imports,c.i.f.; exports f.o.b.)

	1960			
	Imports		Exports	
Commodity Group	Total	Soviet Union and Eastern Europe	Total	Soviet Union and Eastern Europe
Total Trade	362,404	11,979	289,284	21,169
Major Product Categories				
Food products	58,864	771	194,194	21,121
Chemicals	25,819	337		
Manufactured goods	110,345	7,463		
Machinery and transport equipment	94,421	406		
Miscellaneous manufactured articles	35,235	2,934		
Individual Product Breakdown				
Fish and fish preparations	9,806	284		
Sugar and preparations	8,941	362		
Perfume, toilet preparations (soaps)	8,297	357		
Textile yarn fabrics (mainly cotton)	55,163	1,874		
Lime, cement, etc.	12,728	3,139		
Glass and glassware	1,999	353		
Pottery	335	92		
Household equipment	3,942	1,203		
Sanitary plumbing and heating equipment	2,575	370		
Travel goods	1,284	103		
Clothing	10,999	877		
Footwear	6,173	1,220		
Cocoa beans			186,013	21,121
Power generating machinery		..		
Sawlogs, nonconiferous wood				
Iron and steel bars		..		
Iron and steel wire		..		
Agricultural machinery		..		

	1962				1964			
	Imports		Exports			Imports		Exports	
Total	Soviet Union and Eastern Europe	Total	Soviet Union and Eastern Europe		Total	Soviet Union and Eastern Europe	Total	Soviet Union and Eastern Europe
333,557	18,301	281,180	22,561		340,289	47,533	288,071	27,658
64,798	2,671	204,181	22,358		56,138	8,118	207,852	26,730
27,110	641				20,969	1,562	--	--
113,559	10,342				111,106	24,745	--	--
72,510	2,407				99,776	9,414	--	--
24,762	2,093				21,088	3,450	--	--
8,500	80				6,171	36		
7,828	2,314				11,005	6,778		
9,240	473				3,253	1,278		
47,108	1,704				31,154	7,969		
10,488	4,327				11,718	7,891		
2,051	217				2,412	753		
318	110				337	152		
2,889	1,336				1,761	1,177		
1,985	169				1,752	249		
421	105				302	58		
8,575	913				5,126	1,015		
3,851	335				2,771	1,066		
		187,661	22,358				190,727	26,730
	..		..		--	--		
		16,246	94				22,706	871
3,681	1,186				4,398	1,313		
202	119				402	42		
3,044	430				3,519	568		

Sources: U.N., ECA, African Trade Statistics, Series B, Trade by Commodity (E/CN.14/STAT/Ser. B/1-3-6). Figures for 1960: No. 1 (October, 1962), pp. 35-49; 1962: No. 6 (November, 1964), pp. 28-44; and U.N., Yearbook of International Trade Statistics, 1962 (New York: U.N. 1964), pp. 265-270; 1964: No. 9 (February, 1966), pp. 46-77.

1963 and in 1964, the centrally planned economies as
a group constituted Ghana's third largest customer,
and accounted for close to 10 per cent of Ghanaian
turnover of foreign trade.[7]

Furthermore, for each year of the period under
review--except in 1961--Ghana has had a positive
trade balance with the Soviet Bloc. This was more
pronounced in the years up to, and including 1960.
From then on, commodity exchange with the Eastern
trade area has tended to be more balanced. Of the
centrally planned economies, the Soviet Union is by
far Ghana's most important customer and her sixth
largest world-wide off-taker (in 1963).[8] Moreover,
the U.S.S.R. has maintained a constant negative balance in her trade with Ghana: Soviet imports in 1962
and 1963 were only half the size of Ghanaian exports
to the U.S.S.R. (see Table 21).

The remaining centrally planned economies, particularly Czechoslovakia, Eastern Germany, and Poland,
have all been important trade partners for Ghana. In
the case of all these countries their importance has
been more marked in Ghanaian import than in export
statistics. It was not until 1963 that balance of
trade between Ghana and the Eastern European centrally
planned economies took a less negative turn for the
former.

Finally we see from Table 21 that, although commodity exchange between Ghana and the Eastern trade
area increased by about 150 per cent in the 1960-65
period, this increase was very uneven, probably because of sporadic deliveries under Soviet and Eastern
European programs of financial and technical assistanc

The commodity structure of trade between Ghana
and the centrally planned economies is set out in
Table 22.

This follows, by and large, a "conventional"
pattern in commodity exchange between Africa and the
Eastern trade area--large exports of traditional cash
crops with an import structure emphasizing capital
equipment, semimanufactures, and consumer goods.

What is perhaps noticeable in the case of Ghana
is the country's total dependence on one export product in this trade with the centrally planned economies; in each year of the period under review exports
of cocoa beans have accounted for 99 per cent of all
sales to the Eastern trade area.

The structure of imports is more varied, with a
predominance in footwear, household equipment, textile
fabrics, and construction material. It is interesting
to note that Soviet sugar sales to Ghana increased
radically in 1961 and 1962--about the same time the
Soviet Union started her heavy sugar purchases from
Cuba.

Of the main products which Ghana receives from
the centrally planned economies, the capital equipment
group is the smallest. Only in 1961 did this commodity group take on real importance, when imports of
Soviet power-generating machinery accounted for about
one half of total Ghanaian imports of this commodity.
As this was a single operation, these purchases were
presumably made in connection with Soviet-financed
technical assistance projects in Ghana.

Ghana's imports from the centrally planned economies have throughout the period been sufficiently
spread out over a large range of products, so that in
no category can the country be said to be "dependent"
on the Soviet Bloc. At this point, however, it may be
helpful to attach some comments regarding the relative
strength of Ghana's trading position versus the Soviet
Union and the Eastern European centrally planned economies.

As can be expected in any of these contacts, trade
relations are bilateral; but it might be argued that
there are degrees of bilateralism. So far, evidence in
Africa suggests that a bilateral balancing of trade is
not necessarily or invariably the rule.[9] In particular,
payments arrangements are flexible and have, indeed,
been modified from time to time according to the particular circumstances of each country, and in the light
of difficulties confronting it. Egypt has, for instance, been able to insist on settlement of trade

balances in convertible currencies, and not necessarily payable via clearing accounts either.[10] But
then again, it is important to recognize that Egypt,
by sheer weight of the volume of her commodity exchange with the centrally planned economies, is in
an infinitely stronger trading position than is Ghana.

Here we find, that in the case of almost every
trade agreement the country has concluded with the
Soviet Union and Eastern Europe, settlement of balances is in nonconvertible Ghanaian pounds.[11] So
far Ghana has had considerable difficulties in filling
her import requirements from the centrally planned
economies because the centrally planned economies have
delayed completing their planned projects. Ghana consequently has found herself in the uncomfortable position of being an extender of commodities on credit to
the Eastern trade area--a position she can ill afford.

FINANCIAL AND TECHNICAL ASSISTANCE

Over the two-year period 1960-61 Ghana received
altogether $89 million in development assistance from
the Soviet Bloc.[12] This accounted for 4 per cent of
total Soviet and Eastern European financial assistance
to Africa.[13] The major part of the credits to Ghana,
$40 million, was granted by the Soviet Union, while the
remainder was made up of loans from Czechoslovakia and
Poland. In addition to these sums, a reported, but not
confirmed second Soviet credit was granted in March,
1963.[14]

Soviet financial aid has, in the main, been concentrated in two fields: the development of the
Ghanaian fishing industry, and the construction of a
hydroelectric power plant and a dam at Bui on the
Black Volta River. The latter project, which was negotiated only four months after the conclusion of the
August, 1960, protocol to the Ghanaian-Soviet aid agreement,[15] was not even near its completion by mid-1967.
When terminated, however, the Black Volta power station
should have a capacity of 200,000 kws, or twice the
1960 output of all power stations in Ghana.[16]

The most significant Soviet-financed project for the development of the Ghanaian fishing industry will be a $3 million fishing industry complex, for which the foundation stone was laid at Tema on December 23, 1964. The Ghanaian Government will here be responsible for the construction side, while the Soviet Union will supply equipment and materials. The complex will comprise a fish cannery, a fish-smoking, and fish meal plant, as well as auxiliary shops and services.[17] At best, this should be completed by 1968. In addition a Soviet-Ghanaian agreement on technical assistance for the fishing industry was signed in Accra in June, 1961.[18] Under this agreement three Soviet-built trawlers were delivered to Ghana in late 1963 and early 1964.[19] A Soviet-built dry dock of 4,000 tons displacement was towed to Tema in 1966.[20]

Soviet development assistance, however, has not only been limited to the two fields mentioned so far. According to Komsomol'skaya Pravda, the U.S.S.R. will aid Ghana in the construction of a house-building concern for section-built family housing with a capacity of turning out 70,000 cubic meters of space a year.[21] Also, Pravda reported that the Soviet Union had signed a contract to produce 25-30 tons of Ghanaian gold each year.[22] This is part of a May, 1962, protocol, under which more than 200 Soviet and Ghanaian geologists will undertake prospecting in Ghana. This research is expected to last at least three years.[23]

Czechoslovak and Polish aid to Ghana has mainly consisted of the construction of industrial installations of a purely commercial nature. The credits—which are by no means exhausted—have, in the case of Czechoslovakia, financed a sugar refinery, two footwear factories, a tire factory and an aluminum cutlery factory;[24] and Polish credits have been, or will be utilized for the construction of ceramic plants, and shoe and tire factories.[25]

In retrospect then, we find that, up to the present, Soviet economic aid to Ghana has largely been utilized in the development of her infrastructure or capital industries, while Eastern European financial assistance has been directed toward the construction of light and consumer goods industries.

But these projects do not exhaust the list of
Soviet and Eastern European undertakings in Ghana.

In the field of cultural and educational relations we find similar indications of Soviet Bloc
activity. Nearly all of the centrally planned
economies have offered young Ghanaians scholarships
for higher study. In recent years more than fifty
Ghanaians have been studying annually in the Eastern
trade area.[26] In the Soviet Union the most popular
fields of study seem to have been medicine, geology,
and mining engineering. The Soviets have also conducted training programs for Ghanaian pilots for
Ghana Airways which is now operating several IL-18
aircraft on its medium-range flights.[27] Ghana has
also participated in an extensive educational exchange program, mainly with the Soviet Union. Several
prominent Russian teachers--among them the late Professor Pothekin, former director of the Russian Africa
Institute--have taught at Ghanaian Universities. Poland has filled an economics chair at Accra University
with a professor from Warsaw's Central School of Planning and Statistics, while a steady flow of both
Czechoslovak and Polish teachers have taught in Ghana's
secondary school system.[28]

One of the more noticeable programs under these
exchanges has been the agreement between Ghana and
the Soviet Union on peaceful uses of atomic energy,
signed in Moscow on February 28, 1961. According to
this, Soviet organizations will--in the period 1962-66-
design and supply the fuel, equipment, and other necessary materials for an atomic research reactor of 2,000
kws. Soviet specialists will be sent to Ghana to assis
in the construction of the reactor, to train Ghanaian
specialists, and--for a period of one year--supervise
the working of the nuclear plant. Assistance will also
be given in the construction of a laboratory for the
production of isotopes, and in the erection of other
subsidiary buildings, as well as in the formulation of
plans for research and experimental work.[29]

Among those African countries which maintained
economic relations with the centrally planned economies
Ghana has--over the past few years--been one of the mor

important. We find that, in retrospect, the country
has been the Soviet Bloc's second largest trade partner on the continent, and the fourth largest African
recipient of Soviet and Eastern European financial
and technical assistance. Perhaps this position can
be seen in an even better perspective if we report
an earlier finding: Over the period 1960-63 the
Soviet Bloc was Ghana's third largest customer for
her traditional products,[30] and over the same years
she received close to four times as much development
aid from the centrally planned economies as from
official Western sources.[31]

Of the two main types of development assistance--
trade and aid--it is clear that the former has been the
more significant to Ghana. One might, of course, argue
the fact that, even though the Soviet Bloc has been an
important off-taker of Ghana's main export crop, this
has been offset by the generally lower prices the centrally planned economies have paid for this product.
But this must be seen in context with the very real
market deterioration for agricultural cash crops that
are now being felt by developing countries in general.
That the Ghanaian economy has been able to count on the
Soviet Bloc as an importer of close to 10 per cent of
her exports has facilitated Ghanaian foreign trade planning and has made a genuine contribution to the economy.

The impact of financial and technical aid, however,
has been more marginal. Generally, it can be stated
that those Soviet Bloc credits which have so far been
utilized, have financed less important enterprises in
the consumer goods field, many of which are still in
the planning stage. The same can be said of larger
projects--these as well appear to have difficulties in
leaving the blueprint stage.[32]

As such, the whole picture of the economic contribution of the Soviet Bloc to Ghana's economy is somewhat hazy. We must assume that Ghana's exports to the
Eastern trade area are being paid for by the means of
extended credits. Since most projects planned under the
auspices of these are still in an embryonic state, it is
far too early to judge the actual impact they may come
to have on the Ghanaian economy.

Nevertheless, trade ties should persist. The
commodity structure is complementary--particularly
with Eastern Europe which may develop into a major
off-taker of Ghanaian cocoa. Much of this will, of
course, depend on the political relationships between
the two areas. With the ouster of Dr. Nkrumah the
Soviet Bloc has, to a large extent, been discredited
in some of its development efforts and progress on
several projects has been temporarily discontinued.

There is little reason to assume, however, that
relations between Ghana and the centrally planned
economies will forever remain in limbo. After a
reasonable period of stabilization, work on projects
will probably again be taken up although not with the
same fervor as earlier.[33] It should also be noted
that, compared to other countries in Africa, Ghana
has to a far greater extent successfully encouraged
foreign investment from the West, and with the promised return to constitutional rule the country's ties
with the United States, with Britain, and other members
of the Commonwealth should again become relatively
close.

G U I N E A

This country, which became independent after an
unusually stormy divorce from her metropolitan power,
has since 1958 been deeply influenced by reactions to
this break. Because of his dramatic defiance of de
Gaulle, Sekou Touré was one of the more admired African leaders; and--because Guinea soon became a fo-
cal point of the Cold War--this little West African
nation enjoyed international attention all out of
proportion to her size.[34]

In the fall of 1959, Guinea had many problems--
and few resources. As was the case in most of French
Africa, there was a shortage of indigenous administrators and technicians.[35] Most of her population
lived by subsistence agriculture, and her trade balance was in deficit. Although she exported bananas,

coffee, pineapples, and diamonds, her major assets--
deposits of bauxite and iron ore--were just beginning
to be exposed.

The most pressing problem at the time of Guinea's
independence, however, was the almost complete insecur-
ity with which the country was confronted. Angered by
the Guinean refusal to join the newly proposed French
Union, France withdrew abruptly her aid, her technicians,
and administrators, leaving Guinea completely destitute.

The account of how the Soviet Union and the Eastern
European centrally planned economies moved in to fill
this void is now history which has been adequately described elsewhere.[36] Here we shall recollect these
events in miniature.

Partly because of the abrupt break of relations
with France operations of the Soviet Bloc--which went
into effect immediately--probably acquired special importance. Where France persuaded her allies to wait and
see what would develop in Guinea--and thus achieved a
temporary isolation of the country--all the centrally
planned economies joined the Afro-Asian world in recog-
nizing the Republic of Guinea at once. Within the course
of a few weeks Soviet and Eastern European trade delega-
tions began arriving, and on February 13, 1959, the first
trade agreement between Guinea and the Soviet Union was
signed.[37] During the next few months Bulgaria, Czechoslovakia, Eastern Germany, Hungary, and Poland followed
suit.[38] These agreements all envisaged imports of Guinea's
traditional crops--bananas, coffee, and oilseeds.

On a parallel line, the centrally planned economies rapidly extended financial and technical aid. Of
the immediate assistance that was given, mention might
be made of Czechoslovakia's offer to supply 2,000 rifles
and armored cars, so that at least some of Guinea's security troops could be armed and prepared in case of civil
disorder. Commitments of financial aid followed; and in
August, 1959, the Soviet Union extended a 140 million ruble
credit[39] to be used for the construction of factories, a
polytechnical institute, and geological prospecting.[40]
Later Czechoslovakia and Poland extended smaller loans.
Thus, the greatest danger to the survival of the young
state--its economic and political isolation--was removed.

TABLE 23

GUINEA

Value of Trade with the Centrally Planned Economies

Totals and Country Breakdowns

(U.S.$ thousand, imports c.i.f.; exports f.o.b.)

Country Distribution	1959		1960	
	Imports	Exports	Imports	Exports
Total Trade of which:	50,014	36,147	49,872	55,098
Soviet Union and Eastern Europe	9,054	5,245	21,259	12,603
Individual Country Breakdown				
Czechoslovakia	2,957	1,620	8,604	2,447
Eastern Germany	3,897	911	3,500	3,848
Hungary	336	328	1,150	369
Poland	851	1,895	2,483	2,043
Soviet Union	1,013	527	5,242	3,905

1961		1962		1963	
Imports	Exports	Imports	Exports	Imports	Exports
72,886	61,474	65,606	44,913	46,137	55,462
25,136	14,344	23,310	11,805	13,793	12,542

5,035	2,285	3,407	1,912	806	3,889
6,555	3,913	2,224	2,937	875	2,508
2,005	587	794	1,074	348	652
2,645	1,819	2,504	2,795	3,447	2,872
8,458	5,254	13,243	2,532	8,195	2,394

Sources: U.S. Department of Commerce, Bureau of Foreign Commerce, "Exports and Imports of Free World Countries to and from the Soviet Bloc," Value Series, Free World Exports and Imports 1959-62, and Value Series, Free World Exports and Imports January-December, 1963 (Washington, D.C., 1963 and 1964), (mimeographed).

Over the next few years, economic relations with
the centrally planned economies developed along now
familiar lines. If we study the statistics of these
years, it immediately becomes clear that trade relations were far more important to the Guinean economy
than Soviet and Eastern European financial and technical aid.

TRADE

Over the period under review Guinea consistently
had a negative balance of trade with the Soviet Bloc.
Thus, it follows that imports from the Eastern trade
area have been more important to the Guinean economy
than exports. In fact, from 1959 to 1964, the centrally planned economies supplied 35.6 per cent of
total Guinean imports and, purchased 23.2 per cent of
her exports, and accounted for 29.4 per cent--or very
close to one third--of total Guinean turnover of foreign trade. Furthermore, while the volume of Guinean
foreign trade varied considerably from year to year,
trade with the centrally planned economies remained
remarkably stable, with variations of only a few percentage points from year to year.

This stability was not, however, reflected in commodity exchange with the individual centrally planned
economy. Here we find, that although trade varied much
with every country, Poland and the Soviet Union were
among Guinea's more balanced trade partners. Guinean
trade with Czechoslovakia reached a high in 1960 and
declined steadily thereafter. The same tendency marked
trade with Eastern Germany--with the sole exception
that a maximum level here was reached in 1961. Throughout the period the six Eastern European countries accoun
ted for about 55 per cent of total Guinean trade with
the Soviet Bloc, but their role as suppliers of commodities to Guinea was more significant than their role as
purchasers of Guinean products.

The commodity structure of Guinean trade with the
centrally planned economies follows basically familiar
lines: imports of some capital equipment and consumer

TABLE 24

GUINEA

Commodity Structure of Trade with the Soviet Union[a]

1962
(Imports and exports f.o.b.)

Commodity Groups	Units	Quantity	Value
	Imports		
Total Imports from the Soviet Union	Million Dollars		14.0
including:			
Machinery and transport equipment--Total	-		9,165.0
of which:			
Excavators and road-building equipment	-		88.0
Spare parts for road-building machinery	-		67.1
Equipment and materials for projects	-		7,278.0
Spare parts for tractors	-		79.2
Transport and garage equipment	-		865.0
Heavy motor vehicles	Units	132	36.5
Light motor vehicles	Units	43	43.0
Spare parts for vehicles	-		41.2
Aircraft	-		724.0
Tires	1,000 Units	8	321.0
Chemicals--Total			
of which:			
Oil products and synthetic liquid fuel	1,000 tons	74.8	1,661.0
Gasoline	1,000 tons	34.2	924.0
Diesel fuel	1,000 tons	22.2	518.0
Mazut	1,000 tons	18.4	212.3
Manufactured Goods			
including:			
Graded steel	1,000 tons	0.7	63.0
Wire rod	1,000 tons	0.4	36.5
Cotton fibers	Million meters	4.8	645.5
Meal	1,000 tons	5.5	444.0
Refined sugar	1,000 tons	1.2	141.0
Soap	Tons	1,800	296.0
Miscellaneous Manufactured Goods			
including:			
Cultural and household goods	-		316.0
Household refrigerators	Units	350	46.5
Clocks and watches	1,000 Units	8.5	40.8
Printed matter			13.5

Commodity Groups	Units	Quantity	Value
	Exports		
Total Exports to the Soviet Union	Million Dollars		2.75
including:			
Essential oils and fragrant substances	Tons	15	71.5
Palm seeds	1,000 tons	2.4	360.0
Natural coffee	1,000 tons	0.3	118.0
Pineapples	1,000 tons	1.4	600.0
Bananas	1,000 tons	11.8	1,116.0
Husked groundnuts	1,000 tons	0.2	48.0

Sources: Section on Guinea in Vneshnyaya Torgovlya Soyuza SSSR za 1962 god. (Moscow: Vneshtorgizdat, 1964).

Note: [a]All ruble amounts converted to dollars at "new" rate: 1 ruble=$1.11

goods, and exports of agricultural cash crops. Unfortunately, as Guinean statistics on foreign trade
are singularly difficult to obtain, we have information on one trade flow only--that between Guinea and
the Soviet Union.[41]

We find here that in 1962--out of total imports
by Guinea from the Soviet Union--capital equipment
made up 64 per cent, chemicals about 12 per cent, and
manufactured goods and miscellaneous consumer goods
accounted for the remaining 24 per cent. What is
noteworthy is the unusually large proportion of capital goods imports. Within this category we find that
more than 75 per cent was destined for Soviet-financed
development projects in Guinea. Altogether the structure of these imports shows a greater versatility and
variation than we have seen in any African country so
far--with the exception of Egypt. It is questionable,
however, whether 1962 is a typical year. As will be
seen in the discussion on financial and technical aid,
the disbursement pattern of Soviet Bloc credits to
Guinea was very uneven; and 1962 may have been a year
when these were drawn on fairly heavily.

Guinean exports to the Soviet Union were almost
exclusively made up of coffee and tropical fruits.

Very little information exists on the structure
of trade with other centrally planned economies, but
it appears that in both 1962 and 1963 Eastern Germany
and Poland were important customers of Guinean iron
ore. A Paris source gives the following figures for
this trade:[42]

	1962 Thousand Tons	1963 Thousand Tons
Total Guinean iron ore pro- duction	719,970	559,700
Exports to Poland	451,347	348,982
Exports to Eastern Germany	43,354	46,632
Exports to Czechoslovakia	–	14,597

The same source also indicates that sales of
various grades of bauxite to Czechoslovakia have seen
an increase over the past three years.[43] There seems

to be little doubt, however, that exports of coffee and tropical fruits will remain the mainstay of trade with Eastern Europe as well as with the Soviet Union.

Turning to economic assistance it can categorically be stated that in the short history of Soviet Bloc aid to developing countries, hardly any has suffered more bungling and mishandling of project execution at the hands of the donor country than has Guinea.

FINANCIAL AND TECHNICAL ASSISTANCE

The record of Soviet and Eastern European financial and technical assistance to Guinea is a sad story. This is quite possibly due to the inordinate speed with which the aid agreements were negotiated, and probably also the the fact that Guinea, as the first former French colony in Africa to receive Soviet Bloc aid, presented the donors with very unfamiliar situations. This does not, however, justify the repeated cases of poor preplanning and shoddy equipment deliveries to which Guinea has been subjected.

The dismal story begins with the Soviet loan of $35 million in August, 1959.[44] This was intended to finance geological prospecting as well as the construction of a polytechnical institute, factory installations, and a stadium in Conakry. At a later date the agreement was amended to include Soviet assistance in equipping Conakry Airport, in the construction of a 120-room hotel and the laying of tracks for the Conakry-Mamou railway.

Of these commitments the following projects have been completed: the 25,000-seat stadium in Conakry,[45] the hotel,[46] a refrigeration plant in Conakry,[47] a sawmill at Nzérékoré,[48] and a cannery at Mamou.[49]

Also completed is a radio transmission station for Conakry Airport. This station was built on a hill that turned out to be very rich in iron ore. Although this might possibly be a valuable find, the radio station itself is useless for transmission, and Conakry Airport

has been refurnished with American equipment.[50] While
the Soviet Union did not send snowplows to Guinea,[51]
she did provide the tropical country with tractors with
sealed cabs through which an exhaust pipe was passed to
provide extra heat.[52]

Possibly the greatest single failure of the Soviet
development efforts in Guinea, however, was the 700
hectares state rice farm at La Fié, which has so far
yielded no results despite the expenditure of a large
part of the planned investment.[53]

These and other incidents[54] have drawn the entire
Soviet aid program to Guinea into serious disrepute.
Indeed, following Ambassador Solod's expulsion in December, 1961,[55] the program was tuned down and at present few Soviet aid projects are in progress. Work has
been continued on some geological prospecting and on
the Conakry-Mamou railway track-laying, but this latter
is still far from completion.[56]

The record of the Eastern European countries is
somewhat, although not much, better. Here we must, of
course, take into consideration the small amounts grant-
ed--$10 million from Czechoslovakia[57] and $4 million
from Poland[58]--and the rather limited amount of works
that can be undertaken with such sums. In fact, most
of the Czechoslovak credit went toward deliveries of
machinery and equipment--the Czechs state that Guinea
received motor cars, laboratory equipment, small aircraft,[59] and 100 railroad cars which one source states
cryptically--were not measured for Guinea's track
gauges.[60]

Poland has been more successful. Her formation
of a joint fishing company is a form of capital trans-
fer which is distinctly new in Soviet Bloc relations
with developing countries--and could conceivably prove
to be quite effective since it appears on the surface
even better suited to satisfy national pride and the
desire for "economic independence," than the usual
"long-term credits on the basis of mutual equality."[61]
This agreement, so far as is known, assigns 51 per cent
of the shares of the fishing company to Guinea, with
the understanding that the remaining part will be purchased over a period of time.[62] Poland meanwhile,

supplies boats, managerial, and technical equipment,
and much of the refrigeration and canning equipment.
The program became operative in January, 1961. There
is now under study a similar arrangement with Ghana,
and of other African countries conceivably partici-
pating in a Polish-sponsored West African shipping
line.[63]

CULTURAL AND EDUCATIONAL RELATIONS

Probably the most important project in this category will be the 1,500-student polytechnical institute
in Conakry, financed by Soviet credits.[64] The construction of this is in progress--and has been so for
the past five years--but as of now there is no report
on its definite completion.

In addition to the educational facilities which
will be made available once this institute is fully
operational, Guinean students have been offered scholarships for higher study in practically all the centrally planned economies. In 1963, 31 young Guineans
were studying in Bulgaria, 32 in Czechoslovakia, 61
in Eastern Germany, 11 in Hungary, 30 in Poland, 8 in
Rumania, and 60 in the Soviet Union.[65]

Educational exchange has also gone the other way.
In 1962, for example, 45 Czechoslovak physicians, 15
professors, experts in agriculture, geological surveys,
etc. were teaching in Guinea,[66] while in April, 1963,
the Soviet Academy of Sciences presented the Guinea
Institute of Research and Documentation with tape-
recording and modern microfilm equipment.[67]

On the basis of cultural exchange agreements, we
find that, throughout the period, groups of young
Guineans participated in Soviet and Eastern European
sponsored study groups--in Guinea and in the Soviet
Bloc--on topics ranging from "peaceful cooperation between nations" to "socialist planning and development."
It remains to be seen what impact these discussions
will have on Guinean economic development.

Hardly any African country on the receiving end
of Soviet and Eastern European financial and technical
aid has been more thoroughly discussed or more thoroughly disillusioned than Guinea. Whereas trade with the
Soviet Bloc has played, and may continue to play, a
relatively important role in the development of the
Guinean economy, the majority of aid projects have either been poorly planned and executed, or--in a few
instances--they were miserable failures. In addition
to these shortcomings, there were heavy-handed attempts
at political infiltration. Hence, it appears reasonable
to conclude that the whole experience--for the Guinean
Government at any rate--must have been a very sobering
one.

Partly because of this, but also because of a more
reasonable attitude of the French Administration, Guinea
has, since 1961, gradually altered her position from
that of rabid radicalism to one of moderation and de-
liberation. She has rather slowly and painfully re-
established her relations with France and has sought
greater assistance from Western nations. In April,
1962, she promulgated a new investment law designed to
attract private foreign investment--and has attempted
to draw up somewhat more realistic development programs.

The internal front, however--where fewer signs of
change are apparent--has left both Eastern and Western
commentators with deep feelings of mistrust in the future of Guinea. Both Czechoslovakia and Eastern Germany
have expressed doubts on Guinean ability to manage future debt servicing, and both countries are discontented
with Guinea's lack of appreciation for past efforts.[68]
At a speech in Paris, Mr. Jean de Lipkovski, rapporteur
général des questions africaines of the French National
Assembly, noted that, although the Guinean experience
was a courageous attempt to affirm the African person-
ality, economically this policy had been disastrous.
While incompetence and dishonesty in the administration
have contributed to the devaluation of the Guinean franc
to 70 per cent of its preindependence value, for the
past years Guinea has been heavily dependent on U.S.
food aid.[69]

In many respects Guinea provides important and
fascinating lessons for other African countries. Nowher

else has there been a situation more hospitable to
the centrally planned economies, nowhere else have
these countries committed so many errors and so mis-
used their opportunities. No other country has been
Africanized to such a high degree as has Guinea; no
other country has such a crying need for technical and
administrative talent.

But neither the West nor proponents of socialism
can take pride or pleasure from the Guinean experience.
Had France been able to make as rapid adjustments to
Guinea's changing demands as she later proved capable
of doing, much wasted time and anguish might have been
avoided. Instead Guinea might have been functioning
reasonably well rather than chaotically.

As a result, crucial social and economic facts
are not known to anyone--and hence of no value to the
East or to the West in assisting the country in economic planning and development.

M A L I

Mali has, in more ways than one, represented an
enigma in African nation-building. Indeed, in the
judgment of those who were initially sympathetic ob-
servers of African nationalism, but who concluded
shortly after independence that the continent was off
to a bad start, an exception is usually made in the
case of Mali:

> . . . the visitor who lands in Bamako en-
> counters few of the offensive displays that
> confront him elsewhere: there are no sump-
> tious mansions or prestigious glass-and-
> concrete symbols of State supremacy, and
> there is barely talk of corruption in high
> places. Government offices are housed for
> the most part in pre-war French colonial
> structures in the **style soudanais**. Inside
> them there is little self-satisfaction; the
> key words in any conversation with a Malian

official are likely to be austerity and
struggle, construction and watchfulness,
sacrifice and discipline.[70]

This attitude is almost understandable; from a
physical point of view Mali consists largely of desert
and steppe, and this country is one of the poorest
areas of Africa, although it has interesting potentialities in mining and in the further irrigation of the
interior Niger delta.

The modern sector of the economy which Mali in-
herited from the colonial period, was very backward
and completely dependent on France. At independence
(in 1958) the total value of her exports (mainly groundnuts) was 2,703 million CFA francs;[71] of this 97 per
cent went to France where they found a protected market.[72] Imports (90 per cent from France) amounted to
about 8,345 million CFA francs.[73]

In 1961, after deciding to launch "immediately and
vigorously" a program of economic decolonization, a
five-year plan was developed which envisaged an annual
growth rate of 8 per cent--this to be achieved by a total five-year investment as large as the current national
product itself, half of which was to be supplied by foreign aid. The hoped-for increase was to be more or less
evenly allocated between private and public consumption.
Significantly, the planners did not promise their country
men a substantial increase in personal income.[74]

To seek part financing for the realization of these
aspirations, Mali, in the ensuing years, turned toward
the centrally planned economies. By mid-1967, she had
trade ties, and had received financial and technical aid
from a majority of them.

TRADE

Commodity exchange between Mali and the Eastern trad
area first began with the signature of a long-term trade
agreement with Czechoslovakia in February, 1961.[75] This
was rapidly followed by similar arrangements with the
U.S.S.R. By the end of 1962, Mali had commercial ties w

five members of the Soviet Bloc. These are all
strictly bilateral in character and relatively inflexible where payments arrangements are concerned.
On the other hand it appears that Mali has been
granted liberal swing credits from the Eastern partners.[76]

From a very modest beginning (not recorded in
Table 25), trade increased to a peak in 1962, only
to decline again in 1963 and 1964.[77] In spite of
this unevenness trade dependence on the Soviet Bloc
has been high. If we can generalize on the basis of
a three-year experience, the centrally planned economies have been somewhat more important to Mali as a
market for her exports, than as a source of imports.
Based on the 1961-64 period, the Eastern trade area
accounted for 26.0 per cent of total Mali exports
and for 16.3 per cent of her imports.

As expected, the Soviet Union figures very
largely in these relations and accounts for an average of about 60 per cent of Mali trade turnover with
the centrally planned economies, while Czechoslovakia
accounts for about 25-30 per cent. The remainder is
evenly divided between Eastern Germany and Poland.

The commodity structure of this trade can be
illustrated by figures taken from the peak year,
1962. (See Table 26).

These figures are not typical, since 90 per
cent of imports from the centrally planned economies
that year consisted of aircraft deliveries from the
Soviet Union to Mali Airways. The only product the
Eastern trade area buys, and has ever bought from
Mali, is groundnuts.

FINANCIAL AND TECHNICAL ASSISTANCE

In the short period in which Mali has maintained
economic relations with the Soviet Union and Eastern
Europe, she has received close to $76 million worth
of development aid and stands today as the fifth
largest recipient of committed Soviet Bloc aid to

TABLE 25

MALI

Value of Trade with the Centrally Planned Economies

Totals and Country Breakdowns

(U.S.$ thousand, imports, c.i.f.; exports f.o.b.)

Country Distribution	1961		1962		1963		Jan.-Sept., 1964	
	Imports	Exports	Imports	Exports	Imports	Exports	Imports	Exports
Total Trade	35,591	14,063	45,714	10,029	34,246	10,556	27,446	5,708
of which: Soviet Union and Eastern Europe	120	3,214	11,524	3,839	7,502	56	8,183	69
Individual Country Breakdown								
Czechoslovakia	60	1,824	1,623	2,408	1,579	1	654	1
Eastern Germany	-	-	244	-	140	-	16	-
Poland	28	-	250	45	439	-	454	-
Soviet Union	-	1,390	9,374	1,385	5,216	54	6,877	51

Sources: Figures for 1961, 1962, and 1963: U.N., ECA, Foreign Trade Statistics of Africa, Series A,
Direction of Trade (E/CN.14/STAT/Ser.A/5, No. 5)(February, 1965), pp. 22-23; January-
September, 1964: No. 7 (January, 1966), pp. 16-17.

Africa. She has credit arrangements with four centrally planned economies, all concluded in 1961-62.
The Soviet Union accounts for 60 per cent of the total assistance committed,[78] or about one fourth of all
bilateral assistance received by Mali. Most of these
credits have been utilized for financing projects
which can best be classified as belonging to the conventional technical assistance category.

Soviet efforts have been concentrated on large-
scale geological research. _Trud_ reports that Soviet
geologists have discovered significant marble, cement,
limestone, and gold deposits, and are now engaged in
prospecting for oil in the Sahara regions.[79] Altogether some 150 scientists have been sent yearly to
Mali. By the end of 1965, they had covered some
500,000 square kilometers in their work.[80]

Soviet activities, however, are not restricted
only to this--assistance has also been extended to
improving the navigability of the Niger River, to
setting up model farms, to teaching agricultural
techniques, and to building in Bamako a 25,000-seat
stadium which is nearing completion.[81]

What is noticeable about all these projects is
the fact that they seem to have been planned and executed with great thoroughness. Compared to the
Guinean response, relatively few voices of dissatis-
faction have been heard from Mali.

Czechoslovakia has been less fortunate. This
country, which was mostly interested in financing
industry, planned to build in Mali a broadcasting
center and a textile combine.[82] By mid-1967, however, nothing had been heard of the broadcasting
center, while some work has continued on the textile
mill.[83] The only other centrally planned economy to
operate in Mali, Bulgaria, has been interested in
agricultural research and in urban development.[84]

CULTURAL AND EDUCATIONAL RELATIONS

In relative terms, the Soviet Bloc investment
in cultural aid has been more intense in Mali than

TABLE 26

MALI

Commodity Structure of Trade with the Centrally Planned Economies

January-June, 1962

(U.S.$ thousand, imports c.i.f.; exports f.o.b.)

| Commodity Group | 1962--First 6 months | | | |
| | Imports | | Exports | |
	Total	Soviet Union and Eastern Europe	Total	Soviet Union and Eastern Europe
Total Trade	28,710	7,531	6,724	3,032
Major Product Categories				
Food products	1,818	233		
Manufactured goods	7,207	329		
Crude materials--inedible			4,302	3,032
Machinery, transport equipment	14,777	6,876		

Individual Product Breakdown

Sugar	672	233		
Nonmetallic mineral manufacturing	374	189		
Transport equipment (mainly aircraft)	11,533	6,820		
Household equipment	234	138		
Groundnuts			4,032	3,032

Sources: U.N., ECA, Foreign Trade Statistics of Africa, Series B, Trade by Commodity (E/CN.14/STAT/Ser. B/4, May, 1963), No. 4, pp. 33-44.

192

in most other African countries. On the basis of the
1961 agreement, the Soviet Union is now constructing
a National School of Administration, which will, when
completed in 1967, "prepare political and administrative personnel to help build an independent and socialist economy."[85] Moreover, the Soviet Union is also
constructing a Rural Polytechnical Institute for 300
trainees, and this school is now near completion.[86]

Finally, we might mention that both Czechoslovakia
and the Soviet Union have offered scholarships for
young Malians to study in their respective countries.
While the "absorption capacity" here has been fairly
low, there are now about 30 young men from Mali studying at institutions of higher learning in the centrally
planned economies.[87]

With few exceptions, Mali's economic relations
with the Eastern trade area have been smooth and satisfactory, but trade flows between the two areas have
been subjected to heavy fluctuations, a characteristic
which does not facilitate the tasks for Mali planners.
This must, however, be seen in relation to the Soviet
Bloc's apparent willingness to purchase a relatively
large share of Mali's major export product, which is
not easily marketable.

With the usual reservations regarding forecasting,
the future of Mali's relations with the centrally
planned economies seems reasonably stable. On the
basis of current agreements, and arrangements made
for their prolongation, the Soviet Bloc can be expected to maintain its present share of Mali's foreign
trade. With recent mineral finds, the structure of
exports to the Eastern trade area may well become more
varied. Developments in financial and technical assistance will probably be more modest but branch out from
conventional technical aid to heavier participation in
extractive and productive industries.

But throughout all these developments it should
be kept in mind that, despite her allegedly "socialist" leanings, Mali has--since 1958--maintained strong
and relatively cordial ties with France. In September,
1964, in a speech honoring the fourth anniversary of

Mali's independence, President Keita paid tribute to
the French people, heirs to the Great Revolution of
1789, and to their present leader, whose policies
provide "a determining element for the maintenance
of peace and of the independence of the peoples of
Africa, Asia, and Latin America."[88]

T H E   S U D A N

The Sudan has received very little financial
and technical assistance, but is the Soviet Bloc's
second largest trade partner in Africa. This is
mainly due to the willingness of the centrally
planned economies to purchase the Sudan's staple
export crops and has led to the conclusion of trade
agreements with all seven members of the Eastern
trade area, restricting to a degree the country's
policy of free multilateral trade.

TRADE

Having concluded these agreements in the seven-
year period between 1955 and 1962, the Sudan was one
of the first African countries to take up direct relations with the Eastern trade area.[89] All agreements reflect a high degree of bilateralism through
clearing accounts settled in nonconvertible currencies.[90] While there is no indication that the Sudan
has been able to negotiate multilateral payment arrangements providing for settlement of balances in
convertible currencies, it must be admitted that trade
flows between the Sudan and the centrally planned
economies have remained fairly well balanced over the
period.

This statement pertains only to the balance of
trade between the two areas; when we examine trade
flows between the Sudan and the individual centrally
planned economy, we find in every instance considerable imbalance between imports and exports, these
being particularly striking in the case of Sudanese
trade with Eastern Germany and Poland.

Clearly, the Soviet Union is by far the Sudan's most important Eastern trade partner, accounting for an average of between one third and one half of total commodity exchange with the centrally planned economies.

In over-all terms, trade between the Sudan and the Soviet Bloc accounted--in the period 1960 to 1964--for 8.9 per cent of total Sudanese imports; for 10.4 per cent of her exports; and for 9.7, or close to 10 per cent of the Sudan's total turnover of foreign trade.

One might, of course, argue that this is not an alarming dependence on a single, or a group of trade partners, but in relative terms this dependence becomes somewhat more significant when considering the commodity structure of trade between the Sudan and the Eastern area.

The centrally planned economies may well have accounted for an average 10 per cent of Sudanese turnover of foreign trade, but their importance as customers of the Sudan's major product, raw cotton, is greater than that. The Eastern trade area purchased 12.1 per cent of Sudanese cotton exports in 1960 and 14.6 per cent in 1961. Further increases followed in 1962, 1963, 1964, and in 1965,[91] and based on unconfirmed statistics, Soviet Bloc purchases can be expected to reach close to 20 per cent, or one fifth of the Sudan's total cotton exports by the end of this decade.

Sudanese imports from the centrally planned economies cover a relatively wide range of products, with a heavy predominance on imports of cereals, sugar, and cotton fabrics. In no product category, with the sole exception of footwear, do imports from the Eastern trade area constitute a major part of total imports; for the most part they account for anywhere between 5 and 25 per cent of total imports. During the 1960-65 period there was little change in this structure, except that--what is perhaps more important--imports of capital goods declined as a whole.

TABLE 27

THE SUDAN

Value of Trade with the Centrally Planned Economies

Totals and Country Breakdowns

(U.S.$ thousand, imports c.i.f.; exports f.o.b.)

	1955-59		1960		1961	
	Imports	Exports	Imports	Exports	Imports	Exports
Total Trade	..	..	180,900	181,978	237,938	178,54?
of which:						
Soviet Union and Eastern Europe	35,800	38,100	14,383	14,169	19,793	17,15€
Individual Country Breakdown						
Czechoslovakia	14,500	10,100	3,114	4,711	3,621	2,70?
Eastern Germany	5,600	8,000	186	214	1,487	53€
Poland	5,200	4,700	1,011	836	2,584	2,00?
Soviet Union	10,500	13,600	6,541	5,736	8,853	9,81?

1962		1963		1964	
Imports	Exports	Imports	Exports	Imports	Exports
256,520	226,731	285,028	221,498	274,246	192,720
22,955	21,717	29,539	30,736	19,425	18,369

4,574	3,184	3,226	3,516	2,762	1,869
741	2,917	803	2,662	1,141	2,299
3,581	2,524	6,207	2,130	5,119	4,954
8,402	10,306	12,602	15,343	4,221	5,059

ources: Figures for 1955-59: U.N., Yearbook of International
Trade Statistics, 1961, New York: U.N. 1963, pp. 682-83.
U.N., ECA, Foreign Trade Statistics of Africa, Series A,
Direction of Trade (E/CN.14/STATS/Ser. A/1, 2, 4, 6, and
7);1960: No. 1 (May, 1962), pp. 33-40; 1961: No. 2
(November, 1962), pp. 14-15; 1962: No. 4 (February,
1964), pp. 15-17; 1963: No. 6 (December, 1965), pp.
13-15; 1964: No. 7 (January, 1966), pp. 9-11.

TABLE 28

THE SUDAN

Commodity Structure of Trade with the Centrally Planned Economies

(U.S.$ thousand, imports c.i.f.; exports f.o.b.)

| Commodity Group | 1960 | | | |
| | Imports | | Exports | |
	Total	Soviet Union and Eastern Europe	Total	Soviet Union and Eastern Europe
Total Trade	182,949	14,662	174,093	14,175
Major Product Categories				
Food products	28,625	4,303		
Crude materials--inedible	4,711	1,306	153,446	14,150
Manufactured goods	62,734	5,824		
Machinery, transport equipment	44,056	839		
Miscellaneous manufactured articles	11,847	2,166		
Individual Product Breakdown				
Cereals and preparations	6,171	172		
Sugar and preparations	10,763	4,124		
Wood, lumber, and cork	3,804	1,305		
Coal, coke, and briquettes	211	146		
Textile yarn fabrics (mainly cotton fabrics)	39,108	3,396		
Iron and steel (pig iron ferro alloys)	5,052	1,150		
Glass and glassware	1,557	162		
Pottery	713	128		
Finished structural parts	1,611	286		
Household equipment	837	152		
Road motor vehicles	16,495	304		
Footwear	3,961	1,479		
Miscellaneous manufactured articles	1,183	363		
Groundnuts			12,608	1,209
Cotton seeds			7,989	
Raw cotton and linters			95,134	11,485

| 1962 | | | | 1964 | | | |
| Imports | | Exports | | Imports | | Exports | |
Total	Soviet Union and Eastern Europe	Total	Soviet Union and Eastern Europe	Total	Soviet Union and Eastern Europe	Total	Soviet Union and Eastern Europe
260,924	23,085	214,280	22,133	274,337	19,411	192,715	18,368
32,703	6,255	193,491	22,098	61,574	4,663	166,930	18,311
5,996	2,253			6,070	2,095		
87,795	10,503			80,758	9,454		
79,261	1,045			69,021	1,461		
15,639	2,118			14,432	1,292		
7,447	2,860						
8,474	3,325						
4,165	2,155						
154	119						
45,680	4,942						
5,561	1,779						
1,768	318						
828	137						
1,650	224						
1,166	123						
18,594	309						
3,722	1,259						
..	..						
		19,184	4,824			26,372	2,622
		15,688	98			19,136	2,345
		125,018	16,787			92,876	12,423

Continued

Table 28 (Continued)

| Commodity Group | January-June, 1965 | | | |
| | Imports | | Exports | |
	Total	Soviet Union and Eastern Europe	Total	Soviet Union and Eastern Europe
Total Trade	100,663	8,034	100,557	10,976
Major Product Categories				
Food products	22,181	4,056		
Crude materials--inedible	1,793	214	85,946	10,642
Manufactured goods	30,052	2,171		
Machinery, transport equipment	20,539	500		
Miscellaneous manufactured articles	5,939	610		
Individual Product Breakdown				
Cereals and preparations				
Sugar and preparations				
Wood, lumber, and cork				
Coal, coke, and briquettes				
Textile yarn fabrics (mainly cotton fabrics)				
Iron and steel (pig iron ferro alloys)				
Glass and glassware				
Pottery				
Finished structural parts				
Household equipment				
Road motor vehicles				
Footwear				
Miscellaneous manufactured articles				
Groundnuts			17,462	1,862
Cotton seeds			4,316	1,070
Raw cotton and linters			44,219	6,506

Sources: U.N., ECA, Foreign Trade Statistics of Africa, Series B, Trade by Commodity (E/CN.14/STAT/Ser. B/5-7-10). Figures for 1960: No. 5 (October, 1963), pp. 107-23; No. 7, pp. 221-35 (1962); No. 10, pp. 174-201 (1964) and pp. 49-72 (1965).

FINANCIAL AND TECHNICAL ASSISTANCE

Soviet and Eastern European programs of financial and technical assistance have been minimal. We
have frequently seen that deliveries of capital goods
and equipment were made in connection with Soviet
Bloc-financed aid projects. The Sudan, however, has
received development assistance only from the Soviet
Union--a relatively small loan of $22 million in 1961.
This was destined to finance the construction of grain
elevators and various crop-research laboratories.[92]

However, the only report on the utilization of
this credit is a _Tass_ press release to the effect that
a Soviet mission had spent a year in the Sudan studying fish resources in the Upper Nile.[93] By late 1965
about $15 million was still outstanding on the Soviet
credit, and little has been drawn on this amount
since. However, feasibility studies have been made
of several projects including the construction of grain
elevators, canning factories, and a food processing
plant.

In more ways than one, economic relations between
the Sudan and the Eastern trade area are peculiar in
form and in nature. Each area imports from the other
products which are either competitive with local production, or products that can easily be obtained from
other sources. Surely, the large cotton purchases by
the centrally planned economies have eased the Sudanese
market position; but this advantage must be seen in relation to the generally lower cotton prices obtained
from the Soviet Bloc.[94]

All these factors make it extremely difficult to
forecast any future developments. So far, one has the
impression that there is little economic advantage in
this trade--to either side. In such a situation noneconomic factors take on more significance. Assuming
these remain stable over the next few years, commodity
exchange between the two areas should see a reasonable
growth.

                    *   *   *

The seven-year experience of economic relations
between West-Central Africa and the Eastern trade area

is in many respects too short a period from which to
draw firm and abiding conclusions. There is, however, no doubt that the advantage of trade and aid
from the centrally planned economies has lost some
of its former attraction to the region. Economic
aid from the Soviet Bloc has been less than effective and this aid has had only a very small impact
on the recipient economies. True, in the case of
both Ghana and Guinea, large portions of committed
aid are still untouched, and future Soviet Bloc activities in this area must be assumed to improve
over past performances, particularly as the centrally
planned economies have been quick to learn from past
failures.

The record of trade exchanges is more satisfactory. Particularly, West Africa produces today commodities that are eminently marketable in the Eastern
trade area; in fact, few other regions of Africa offer
the Soviet Bloc more attractive commodities for exports. Consequently, trade exchange should increase
between West Africa and the centrally planned economies in Eastern Europe.

NOTES TO CHAPTER 6

1. William A. Hance, The Geography of Modern Africa (New York: Columbia University Press, 1964), p.

2. U.N. Yearbook of National Account Statistics,
1965, Table 9a, p. 493.

3. Ghana - Seven Year Development Plan, 1963/64-
1969/70 (Accra: Ministry of Finance, 1962).

4. U.N., ECA, Outlines and Selected Indicators
of African Development Plans (E/CN.14/336, January 14,
1965) (Addis Ababa, 1965), p. 25.

5. See Chapter 3, Table 9, "Africa--Country
Distribution of Credits," pp. 81-89.

6. Ibid.

7. U.N., ECA, Foreign Trade Statistics of Africa
Series A, Direction of Trade, No. 5 (January, 1965), p

8. *Ibid.*, pp. 36-37.

9. See Chapter 8, pp. 243-48, for a discussion of bilateral balancing of African trade with the Soviet Bloc.

10. See Chapter 2, Table 4, "Africa--Trade and Payments Agreements," pp. 37-51.

11. *Ibid.*, pp. 41-42.

12. See Chapter 3, Table 9, "Africa--Country Distribution of Credits," pp. 81-89.

13. See Chapter 3, Table 8, "Africa--Credits Received from the Centrally Planned Economies in Proportion to Total Soviet Bloc Credits to all Developing Areas, 1957-65," p. 80.

14. *Pravda*, March 5, 1963.

15. *Ibid.*, December 12, 1960.

16. *Ibid.* This project is independent of the U.S.-financed Volta River scheme for reduction of alumina, and power production.

17. Accra Radio Press Release, December 23, 1964, and *Pravda*, April 28, 1964.

18. *Pravda*, June 15, 1961.

19. *Tass* Press Release, February 12, 1964.

20. Moscow Radio Press Release, December 2, 1966.

21. December 20, 1962.

22. May 19, 1963.

23. *Tass* Press Release, May 16, 1962.

24. *Czechoslovak Foreign Trade*, Vol. 2, No. 9 (September, 1962), p. 9.

25. West Africa (London), March 24, 1962.

26. Pravda, March 6, 1966.

27. Ibid.

28. Czechoslovak Foreign Trade, Vol. 3, No. 4 (April, 1963).

29. Vedomosti Verkhovnogo Soveta SSSR, No. 25, p. 1060 (Moscow: June 22, 1964).

30. See Table 21, pp. 166-67.

31. In the period 1960-63 Ghana received a total of $17.4 million in grants, loans, and resource transfers from the member countries of the OECD group. (OECD, The Flow of Financial Resources to Less-Developed Countries, 1956-63, Table V-3, p. 172). This amounts 16 per cent of total aid from Eastern and Western sources. However, the contribution of member countries of the OECD group has been more significant than this might indicate. For one thing, the $17.4 million represent aid delivered, whereas the $89 million from the centrally planned economies represent commitments. Disbursements run far below this. Secondly, several members of the OECD group have large private investment programs under way in Ghana, and many of these projects have received governmental investment guarantees. The Volta River scheme, which involves total investments of $300-400 million, completely overshadows any development project undertaken by the Eastern group. Furthermore, Ghana reportedly received a Chinese credit of $19.6 million in August, 1961, (NCNA Press Release, August 18, 1961).

32. U.N., TAB, Technical Assistance Activities in Ghana, Report of the U.N. TAB Resident Representative for the period January-July, 1964 (res. TAB/GHA/R.14, September 29, 1964)(New York: 1964), p. 8.

33. Ghanaian Times reported on September 29, 1966 that a Soviet mission had arrived in Ghana to undertake a general review of Soviet-financed projects. The purpose would be to assess their feasibility and to determine whether they be worth continuing.

34. The population of Guinea in 1964 was estimated at 3.4 million inhabitants (U.N., Statistical Yearbook, 1964), Table 19, p. 81.

35. In 1957, there were 7,000 French in Guinea. By 1960 this number had dwindled to fewer than 2,000 (The World Mark Encyclopedia of Nations, New York: Harper and Brothers, 1960), p. 406.

36. See, for instance, Alexander Dallin in Brzezinski, Z., ed., Africa and the Communist World, pp. 7-48; and Billerbeck, K., Die Auslandshilfe des Ostblocks für die Entwicklungsländer, pp. 76-78.

37. Vneshnyaya Torgovlya, No. 10 (October, 1959).

38. See Chapter 2, Table 4, "Africa--Trade and Payments Agreements," pp. 37-51.

39. It is interesting to note that this credit (140 million rubles=$35 million) was not revalued according to the new ruble to dollar rate which went into effect on January 1, 1961. Other African recipients of Soviet financial assistance, e.g., Ethiopia, which received a 90 million ruble credit ($22.5 million--old rate), had this amount adjusted to the new rate ($100 million) even though the Ethiopian loan was granted one month prior to the loan to Guinea. (See Chapter 3, Table 9, "Africa--Country Distribution of Credits," pp. 81-89.) Furthermore, any significant disbursements from the Soviet loan to Guinea did not commence until 1961-62, i.e., not until after the new rate had come into effect. Of course, this point is purely academic. On the face of it the Soviet Union has no reason to care what foreign exchange rate is applied to her loans-- these will have to be utilized for the purchases of Soviet goods at any rate; but since most international aid comparisons are made in U.S. dollars, one would think it would be in the interest of the Soviet Union to have her development loans quoted in as favorable a rate as possible.

40. Sovremennyy Vostok, No. 5 (May, 1960).

41. Guinean statistics are not reported in any of the current sources on African trade information. What remains for the researcher to do is to gather whatever information can be gleaned from trade news published by the partner countries. Helpful here has been Vneshnyaya Torgovlya soyuza SSSR za 1960, 1961, 1962, etc. gody, which publishes detailed breakdowns on the foreign trade of the U.S.S.R. Another important source for economic information on former French Africa is: Marchés Tropicaux et Méditerranéens (Paris).

42. Marchés Tropicaux et Méditerranéens, No. 948 (January 11, 1964), p. 85.

43. Ibid., No. 952 (February 8, 1964), p. 279.

44. Sovremennyy Vostok, No. 5 (May, 1960), and Pravda, March 3, 1960.

45. Tass Press Release, December 13, 1964.

46. Pravda, October 2, 1964.

47. Trud, March 22, 1963.

48. Tass Press Release, December 13, 1964. This mill is the first major industrial enterprise in the forest area of Guinea, and will produce annually up to 50,000 cubic meters of timber.

49. Ibid., December 31, 1963. This cannery has a capacity of 5 million cans a year, enough to meet home demand with a surplus for export.

50. Marchés Tropicaux et Méditerranéens, No. 874 (August 11, 1962), p. 1705.

51. They were large tractors equipped with shovel for brush-clearing, a method which had proved successf in Kazakhstan.

52. Marchés Tropicaux et Méditerranéens, No. 975 (March 14, 1964), p. 515.

53. Economist Intelligence Unit, "Three-Monthly Economic Review of the French African Community," No. 8 (March, 1962), p. 16.

54. An old story, and a sad story, which seems to repeat itself in several countries on the receiving line of Soviet aid, was The New York Times (August 20, 1960) account of a Soviet cement shipment to Guinea. Because of the then inadequate storage facilities at Conakry, the shipment was rerouted to Monrovia and left unsheltered on the docks just before the rainy season.

55. For a good account of Soviet political activity in Africa, see Alexander Dallin, "The Soviet Union--Political Activity," in Brzezinski, Z., ed., Africa and the Communist World, pp. 7-48.

56. Moscow Radio Press Release, January 17, 1964.

57. Czechoslovak Foreign Trade, Vol. 2, No. 10 (October, 1962), pp. 14-15.

58. Marchés Tropicaux et Méditerranéens, No. 880 (September 22, 1962).

59. Czechoslovak Foreign Trade, Vol. 2, No. 10 (October, 1962), p. 15.

60. Marchés Tropicaux et Méditerranéens, loc. cit.

61. Robert and Elizabeth Bass, "Eastern Europe," in Brzezinski, Z., ed., Africa and the Communist World, p. 98.

62. This period is probably eight years, or the length of the amortization period for the Polish credit. Marchés Tropicaux et Méditerranéens, No. 810 (May 28, 1961), p. 1317.

63. Radio Warsaw, December 28, 1960, and Polish Press Agency PAP, January 11, and October 25, 1961.

64. Pravda, October 2, 1964.

65. Marchés Tropicaux et Méditerranéens, No. 936 (October 19, 1963), p. 2515.

66. Czechoslovak Foreign Trade, Vol. 2, No. 10 (October, 1962), p. 15.

67. Izvestiya, May 30, 1963.

68. Marchés Tropicaux et Méditerranéens, No. 880 (September 22, 1962), p. 1962.

69. Ibid.

70. Aristide R. Zolberg, "The Political Revival of Mali," The World Today (April, 1965), p. 151.

71. Mali, Comptes Economiques de la République du Mali, 1959, pp. 133-35.

72. Ibid.

73. Ibid., p. 137.

74. Mali, Rapport sur le Plan Quinquennal, 1961-65 (Paris: Imprimerie Maubert, 1961), pp. 12-13.

75. Czechoslovak Foreign Trade, Vol. 1, No. 4 (April, 1961). Czechoslovakia has frequently been the first centrally planned economy to initiate relations with former French colonies in Africa.

76. Vneshnyaya Torgovlya, No. 5 (May, 1961), and Czechoslovak Foreign Trade, Vol. 1, No. 4 (April, 1961).

77. Incomplete figures for the first six months of 1964 indicate a general decline over the whole year (U.S. Department of Commerce, Value Series, Report of March, 1965).

78. U.N., TAB Report of the Resident TAB Representative to Mali (res. TAB/MALI/R.2, October 30, 1964) (New York, 1964), p. 8.

79. March 18, 1964.

80. *Tass* Press Release, December 12, 1965.

81. *Pravda*, January 6, 1964.

82. *Czechoslovak Foreign Trade*, Vol. 2, No. 9
(September, 1962), p. 7.

83. U.N., TAB, *op. cit.*, p. 8.

84. *Ibid.*, p. 9.

85. *Pravda*, January 6, 1964.

86. *Trud*, March 18, 1964, and TAB, *op. cit.*, p. 8.

87. *Pravda*, January 27, 1964, which stated the
expected figures for the academic year 1964-65, without, however, giving country breakdowns. This figure
should be seen in the perspective of the more than
200 Mali students that annually attend French universities (Zolberg in *The World Today*, *op. cit.*, p. 159).

88. *L'Essor* (Bamako), September 28, 1964, as
cited by Zolberg in *The World Today*, *op. cit.*, p. 160.

89. "Direct commercial relations" here are understood as a contradistinction to indirect ties, i.e.,
trade conducted through the former metropolitan country.

90. See Chapter 2, Table 4, "Africa--Trade and
Payments Agreements," pp. 37-51.

91. U.N., ECA, *Foreign Trade Statistics of Africa*,
No. 10 (July, 1966), pp. 49-71.

92. *Pravda*, November 23, 1961.

93. January 7, 1961.

94. See Chapter 8, pp. 249-55.

CHAPTER 7 EAST AFRICA

Over the short period of Soviet and Eastern European economic relations with Africa it is quite possible to detect shifting trends in the degree of their involvement with individual countries. While as of mid-1967, upward of twenty-nine African countries were maintaining some form of economic relations with the Eastern trade area, only ten of these--countries discussed so far--were trading with and receiving aid from the centrally planned economies to the extent that this trade aid has had, or may come to have, a definite impact on their rate of economic growth.

But this should not lead one to believe that the number of these trade and aid flows will forever remain stagnant. Chapter 1 discussed the general decline in agricultural commodity prices and the need evidenced by developing African countries for investment capital, which constantly leads to an exploration of all possible sources of trade outlets and of economic aid. This search will no doubt tighten up many presently loose connections between Africa and the Soviet Bloc, but also cause an expansion of what can best be termed as embryonic relations between the two areas.

In clear evidence here stands East Africa. As we define the region, it includes Ethiopia, Somalia, and the three countries cooperating in the East African Common Services Organization--Kenya, Tanzania, and Uganda.

With the possible exception of Ethiopia, this area presents today a relatively promising picture of Soviet Bloc economic aid to Africa.

210

There are many reasons for this, the foremost
probably being the fact that relations are recent and
the centrally planned economies have had time to learn
from past errors. Moreover, it should not be forgotten
that Chinese economic aid activities are relatively
strong in this area and the specter of competition cannot but sharpen Soviet Bloc performance.

Trade between the two areas has been more laggard.
This is due not only to the present inability of the
East African region to supply centrally planned econo-
mies with desired products, but the insignificant trade
flows also stem from the novelty of these relations.
Commodity exchange may increase not only as aid projects
in progress are completed, but gradual changes in East
African primary commodity production may render exports
more accessible to markets in the Eastern trade area.
This assumption, however, is a generalization which does
not hold true for each individual country in the area.
A pertinent exception is Ethiopia.

E T H I O P I A

Ethiopia has existed as an independent country
longer than any other African nation. It cannot be said,
however, that the old traditions this independence has
fostered have brought it to a more advanced stage than
younger African countries; it stands today as one of the
least developed nations on the continent, a country whose
complex customs and institutions are incrustations which
have inhibited economic, social, and political advance.[1]

In no better way can this be illustrated than by
the telling figures of Ethiopian economic activity.
About 90 per cent of the population[2] are engaged in agriculture, which accounts for over 90 per cent of exports
by value. In 1961 it provided an estimated 62 per cent
of the gross domestic product.[3] In 1958 the annual per
capita income of the Ethiopians was $33, the lowest re-
corded figure for any African country.[4] This figure has
since increased neither absolutely nor relatively.

To help this society move more rapidly into the
modern world, a veritable "united nations" of assisting

TABLE 29

ETHIOPIA

Value of Trade with the Centrally Planned Economies

Totals and Country Breakdowns

(U.S.$ thousand, imports c.i.f.; exports f.o.b.)

Country Distribution	1955-59		1960	
	Imports	Exports	Imports	Exports
Total Trade	..	..	88,253	78,033
of which:				
Soviet Union and Eastern Europe	5,800	3,000	4,375	501
Individual Country Breakdown				
Czechoslovakia	3,700	..	2,346	493
Eastern Germany	900	..	-	-
Poland	..	..	48	-
Soviet Union	2,100	2,500	1,520	-

1961		1962		1963		1964	
Imports	Exports	Imports	Exports	Imports	Exports	Imports	Exports
94,413	96,058	102,247	80,316	111,145	88,330	123,843	104,308
3,903	1,264	4,427	1,303	5,327	1,375	5,622	1,224

1,715	649	1,984	433	2,392	104	2,844	484
804)	..	1,033)	..	5	..	9	..
) 162)	106 ..	) 362)	66 ..	505	..	558	..
1,122	509	1,043	804	1,149	1,222	1,162	660

Sources: Figures for 1955-59: U.N., Direction of International Trade, Statistical Papers, Series T, Vol. X, No. 8, and Vol. XI, No. 9; U.N., ECA, Foreign Trade Statistics of Africa, Series A, Direction of Trade (E/CN.14/STAT/ Ser. A/2, 4,and 7); 1960: No. 2 (November, 1962), pp. 62-63; 1961: No. 4 (February, 1964), pp. 81-83; 1962, 1963, and 1964: No. 7 (January, 1966), pp. 78-80.

groups and countries have offered their help. The
OECD group extended over $80 million in loans, grants,
and private export credits to Ethiopia over the three-
year period 1960-63.[5] Israel, Norway, Sweden, West
Germany, and Yugoslavia have all assisted in one way
or another, while the IBRD and its International Development Association granted loans totalling $39
million up to mid-1963--mainly for transport development, but also to cover foreign exchange requirements
for small industries.[6] Ethiopia hopes that one third
of the $1,062 million expenditures of the Second Plan
will be provided by foreign sources, public, and private.[7]

The aid effort has also been shared by the centrally planned economies. Although the impact of the
assistance from these countries on the Ethiopian econom
is minimal, it is possibly less so in the field of trad
than aid.

TRADE

Ethiopia has traded with the centrally planned
economies since the mid-1950's and is assumed to have
signed trade agreements with a number of Eastern European countries. The only one fully confirmed, however,
is a trade agreement with the Soviet Union signed in
Moscow on July 11, 1959, with a validity of three years

From Table 29 we see immediately that these trade
relations have been modest in scope and, for the period
under review, have not amounted to more than an average
of 3 per cent of Ethiopia's turnover in foreign trade.
This figure is a relative one for, while the volume of
Ethiopian foreign trade has increased by some 4 to 5 pe
cent each year, the proportionate share of trade with
centrally planned economies has declined.

It is interesting to note that, contrary to what
usually is the case, Czechoslovakia has, throughout the
period, remained Ethiopia's most important partner in
the Soviet Bloc, accounting for about 50 per cent of
trade transacted with this area.

The trade balance with the centrally planned economies has always been negative, and while it can be estimated that annual imports from this group have, over the period, amounted to an average of 4 per cent of total Ethiopian commodity purchases from abroad, annual exports to the Eastern trade area accounted for a mere 1.5 per cent.

No details of commodity composition of trade between Ethiopia and the Soviet Bloc have ever been specified in the trade agreements, but from statistics released by the Economic Commission for Africa we can get some idea of the pattern of commodity exchange between the two areas.

Not surprisingly, Ethiopian exports to the Eastern trade area consist exclusively of agricultural raw materials and animal products. In a typical year, 1964, 60 per cent of commodity sales to the centrally planned economies were made up of consignments of raw and roasted coffee--all of which went to the Soviet Union[9]-- and oilseeds and hides--most of which were purchased by Czechoslovakia.[10]

The import pattern is slightly more varied, but with a heavy predominance of imports of manufactured goods and articles. Most of these were in the clothing or footwear field, with small purchases of metals and tools complementing the picture. Altogether, consumer goods and semimanufactures accounted for more than 80 per cent of Ethiopian imports from the Eastern trade area, with capital goods not exceeding 10 per cent of the total.

FINANCIAL AND TECHNICAL ASSISTANCE

The record of the centrally planned economies shows that their financial and technical assistance has centered around the construction of an oil refinery at the Red Sea port of Assab. This is to cost $12 million and is financed by a $100 million credit, which was granted to Ethiopia by the Soviet Union in July, 1959.[11] Agreement for constructing the refinery, however, was not concluded until December, 1963, in Addis Ababa. The

TABLE 30

ETHIOPIA

Commodity Structure of Trade with the Centrally Planned Economies

(U.S.$ thousand, imports c.i.f.; exports f.o.b.)

	1962				1964			
	Imports		Exports		Imports		Exports	
	Total	Soviet Union and Eastern Europe	Total	Soviet Union and Eastern Europe	Total	Soviet Union and Eastern Europe	Total	Soviet Union and Eastern Europe
Total Trade	103,077	4,430	78,955	1,276	123,112	5,577	103,668	1,217
Major Product Categories								
Food products	4,924	309	55,021	725	5,594	191	80,053	393
Chemicals	6,717	592	--	--	9,208	855	22,806[a]	768[a]
Manufactured goods	31,792	1,743	--	--	34,064	1,937	--	--
Miscellaneous manufactured articles	10,880	1,411	--	--	14,978	1,808	--	--

Sources: U.N., ECA, Foreign Trade Statistics of Africa, Series B, Trade by Commodity, No. 6 (November, 1964), pp. 169-85; and No. 10 (July, 1966), pp. 291-309.

Note: [a]Crude inedible materials.

complex will process 500,000 tons of crude oil a year,
thus providing for all domestic requirements, with a
surplus for exports. According to Soviet sources,
this refinery will be the largest in Africa.[12] Earlier,
in March, 1960, a protocol was signed between Ethiopia
and the Soviet Union providing for Russian assistance
in mineral prospecting and in the construction of a
gold mine.[13] No progress has been reported on the
latter projects, although the oil refinery was partial-
ly commissioned in late 1966.[14] Additionally, _Pravda_
notes that a contract was signed in June, 1964, for
Soviet assistance in constructing a thermoelectric
power station at Assab.

In order to control the execution of aid projects,
the Soviet may have set an interesting precedent in
Ethiopia by establishing in Addis Ababa a Soviet-
Ethiopian trading company for the delivery of Soviet
machinery and for Soviet imports of traditional Ethiopian commodities. Fifty-one per cent of the capital of
this company is Soviet, represented by the foreign trade
corporation.[15]

Czechoslovakia is the only Eastern European country known to have been active in Ethiopia. A credit,
reportedly amounting to $14 million, was extended in
connection with the signature of a Czechoslovak-
Ethiopian Treaty of Friendship and Cooperation on
May 11, 1960.[16] It is known that part of this loan
provides for the construction of a canvas shoe factory and assistance in the development of cotton and
sugar plantations.[17] The major part of the loan, however, has apparently been earmarked for vocational
training and scholarships for young Ethiopians to
undertake studies in Czechoslovakia.[18]

In the field of cultural and educational relations the only noticeable project is the construction
of a technical school for 1,000 students at Bahr Dar,
which was completed in May, 1963, and turned over to
Ethiopia as a gift from the Soviet people.[19] This
school will educate technical personnel for industry
and agriculture, as well as technicians for the Assab
refinery. In December of the same year, the Soviet
Ambassador presented the Ethiopian Minister of Education with a complete library of scientific, technical,
and educational literature for the Bahr Dar school.

What this adds up to is that there is no distinctive pattern of Ethiopia's economic relations with
the centrally planned economies. Trade is minimal in
both directions; and besides the Bahr Dar technical
school, it is difficult to pinpoint any positive impact of Soviet Bloc financial and technical aid--in-
asmuch as projects are either still in the planning
stage, or at any rate, a long way from completion.

This should not be taken as an indication of the
failure of Soviet Bloc development aid to Ethiopia.
The lack of activity in that country may equally well
have resulted from Ethiopia's neglect in suggesting
suitable development projects to the centrally planned
economies. Until we see increased activities on this
point, trade and aid relations between Ethiopia and
the Eastern trade area will probably remain at their
present low level.[20]

S O M A L I A

In contradistinction, Somalia presents a more
positive picture of Soviet Bloc economic assistance.
A characterization of this country's economy cannot
be anything but negative. It is poor from the point
of view of natural resources; its population[21] is
illiterate and clannish, and saddled with a very high
rate of venereal disease. Compounding these difficulties is the sad fact that the Somalis--who are
basically nomadic--have long had strong prejudices
against certain manual occupations, considering them
as undignified and fit only for inferior people. As
a rationale for this prejudice, they believe that
Allah will provide--an attitude which treats the
economic motive with obvious contempt.[22]

It is not surprising then that the annual per
capita income of Somalia is among the lowest on the
continent--approximately $45 in 1962-63--but 80 per
cent of the population live outside the money economy.[23]

Bearing these difficulties in mind, it is not easy
to agree with the highly optimistic views of a Soviet

writer who states that "everything in Somalia is now
to be seen as suggesting the contours of the future,
of a time when having conquered all its difficulties,
it will have developed into a flourishing state."[24]
But possibly the belief that Somalia can compress all
of her difficulties within the foreseeable future, is
one of the factors motivating the Soviet Union to engage herself so actively in Somalia's future. In this
endeavor, however, she is not alone. In the field of
trade Somalia has to date concluded two known agreements with the centrally planned economies--Czecho-
slovakia and the Soviet Union.[25] Both provide for exports of Somalia's traditional products, meat and
fruits, and for imports of industrial products. No
information was given in these agreements either on
the quantity of commodities to be exchanged or on
their value.

TABLE 31

SOMALIA

Value of Imports from the Centrally Planned Economies

Totals and Country Breakdowns

(U.S.$ thousand, imports c.i.f.)

	1960	1962	1964
Total imports	30,358	37,870	44,497
Total imports from Soviet Union and Eastern Europe	130	1,748	6,935
Individual product break-down			
Czechoslovakia	130	521	681
Soviet Union	0	1,227	6,254

Source: U.N., Yearbook of International Trade
         Statistics, 1964, New York: United Nations,
         1966, p. 662.

From the preceding table we find, however, that whereas Somalian trade with the centrally planned economies still is relatively small, it has grown from an almost nonexistent base in 1960 to account for 13 per cent of imports in 1964. Exports to the Soviet Bloc countries are still negligible.

No official statistics are available on the commodity structure of these imports, but here we must assume that most are deliveries of materials and equipment made in connection with Soviet and Czechoslovak aid programs.

FINANCIAL AND TECHNICAL ASSISTANCE

Aid agreements were signed simultaneously with the trade agreements. To date Somalia has received $74 million in development loans--$30 million from Czechoslovakia and $44 million from the Soviet Union.[26]

While the Czechoslovak program has received little publicity, that of the Soviet Union has been more apparent. Included in the original agreement of June, 1961, were commitments to build three state agricultural enterprises, including a grain and stock-breeding farm with a school for preparing agricultural specialists; a cotton farm with irrigation facilities; and a farm for growing oil-yielding crops. Further-more, the Soviet Union undertook to construct a dam with a 25,000 kilowatt hydroelectric station; a deep-water port; and three food-processing factories. There was also to be geological prospecting for tin and lead, and the drilling of water wells to aid in development of cattle raising. The Soviet Union would give free assistance to the Somali Government in the construction of two hospitals, a secondary school, a printing plant, and a radio station; and a group of Soviet physicians and teachers would be sent to work in Somalia, while doctors and other professional personnel would be trained in the U.S.S.R.[27]

In March, 1962, a protocol attached to this agreement specified the above commitments and fixed the location of the deep-water port at Berbera on the Red Sea.[28]

In both relative and absolute terms these commitments are impressive--and it might be interesting to follow them up to see where they stand at present.

The projected state grain and dairy farm will be built at Tug Wajakh in the Northern region.[29] When completed, it will have an output of 5,000 to 7,000 tons of grain, and will include an agricultural school, workers' homes, a hospital, a club, silos, and repair shops.[30] By mid-1963, Soviet specialists had undertaken preparatory and planning work, and Soviet ships had arrived with tractors and other necessary machinery. The other two state farms, one of them growing cotton and the other oil-yielding crops--each consisting of 5,000 hectares--are located near the town of Telib in the Lower Juba region.[31]

Radio Mogadishu reported in August, 1964, that the first stage of the Jelib project had been completed, that the second stage was nearing completion and that both farms would be ready for planting by late-1965.[32] These farms have modern irrigation facilities since the project provides for damming the Juba River and building a 5,000 kilowatt power station.[33] Closely connected to the farms will be a cotton-ginning plant, designed by Uzbek experts. With a planned output of up to 10,000 tons of cotton a year, this plant will be operated by centrally controlled mechanized process.[34] Work on this was started in 1964.

As to the deep-water port at Berbera, Soviet engineers did extensive surveys of the land forms of the region in late 1962, and preparatory work commenced in early 1963;[35] building materials and earthmoving equipment were arriving by Soviet ships in October of the same year.[36] The port should be completed by 1968.

The fish processing factory to be built at Las Khareh is designed to process 14 tons of fish daily, 6 million cans yearly. It will include an 80-ton capacity refrigeration plant, repair workshops, and a Diesel power plant.[37] It will also provide large quantities of fish meal and oil. Since plans for this factory had already been compiled, Soviet specialists left Moscow in October, 1963, to supervise the construction.[38]

The foundation stone of the meat-packing plant at Kismayo was laid on March 24, 1964. When completed, this plant will produce 6,000 tons of meat produce a year.[39]

The construction of one of the two hospitals, which the Soviet Union is donating to Somalia, began late in 1962.[40] Located in the Upper Juba region, this will be for the benefit of tuberculosis patients,[4] with a clinic and beds for 50 persons. Soviet doctors will staff both hospitals--in 1963-64, there were an estimated 30 Soviet physicians at work in Somalia.[42]

A printing press located near the harbor of Mogadishu will be able to print 6.6 million newspapers a year. After a ceremony marking the beginning of the construction in March, 1963, the building was completed in four months--by July of the same year.[43] A radio station was also planned and is now under construction.

As to future Soviet financial and technical assistance, a protocol to this effect was signed on July 13, 1964. It provides for the construction of a dairy plan with a daily output of 10 tons of milk; a bakery; two 3,000-ton grain stores; a leather tannery at Kismayo with a capacity for tanning 600,000 tons of skins annually; and water supply projects throughout the country.[45]

CULTURAL AND EDUCATIONAL RELATIONS

Perhaps the most important project in this category is the secondary school located at Mogadishu,

completed in mid-1964. This institution, which was
a gift, includes the school proper, gymnasiums, dorm-
itories, and a medical center.[46]

The headmaster, Nur Hajj Alinjan, left in late
1963 to study educational methods in Moscow. Ten
Soviet secondary school teachers, who will teach at
this school, left for Somalia in March, 1964, to practice in local schools.[47]

An indication of the number of Somali students
studying in the Soviet Union was given by an announcement stating that the Second Congress of Somali Students in the U.S.S.R., which convened at Moscow University on January 29, 1963, was attended by delegates
representing more than 400 students.[48] Indeed, the
Director of cultural relations of the Somali Department of Education stated that "in the course of one
year the Soviet Government had granted Somali more
scholarships for higher studies than either France,
Great Britain, or Italy had offered in 60 years of
colonial rule."[49]

By any standards, it is an undeniable fact that
economic aid received by Somalia from the Soviet Bloc
has been comprehensive in scope and significant in
nature. Based on the purely committed amounts, Somalia
has received more aid from the centrally planned economies per capita than any other country in Africa, except Egypt. If we consider the rate of disbursement
of these loans, it is quite possible that the primary
impact of Soviet Bloc aid has been more pronounced in
Somali than anywhere else on the continent.

What is interesting about the Soviet program is,
however, that in the Somalian case it appears to have
been reasonably well planned with a view to the basic
needs of the country; prestige projects, such as
stadiums, or super-highways, seem to have been avoided.
Once planned, these projects have been, or are being
completed within tightly set time limits that quite
belie past Soviet performances in project execution.

Barring unforeseen noneconomic incidents, the
future of Somali-Soviet Bloc economic relations looks

relatively bright. Here it should be recalled that
most of the $30 million Czechoslovak loan is still
outstanding, while the Soviet Union is under commitment to assist Somalia at least until 1968.[50]

Very little has been said about the payments for
these services, which will probably be effectuated
through commodity deliveries. As credits become ready
for amortization, we can expect commodity flows from
Somalia to the Eastern trade area to take on more
meaningful dimensions than is the case today.

K E N Y A,   T A N Z A N I A,   A N D   U G A N D A

Foremost among the potentially important new relations with the Eastern trading area are those of the
three main countries of East Africa--Kenya, Tanzania, and
Uganda. Populated by about 26.8 million people (in 1964)
they have one characteristic in common: All three have,
since their independence, been severely plagued by internal disunity, which has no doubt complicated the
formulation of a coherent development policy.

In foreign economic policies the area has strongly
tried to diversify its trade flows. As an appendix to
the budding Sino-Soviet strife in Africa, it is interesting to note that this group of countries trade much more
with the Chinese People's Republic than with the Soviet
Union and Eastern Europe.[52]

Commercial relations between Kenya, Tanzania, and
Uganda on the one hand, and Bulgaria, Czechoslovakia,
and the Soviet Union among the centrally planned economies on the other, were initiated in 1963 and 1964--in
all cases only a few months after their independence.
Although it is far too early to undertake any coherent
analysis of this trade, figures for 1963 indicate that,
so far, East Africa's imports from the centrally planned
economies have mainly been consumer goods and household
articles, while exports have largely consisted of local
primary products--coffee, some sugar, and jute.[53]

In terms of volume, this commodity exchange is
still very small, and in no case does it amount to
more than 1 per cent of the turnover of foreign
trade.[54]

This situation, however, might be in for a change.
During the past two years, the centrally planned economies announced long-term development credits to East
Africa totalling $100.5 million, or about 4.5 per cent
of the total Soviet and Eastern European aid to Africa.[55]
Understandably, most projects to be financed with this
aid are still in the early planning stage, but from
credit announcements, on-the-spot visits, and subsequent press releases it is possible to form an idea
as to how this financial assistance is likely to
develop.

In K E N Y A, the Soviet Union has "agreed in
principle" to assist in the construction of certain
agricultural installations; a textile factory, a fish
cannery, a fruit processing plant, and a sugar refinery.
As some evidence of the alleged caution with which the
centrally planned economies now claim they approach
aid projects in developing countries, a Soviet source
mentions that: "Soviet specialists would also study
the advisability of building a saw mill and a paper
factory in Kenya."[56]

The Soviet Union will also build and present as
a gift a 200-bed hospital with an adjoining polyclinic,
and a technical institute for 1,000 students.[57] In
the field of educational aid, the above source also
mentions that in 1964 more than 500 Kenyan students
were studying in the U.S.S.R.[58] Assuming this figure
to be reliable, Kenya is clearly the African country
with the largest number of students in the Soviet Union.

Czechoslovakia will probably also become involved
in technical aid to Kenya. Although no formal loan has
been granted, she will, under terms of the trade agreement, export to Kenya engineering equipment of all kinds,
complete industrial plants and heavy agricultural machinery. This will be repaid by Kenyan exports of her traditional products, i.e., fodder, corn, coffee, etc.[59]

T A N Z A N I A has received a Soviet loan of $20 million,[60] and unspecified assistance from Eastern Europe.[61] Pravda states here that the U.S.S.R. had agreed to provide technical aid for industrial construction, for prospecting minerals, for the construction of two hospitals, and for the development of the Tanzanian telephone network.[62]

The Soviet Union will also supply laboratory equipment for veterinary stations and dispatch veterinary surgeons to Tanzania. Agreement was reached on the cooperation in the development of marine fisheries and on permitting Soviet organizations to use Tanganyikan-Zanzibar ports as bases for fishing vessels and research ships.[63]

Both Czechoslovakia and Poland will assist Tanzania in constructing a sugar refinery and in developing the fishing industry. Both countries will extend scholarships for young Tanzanians to study in their respective institutions of higher learning.[64]

U G A N D A has, to date, received a Soviet loan of $15.5 million. According to the announcement, the U.S.S.R. will cooperate with Uganda in constructing a textile factory, a training center specializing in mechanized agriculture, meat refrigerating installations, and a dairy plant.[65]

Repayments by the Uganda Government will be used by the Soviet Union for the purchase of coffee, cotton, copper, tea, and fruit--all under the terms of the trade agreement between the two countries.[66] Under a cultural exchange agreement, 54 Uganda students were studying in the Soviet Union during the academic year 1964-65.[67]

* * *

It would be completely unrealistic should one pretend to establish--on the basis of the foregoing survey--any definite lines along which African countries will conduct their economic relations with the centrally planned economies, or vice versa, determine the exact nature of Soviet and Eastern European trade and aid flows to developing countries.

The only conclusion that can be drawn at this
point, from an interim survey of this nature, is that
there is as yet no definite pattern for African economic relations with the Soviet Bloc. However, this
does not mean that there are no lessons to be learned
from the past ten-year experience. Soviet and Eastern
European trade and economic aid have--in that period--
covered almost every conceivable field of development
assistance.

It would be closing our eyes to reality not to
admit the effect this has had on African economies.

It is of course difficult--or well-nigh impos-
sible--to determine the impact of development aid to
its fullest extent; but what remains beyond doubt is
the fact that the Soviet Bloc has begun a many-sided
and very intense activity, which may come to have significant implications on the process of economic growth
in Africa.

On the basis of experience gained during the past
decade, the concluding chapters of this study will examine the immediate effects of these new relations.
We will continue to distinguish between trade and aid,
and while it is far too early to uncover their many-
faceted effects, an attempt will be made to discuss
whether economic relations with the Eastern trade area,
in their initial stages, have contributed to an acceleration of the development process in Africa.

NOTES TO CHAPTER 7

1. William A. Hance, The Geography of Modern
Africa (New York: Columbia University Press, 1964), p. 351.

2. U.N., Statistical Yearbook, 1965, Table 19, p. 80,
estimates Ethiopia's population in 1964 at 22 million, but
this figure (as all African population statistics) is
questionable.

3. Hance, op.cit., p. 356.

4. U.N., ECA, Industrial Growth in Africa, Annex I,
p. 83.

5.   OECD, The Flow of Financial Resources to Less-Developed Countries, 1956-63, Table V-3, p. 172.

6.   IBRD, The World Bank Group in Africa, 1964 (Washington, D.C.: 1964).

7.   Hance, op. cit., p. 352.

8.   Vneshnyaya Torgovlya, Nos. 8 and 9, 1959.

9.   U.N., ECA, Foreign Trade Statistics of Africa, Series B, Trade by Commodity, No. 10 (July, 1966) (E/CN.14/STAT/Ser.B/10), pp. 291-307.

10.   Ibid.

11.   Vneshnyaya Torgovlya, Nos. 8 and 9, 1959.

12.   Tass Press Release, December 24, 1963.

13.   Vneshnyaya Torgovlya, No. 9, 1960.

14.   Le Moniteur Africain, May 18, 1966.

15.   Press Release, Ethiopian Embassy, London, March 9, 1967.

16.   Czechoslovak Foreign Trade, Prague, Vol. 1, No. 4 (April, 1960).

17.   "L'Evolution de l'Economie tchécoslovaque en 1960," La documentation française--Notes et Etudes Documentaires, Report No. 2833, (Paris, November 1, 1961), p. 39.

18.   U.S. Department of State, Mutual Security Presentation, "Credits and Grants Extended by the Sino-Soviet Bloc to Less-Developed Countries of the Free World," Background Paper B-8 (mimeographed) (Washington, D.C.: Government Printing Office, March, 1961), p. 16.

19.   Pravda, June 4, 1963.

20.   The combined effect of Soviet Bloc trade and development aid may have had some political ramificatio

A study of the U.N. General Assembly voting in 1959, shows a definite shift in Ethiopia's vote for the Soviet position on several issues (Robert B. Stauffer and Mulford J. Colebrook, "Economic Assistance and Ethiopia's Foreign Policy," Orbis, Vol. V, No. 3, fall, 1961, pp. 320–41). However, it is by no means certain that economic assistance, rather than the Emperor's view of a changing world situation, was the motive force behind Ethiopia's actions. This may also have been the reason for difficulties the United States have had, over the past three years, in renewing radio base agreements with Ethiopia.

21. Estimated at two million in 1962. U.N., Statistical Yearbook, 1963, Table 2, p. 25.

22. Hance, op. cit., p. 366.

23. U.N., ECA, Industrial Growth in Africa, Annex I, p. 83.

24. Yuri Bochkarev in New Times (Moscow), No. 30, 1963, p. 28.

25. See Chapter 2, Table 4, "Africa--Trade and Payments Agreements," pp. 37-51.

26. Vneshnyaya Torgovlya, No. 7, July, 1961, Supplement pp. 8-9.

27. Ibid.

28. Yezhegodnik Bolshoy Sovetskoy Entsiklopedii, 1963 (Moscow, 1963), p. 354.

29. Moscow Radio, May 26, 1963.

30. Ibid., June 3, 1963.

31. Tass Press Release, February 2, 1963; and Pravda, June 27, 1963.

32. A.R.L., Vol. 1, No. 9, August 27, 1964.

33. Tass Press Release, June 18, 1964.

34. Ibid., April 3, 1963.

35. Pravda, November 22, 1963; and Tass Press Release, January 30, 1963.

36. Moscow Radio, October 13, 1963.

37. Ibid., April 24, and October 2, 1963.

38. Ibid., May 19, 1964.

39. Radio Mogadishu (A.R.L., Vol. 1, No. 3), March 16, 1964.

40. Pravda, November 28, 1962, and April 16, 1963.

41. Hance, op. cit., p. 366. Tuberculosis is a prevalent disease in East Africa.

42. Pravda, May 5, 1963.

43. New Times, No. 30, 1963, p. 38.

44. Izvestiya, June 29, 1963.

45. Radio Mogadishu (A.R.L., Vol. 1, No. 8), July 30, 1964.

46. New Times, No. 30, 1963, p. 28, and Izvestiya July 30, 1964.

47. Ibid.

48. Moscow Radio, January 30, 1963.

49. Tass Press Release, December 1, 1964.

50. $74 million. See Chapter 3, Table 9, "Africa Country Distribution of Credits," pp. 81-89.

51. U.N., Statistical Yearbook, 1965, Table 19, pp. 81-82.

52. Kenya, Tanzania, and Uganda--Trade with
the Sino-Soviet Group:

	1964		
	Kenya	Tanzania	Uganda
Imports--Total	214,286	123,087	91,799
From China (P.R.C.)	1,940	2,194	13,204
From Soviet Union and Eastern Europe	4,711	1,590	1,409
Exports--Total	131,530	193,043	180,411
To China (P.R.C.)	1,103	12,492	9,086
To Soviet Union and Eastern Europe	3,238	3,613	2,047

Source: U.N., ECA, Foreign Trade Statistic of Africa,
Series B, No. 10 (July, 1966), pp. 202-290.

It is noteworthy that the P.R.C.'s importance as a
buyer of East African products is counterweighted by
Soviet and Eastern European relatively higher imports
into the area. This is possibly due to the fact that
China (P.R.C.) has difficulties in supplying Kenya,
Tanzania, and Uganda with desired products, but has
probably expressed more willingness than the Eastern
trade area in purchasing East African primary commodities.

53. U.N., ECA, Foreign Trade Statistics of Africa,
Series B, Trade By Commodity, No. 7 (April, 1965).

54. Ibid., and Value Series (January-December,
1963).

55. See Chapter 3, Table 9 "Africa--Country Distribution of Credits," pp. 81-89.

56. Pravda, May 18, 1964, and East African
Standard, May 18-20, 1964 (A.R.L., Vol. 1, No. 5).

57. Ibid. The status of this technical institute
is unclear. It has been reported, but not confirmed,
that the U.S.S.R. was planning a school for propaganda
and subversionary techniques to be constructed in Kenya.

When this came up in the Kenyan Parliament, President Kenyatta promptly threw the Soviet project out, but it is unclear whether this "school" was identical with the technical institute mentioned in the original credit announcement.

58. Ibid., November 16, 1964. However, according to The New York Times reports, this program was not entirely successful, and an unspecified number of students left the Soviet Union because of apparent mistreatment.

59. Czechoslovak Foreign Trade, Vol. 4, No. 7 (July, 1964). The trade agreement between Kenya and Czechoslovakia came into force on January 1, 1964.

60. Tanzania Standard, May 28, 1966.

61. According to a statement made by Tanzanian Vice President Kawawa (but not confirmed in Soviet papers) Czechoslovakia, Poland, and the Soviet Union committed $15 million in machinery and technicians to specified projects in Tanzania. Tanzania Standard, August 31, 1964 (A.R.L., Vol. 1, No. 8).

62. Pravda, August 25, 1964.

63. Ibid., and Tanganyika Standard, March 26, 1964 (A.R.L., Vol. 1, No. 3).

64. Radio Dar-es-Salaam, December 17, 1964 (A.R.L., Vol. 1, No. 12).

65. Tass Press Release, December 1, 1964.

66. Uganda Argus, February 2, 1965 (A.R.L., Vol. 2, No. 1). The trade agreement was concluded in April, 1964.

67. Kampala Radio, December 18, 1964 (A.R.L., Vol. 1, No. 12).

PART III

AFRICA AND THE CENTRALLY PLANNED ECONOMIES--
THE PRESENT AND THE FUTURE

8

GROWTH OF TRADE

In attempting to place the information we have into a coherent picture of all African trade with the centrally planned economies, it may be helpful, first, to consider the volume and growth of these flows as they have developed over the past ten years.

In 1954--the base year--global turnover of African foreign trade amounted to $10.4 billion.[1] As has been seen, commercial relations with the Eastern trade area were at that time in an embryonic stage, and total turnover of trade with the Soviet Union and Eastern Europe did not amount to more than $142 million[2]--or 1.37 per cent of global African trade.

By the end of 1964 the situation had changed. In that year the turnover of African trade totalled some $17.9 billion, out of which the centrally planned economies accounted for $904 million[3]--or 5.05 per cent. In the same year, African exports to the Soviet Bloc accounted for 5.71 per cent of the total, and imports for 3.96 per cent.[4] What is interesting about these trade flows is that they may be small, but over the period they have also represented the fastest growing commercial relations Africa has maintained with any developing area.

We get an idea of how this growth has developed from Table 32. Here we have computed trade with the centrally planned economies as expressed in millions of dollars for each relevant African country.

235

TABLE 32

AFRICA

Pattern of Growth of Trade with the Centrally Planned Economies;

Expressed in Millions of U.S. Dollars, 1954-64

Country of Origin for Imports and Destination for Exports	Bulgaria		Czecho-slovakia		Eastern Germany		Hungary		Poland		Rumania		Soviet Union	
	I	E	I	E	I	E	I	E	I	E	I	E	I	E
Algeria														
1954		0.1	0.6	0.3			0.2	1.2		0.8		0.1	0.3	2.1
1955			0.4	2.8			0.9	1.7		0.7	0.1		0.2	2.2
1956			0.2				0.3	0.1	0.4	0.6	0.5	0.3	0.2	3.5
1957			0.5				0.2		0.2	0.9	1.6	0.2	1.4	2.7
1958		0.2	0.7		0.1		0.3		0.8	0.4	1.7	0.5	2.3	2.8
1959		3.1	0.6		3.8		3.3		2.0	0.3	3.9	0.7	3.9	3.2
1960		0.7	0.2		0.1		1.3		2.0		3.7	0.4	1.9	1.6
1961	0.2	0.1	0.8				0.7		0.7		0.6		0.6	1.6
1962							0.3		0.2				3.9	
1963														
1964a														
Congo (K)														
1954			1.0	0.1			0.1		0.1					
1955			0.9				0.4		0.1					
1956			1.3				0.7		0.1					
1957			2.0				0.8		0.3					
1958			1.7		0.1		0.7		0.2					
1959			2.0		0.2		0.4		0.4					
1960			1.1		0.2		0.4		0.3					
1961			0.1						0.2					
1962														
1963														
1964a														

Country of Origin for Imports and Destination for Exports	Bulgaria I	Bulgaria E	Czecho-slovakia I	Czecho-slovakia E	Eastern Germany I	Eastern Germany E	Hungary I	Hungary E	Poland I	Poland E	Rumania I	Rumania E	Soviet Union I	Soviet Union E
Egypt (U.A.R.)														
1954	0.3	0.3	7.9	17.3	1.4	2.1	4.0	5.3	1.4	6.9	5.0	7.7	6.7	5.4
1955	0.5	0.3	10.6	25.4	2.5	4.0	2.0	11.9	1.4	8.3	11.0	11.6	6.6	20.2
1956	1.6	4.3	11.0	59.1	8.4	9.6	4.6	4.2	3.0	11.2	14.4	9.4	22.7	16.0
1957	2.7	3.8	18.0	42.0	18.7	19.9	6.7	3.0	7.9	19.5	5.7	9.6	53.4	89.8
1958	5.0	3.6	29.0	43.0	26.1	22.5	13.6	10.2	12.4	13.8	17.8	10.7	90.2	82.1
1959	3.7	3.9	23.2	46.6	25.5	30.2	9.7	7.2	7.7	16.5	12.9	8.3	77.1	81.4
1960	4.0	5.5	23.0	37.2	25.3	29.1	6.9	6.2	8.2	22.1	8.3	10.8	65.8	88.7
1961	3.2	3.7	17.1	68.5	22.8	17.4	7.9	8.8	8.0	9.8	8.7	13.1	79.4	72.9
1962	5.6	2.8	25.6	31.6	20.1	15.5	10.8	6.9	14.0	8.7	11.4	12.6	60.2	62.7
1963a	3.7	4.0	25.2	50.7	17.1	15.0	15.2	12.2	13.3	10.9	9.8	12.5	49.0	101.2
1964a	2.4	4.0	14.3	32.8	6.7	10.6	2.9	7.0	7.3	11.2	4.2	9.6	21.0	48.9
Ethiopia														
1954													0.2	0.3
1955													0.4	0.2
1956													0.6	0.5
1957			0.8	0.1									1.5	
1958			1.2	0.2			0.3						1.0	0.5
1959			1.1				0.4						1.0	0.8
1960			2.3	0.5			0.6							
1961			2.0	0.6			0.9		0.1					
1962	0.1		2.0	0.4					0.4					
1963														
1964a			1.5	0.5			0.5	0.1	0.2				0.6	0.1

Continued

TABLE 32 (Continued)

Country of Origin for Imports and Destination for Exports	Bulgaria I	Bulgaria E	Czecho-slovakia I	Czecho-slovakia E	Eastern Germany I	Eastern Germany E	Hungary I	Hungary E	Poland I	Poland E	Rumania I	Rumania E	Soviet Union I	Soviet Union E
Ghana														
1954			2.4				0.2		0.1					20.4
1955			3.5		0.8		0.2		0.3					11.5
1956			3.2		1.1		0.4		0.2					5.7
1957			4.0		1.9		0.4		0.3					17.5
1958			3.7		1.6	0.7	0.3		0.5					1.1
1959			4.5		2.1	0.8	0.3		1.1					5.5
1960			4.9		3.2		0.6		1.8				1.6	20.4
1961	0.1		4.3		3.8		0.9		3.4	1.5			6.2	8.6
1962	0.4	0.5	4.0	0.2	2.4	2.1	1.5	2.1	4.8	4.0			5.1	13.5
1963	0.2	0.5	8.6	1.7	4.1	6.0	3.5	0.8	5.8	4.3			9.1	20.6
1964a	0.4	0.5	6.9	1.8	2.7	1.6	3.1		5.2	5.1	0.4		13.0	17.6
Guinea														
1954														
1955														
1956														
1957														
1958														
1959			3.0	1.6	3.9	0.9	0.3	0.3	0.9	1.9			1.0	0.5
1960	0.3		8.6	2.4	3.5	3.8	0.1	0.4	2.5	2.0			5.2	3.9
1961	0.4	0.5	5.0	2.3	6.6	3.9	2.0	0.6	2.6	1.8			8.5	5.3
1962	1.1	0.6	3.4	1.9	2.2	2.9	0.8	1.0	2.5	2.8			13.2	2.5
1963	0.1	0.2	0.8	3.9	0.9	2.5	0.3	0.7	3.4	2.9			8.2	2.4
1964a														

Country of Origin for Imports and Destination for Exports	Bulgaria		Czecho-slovakia		Eastern Germany		Hungary		Poland		Rumania		Soviet Union	
	I	E	I	E	I	E	I	E	I	E	I	E	I	E
Mali														
1954														
1955														
1956														
1957														
1958														
1959														
1960														
1961														
1962			1.6	1.8	0.2								9.4	1.4
1963			1.7	2.4	0.1						2.8		7.0	1.4
1964a	0.1		0.5										2.8	
Morocco														
1954			1.8	0.6			0.4		0.3	1.7			0.3	0.6
1955	0.1	0.3	2.1	0.4	0.1	0.2	0.4	1.5	0.9	5.5	0.3		0.2	1.7
1956	0.3		1.6	0.3			0.3	0.6	2.5	3.5				0.2
1957	0.2		1.3	0.4	0.1		0.5	0.5	1.6	3.2	0.3		1.4	2.4
1958		0.3	1.7	2.6		1.2	0.5	1.1	2.5	4.4			1.2	1.5
1959		0.2	1.9	1.9		1.1	0.6	0.5	2.3	2.7			2.5	1.3
1960	0.3	0.1	2.2	1.8	1.1	0.8	0.9	0.2	3.3	2.9	1.5		6.5	3.3
1961	0.4	0.6	3.2	3.2	0.6	0.7	1.5	0.2	5.1	4.6	3.4	0.1	4.1	4.7
1962	0.5	0.8	3.8	5.7	1.0	0.5	0.7	1.7	4.2	6.0	4.1		5.2	4.7
1963	0.8	0.4	5.9	5.9	1.5	0.7	1.2	3.4	6.5	6.5	2.8		7.1	8.0
1964a	0.3	0.8	4.8	8.1	1.2	1.5	1.5	2.1	4.2	6.3	0.1		8.5	4.5

Continued

TABLE 32 (Continued)

Country of Origin for Imports and Destination for Exports	Bulgaria		Czecho-slovakia		Eastern Germany		Hungary		Poland		Rumania		Soviet Union	
	I	E	I	E	I	E	I	E	I	E	I	E	I	E
Nigeria														
1954			3.7	0.6	0.8		0.7	1.5	0.5	1.7				0.6
1955		0.3	4.3	0.4	2.1	0.1	0.7	0.6	0.5	5.5			0.1	1.7
1956			5.1	0.3	3.6		0.8		0.5	3.5				0.2
1957			5.4	0.8	3.8		0.4		0.6	0.2				
1958			5.4	2.0	3.1		0.6		0.5	0.9				
1959			5.4	1.5	3.8		0.2		0.1	2.5				6.2
1960			6.6	1.8	4.5		0.3		0.2	1.2				
1961			7.5	1.7	5.4		0.5		0.9	1.3				
1962			7.4	1.2	4.5		0.8		2.5	3.1			0.1	
1963	0.5		8.3	0.1	3.9	0.2	0.7		3.8	3.0	0.2		0.3	
1964a	0.3		4.1		2.0	0.6	1.0		2.4	4.6				0.6
South Africa														
1954		0.2	2.7	0.3	0.4		1.5		0.3	1.2			0.2	0.3
1955		0.4	3.7	0.5	0.9		1.3		0.4	0.8				12.3
1956		0.5	4.9	0.5	1.2		1.5		1.0	1.3			0.5	2.1
1957		0.3	5.3	0.2	1.7		1.0		0.8	1.8			0.5	29.9
1958		0.1	4.3	0.1	2.4	0.1	1.0		0.5	0.6			0.3	8.4
1959			3.0	0.3	1.9	0.4	0.7	0.2	0.6	2.1	0.4		0.3	4.1
1960			4.7	1.7	2.0	0.1	0.9	0.2	0.7	3.1			3.8	4.3
1961			3.8	1.7	1.4	2.5	1.0	0.1	0.6	4.6		0.1	0.7	
1962			3.8	0.8	1.3	2.3	1.1	0.5	0.6	3.0		0.2	0.4	
1963			4.9	1.1	2.5	2.9	1.3	0.2	1.0	3.5		0.1	0.2	
1964a														

Country of Origin for Imports and Destination for Exports	Bulgaria I	Bulgaria E	Czecho-slovakia I	Czecho-slovakia E	Eastern Germany I	Eastern Germany E	Hungary I	Hungary E	Poland I	Poland E	Rumania I	Rumania E	Soviet Union I	Soviet Union E
Sudan														
1954			3.5	2.0	1.7		0.5	0.4	5.1	0.3	0.2		0.2	
1955			1.8	1.0		0.1	0.6	0.9	1.4	0.4	0.1		0.2	
1956		0.2	4.8	1.7			0.8	0.7	0.9	1.6			0.4	
1957	0.4		3.8	3.5	0.1	0.7	0.3	0.9	0.5	0.3	0.2		0.8	2.9
1958			2.7	2.8	0.1	1.0	0.4	0.5	2.4	1.6			0.5	
1959	0.1	0.1	3.6	4.7	1.5	0.3	2.2	2.0	1.2	1.2	1.0	0.2	2.9	4.3
1960	0.3		3.1	2.7	0.2	0.2	1.8	1.8	1.0	0.8	1.7	0.8	6.6	5.8
1961	1.1	0.3	3.6	3.2	1.5	0.5	0.5	0.4	2.6	2.0	1.6	1.4	8.9	9.8
1962	2.4	2.4	4.6	3.2	0.7	2.9	1.6	0.4	3.6	2.5	1.7		8.5	10.8
1963	1.6	1.9	3.0		0.7	2.7	1.2	0.9	5.8	2.0	2.8	4.3	11.1	15.3
1964[a]	0.5	0.3	1.9	1.3	0.6	2.3	1.0	1.1	2.1	3.2	1.9	2.4	2.3	4.3
Tunisia														
1954			0.2	0.4			0.2	0.1	0.1	0.6				
1955		0.2	0.3	0.5			0.3	0.1	0.1	0.5				
1956		0.6	0.3	0.2			0.3		0.1	0.5			0.1	0.5
1957	0.4	0.4	0.4	0.1			0.1		0.4	0.4	0.2		1.3	0.7
1958	0.4	0.4	0.6	0.8	0.1		0.2	0.5	0.1	0.9			0.6	1.0
1959	0.2	1.2	0.8	0.7			0.2	0.3	0.5	0.6			1.0	1.6
1960	0.2		1.5	1.0			0.3	0.1	0.9	1.1			2.9	2.5
1961	1.3	0.7	2.2	2.3	0.2	0.3	0.4	0.2	2.0	1.3			2.7	2.3
1962	0.5	1.0	1.2	1.0	0.2	0.2	0.3		1.6	1.5			2.2	2.3
1963	0.8	1.3	3.0	1.6	0.5	0.1	0.5		3.7	2.0			4.4	2.6
1964[a]	0.5	2.2	3.7	1.4	1.8	0.2	0.5		4.0	1.7			2.9	0.4

241

Sources: U.N., ECA, Foreign Trade Statistics of Africa, Series A, Direction of Trade, No. 1-7 (May, 1962 - January, 1966), and U.S. Department of Commerce, Value Series, "Exports and Imports of Free-World Countries to and from the Soviet Bloc," 1954-March, 1965, and National Trade Statistics.

Note: [a]Figures for 1964: January-June only.

Apart from underlining the relatively modest nature of these trade flows in almost every case except
Egypt, Ghana, and Mali, Table 32 points up another
curious, but perhaps not unexpected fact. Bearing in
mind that here one is dealing with very small percentage changes, it appears--in the case of practically every country--that commodity exchange with the
centrally planned economies, from the mid-1950's enjoyed a small but steady increase per year. However,
this increase took on more significant proportions the
year, or the year after the respective African country
gained independence, thereafter resuming the moderate
pre-independence growth rates.

This development, of course, could imply two different lines of action on the part of the centrally
planned economies, inasmuch as they--far more than the
African countries--are the determinants of these trade
flows.

If it is assumed that prior to independence, commodity exchange between Africa and the Eastern trade
area was conducted through the metropolitan countries,
then it is only natural that, with independence and th
establishment of direct trade relations, these trade
flows should increase. However, a case may also be ma
for the political impact of these commercial relations
The first argument would have been easily acceptable,
provided growth had developed at a steady rate. With
the sudden increase in the year of independence, or th
following year, the simple transfer-of-trade argument
is not acceptable; one must also assume that the Sovie
Bloc countries may have seen political advantage stemm
from a more rapid increase in trade with Africa.

Regardless of the reasons for this growth, it can
be seen from Table 32 that: From 1954 to 1958 African
trade with the centrally planned economies increased a
a very modest rate; from 1958 to 1961 this growth was
far more marked; in 1961, 1962, and early 1963, trade
suffered a slight decline--but not below 1958 levels--
and picked up again in the second part of 1963 and 196
and this growth continued into 1965 and 1966.[5]

THE DEGREE OF BILATERAL BALANCING OF
AFRICAN-SOVIET BLOC TRADE

The question of growth brings up the point to
what extent African-Soviet Bloc commodity exchange--
conducted on the basis of long-term agreements--has
affected the degree of bilateral balancing of the
trade flows.

In Tables 33a and 33b an attempt has been made
to demonstrate the degree of bilateralism in African
commodity exchange with the centrally planned economies in the 1954-64 period. But before turning to an
examination of these calculations the information they
contain must be qualified on several counts. Above all,
it is important to note that the available material does
not provide an entirely accurate picture. African trade
data have been used, showing f.o.b. values for exports
and c.i.f. values for imports. Import figures therefore
include a freight element, which over the relatively
long hauls in African trade with the Eastern group is
quite substantial for certain bulky commodities. This
part of the import values does not necessarily represent
income for the centrally planned economies and it has
varied with the sharp fluctuations in freight rates over
the period.

A second, and perhaps more important qualification,
is strongly linked to the growth pattern of trade. Since
any meaningful commodity exchange between the two areas
did not get under way until the end of the last decade,
the following analysis will only be based on trends manifested in the 1958-64 period.

The development throughout these years has been a
pronounced decline in the degree of bilateral balancing
of trade between Africa and the centrally planned economies. This means that trade expansion between the two
areas has involved an increase in export and import surpluses relative to reciprocal exchanges.

In the case of African trade with the Soviet Union
and Eastern Europe one general, but incomplete explanation

Degree of Bilateral Balancing of Commodity Trade

Between Africa and the Centrally Planned Economies, 1954-64

(U.S.$ million, exports c.i.f.; imports f.o.b.)

A = Sum of bilaterally balanced element in each trade exchange; B = Sum of import surpluses; C = Sum of export surpluses; D = Total of A to C; E = A as a percentage of D, e.g., the sum of the bilaterally balanced element in each trade exchange as a percentage of the sum of the highest flow (i.e., actual value of imports or exports, whichever is the greater) in each trade exchange.

Country		1954	1955	1956	1957	1958	1959	1960	1961	1962	1963	1964
Bulgaria	A	0.5	0.5	1.7	3.8	5.6	4.0	4.8	5.8	8.1	7.6	4.4
	B	0.1	0.2	0.1	0.5	1.4	0	0.5	1.8	3.5	0.9	0.6
	C	0.3	0.9	3.5	1.4	3.2	1.4	1.6	0.8	0.8	1.3	3.9
	D	0.8	1.6	5.3	5.7	10.2	5.4	6.9	8.4	12.4	9.8	8.9
	E	63	31	32	67	55	74	70	69	65	78	49
Czecho-slovakia	A	19.6	27.6	32.4	41.5	51.0	49.1	51.1	49.6	48.0	61.4	37.7
	B	10.2	13.2	19.2	19.9	14.7	17.1	22.5	17.9	16.2	21.8	15.4
	C	9.6	15.2	40.1	14.0	15.7	23.4	15.8	53.3	8.7	28.8	21.8
	D	39.4	56.0	91.7	75.4	81.4	89.6	89.4	120.8	72.9	112.0	74.9
	E	50	49	35	55	63	55	57	41	66	55	50
Eastern Germany	A	2.1	4.4	9.6	20.6	24.8	33.6	34.8	25.3	26.4	30.1	15.0
	B	2.9	3.7	6.0	7.4	10.9	14.9	9.4	18.3	9.9	7.1	4.1
	C	0.7	1.8	1.2	1.8	2.0	5.8	4.1	1.3	2.9	5.9	5.9
	D	5.7	9.9	16.8	29.8	37.7	54.3	49.3	44.9	39.2	43.1	25.0
	E	37	44	57	69	66	62	71	56	67	70	60
Hungary	A	7.0	7.0	6.1	4.0	12.3	10.5	8.9	10.3	12.2	18.2	10.0
	B	3.1	2.1	3.9	6.5	6.3	7.8	5.9	6.6	8.8	8.3	5.0
	C	2.3	11.2	0.3	0.6	0.7	0.1	0	0.9	1.8	2.6	5.2
	D	12.4	20.3	10.3	11.1	19.3	18.4	14.8	17.8	22.8	29.1	20.2
	E	56	34	59	36	64	57	60	58	55	63	50
Poland	A	11.5	5.1	7.8	12.8	19.9	16.8	20.9	26.3	31.6	35.1	25.4
	B	5.6	1.4	0.3	1.7	1.9	3.0	5.2	6.7	9.0	11.1	2.8
	C	9.5	18.0	13.8	14.9	5.4	13.3	16.9	6.2	5.5	2.4	9.3
	D	22.9	24.5	21.9	29.4	27.2	33.1	43.0	39.2	46.1	48.6	37.5
	E	34	21	36	43	73	51	49	67	69	72	68

ountry		1954	1955	1956	1957	1958	1959	1960	1961	1962	1963	1964
umania	A	5.0	11.0	9.4	8.0	10.9	9.0	12.4	15.3	12.8	15.4	6.6
	B	0	0.4	5.6	2.5	9.1	7.0	5.5	6.9	6.4	2.8	0.7
	C	2.7	0.6	0	3.9	0	0	2.5	4.5	1.4	4.3	5.9
	D	7.7	12.0	15.0	14.4	20.0	16.0	20.4	26.7	20.6	22.5	13.2
	E	65	92	63	56	55	56	61	57	61	68	50
oviet	A	7.5	7.4	23.8	58.3	95.5	89.3	97.8	105.4	98.7	96.4	51.1
Union	B	1.5	0.2	7.1	1.0	8.8	2.5	18.4	12.4	24.1	15.6	9.8
	C	23.3	42.5	10.9	86.5	10.1	15.0	48.5	6.3	13.3	69.0	35.1
	D	32.3	50.1	41.8	145.8	114.4	106.8	164.7	124.1	136.1	181.0	86.0
	E	23	15	57	40	83	84	59	85	73	53	59
otal of	A	53.2	63.0	90.8	149.0	220.0	212.3	230.7	238.0	241.3	260.7	150.2
Centrally	B	23.4	21.2	51.8	39.5	53.1	51.7	67.4	70.6	80.0	65.5	38.4
Planned	C	48.4	90.2	56.3	123.1	37.1	59.0	89.4	73.3	31.3	117.4	87.1
Economies[a]	D	121.3	174.4	198.9	311.6	341.0	323.0	387.5	318.9	352.6	443.6	275.7
	E	41	64	54	52	65	66	60	75	68	59	54

ources: Table 32, pp. 236–41, and similar calculations in U.N. Economic Bulletin for Europe, Vol. 12, No. 2 (September, 1960), pp. 46–49, and Ibid. Vol. 17, No. 1 (October, 1965, manuscript version), pp. 58–61.

ote: [a]In computing Table 33b some trade flows between Africa and the centrally planned economies were so minuscule that no meaningful results could be obtained (Congo and Mali). In the case of other countries (Ethiopia, Ghana, Guinea, the Sudan, and Tunisia) no meaningful commodity exchange took place prior to 1957-59, and consequently computations have been omitted for years preceding these. These omissions account for the disparate totals in Tables 33a and 33b. In Table 33a, all trade flows from 1954 to 1964 with all relevant African countries have been included.

TABLE 33b

Degree of Bilateral Balancing of Commodity Trade

Between Africa and the Centrally Planned Economies, 1954-64

(U.S.$ million, exports f.o.b.; imports c.i.f.)

Country		1954	1955	1956	1957	1958	1959	1960	1961	1962	1963	1964
Algeria	A	1.1	1.6	1.6	3.9	6.3	4.7	2.4	2.0			
	B	0.3	0.1	1.0	1.9	3.5	11.3	7.1	5.7			
	C	3.7	5.2	3.5	2.2	3.6	0.7	0.1	1.0			
	D	5.1	6.9	6.1	7.0	13.4	16.7	9.6	8.7			
	E	22	23	26	56	47	28	25	23			
Egypt	A	26.7	34.6	65.7	113.1	185.9	194.1	141.5	147.1	140.8	133.3	58.8
(U.A.R.)	B	1.3	0.2	12.1	3.7	23.6	6.6	0.7	11.9	15.4	7.5	0
	C	19.6	47.3	57.5	78.2	15.4	41.4	58.8	59.0	8.5	80.7	65.3
	D	47.6	82.1	135.3	195.0	223.9	242.1	201.0	218.0	164.7	221.5	124.1
	E	56	42	49	58	83	80	70	67	85	60	47
Ethiopia	A				0.4	0.4	0.5	0.5	1.1	1.2		0.7
	B				0.7	1.2	2.0	3.7	2.6	3.2		2.0
	C				0.1	0	0	0	0	0		0
	D				1.2	1.6	2.5	4.2	3.7	4.4		2.7
	E				33	25	20	12	30	27		24
Ghana	A						6.6	12.1	10.3	18.2	31.3	24.8
	B						7.3	9.7	10.8	3.4	11.1	11.6
	C						5.5	18.8	2.4	9.1	13.7	4.7
	D						19.4	30.6	23.5	30.7	56.1	41.1
	E						34	39	44	59	56	60
Guinea	A						5.2	12.5	14.4	11.7	12.6	
	B						4.9	8.3	10.8	12.7	6.3	
	C						0.9	0.6	0.1	1.2	5.2	
	D						11.0	21.4	25.3	25.6	24.1	
	E						47	58	57	46	52	

Country		1954	1955	1956	1957	1958	1959	1960	1961	1962	1963	1964
Morocco	A	2.8	3.9	4.5	5.4	6.2	7.3	9.2	14.0	19.4	24.9	20.5
	B	1.6	1.7	1.5	1.5	0	1.3	6.6	5.2	5.6	4.0	4.1
	C	1.7	7.7	1.5	2.6	4.9	1.7	0	0.9	5.0	3.1	6.8
	D	6.1	13.3	7.5	9.5	11.1	10.3	15.8	20.1	30.0	32.0	31.4
	E	46	29	60	57	56	71	58	70	65	78	65
Nigeria	A	2.9	7.7	4.6	1.0	2.9	4.0	9.2	3.0	4.3	3.4	5.8
	B	4.6	5.9	8.6	9.2	7.1	6.9	9.6	11.7	11.6	14.1	7.0
	C	1.4	7.7	3.4	0	0.4	2.4	7.2	0.4	0.6	0	3.0
	D	8.9	21.3	16.6	10.2	10.4	13.3	26.0	15.1	16.5	17.5	15.8
	E	33	36	28	10	28	30	35	20	26	20	37
South Africa	A	1.8	6.3	4.4	9.3	8.9	6.9	9.4	8.5	6.8	7.8	
	B	4.3	5.4	7.1	7.8	7.5	5.1	5.6	3.7	4.0	5.1	
	C	1.4	13.1	2.4	30.7	8.3	5.6	2.9	5.2	3.6	3.0	
	D	7.5	14.8	13.9	47.8	24.7	17.6	17.9	17.4	14.4	15.9	
	E	24	43	32	20	36	39	53	49	47	49	
Sudan	A				6.1	6.1	10.9	14.1	17.1	22.2	26.2	10.3
	B				2.9	1.3	2.9	2.0	5.1	5.4	4.1	0.8
	C				3.3	1.8	1.4	1.6	0.9	4.5	8.2	5.4
	D				12.3	9.2	15.2	17.7	23.1	32.1	38.5	16.5
	E				50	66	70	80	74	69	68	62
Tunisia	A				1.4	2.0	3.8	3.8	7.3	6.0	7.6	5.9
	B				1.8	0.1	0.1	1.3	4.5	0.6	6.8	9.2
	C				0	1.4	1.2	0.2	0.1	0.6	0.5	1.7
	D				3.2	3.5	5.1	5.3	11.9	7.2	14.9	17.8
	E				44	57	75	72	62	83	51	33
Total of 10 African Countries[a]	A	35.3	54.1	80.8	139.2	218.7	244.0	214.7	214.8	234.4	247.1	126.8
	B	12.1	13.3	30.3	30.5	44.3	48.4	54.6	72.0	54.0	59.0	34.7
	C	27.8	81.0	58.3	117.1	37.2	60.8	94.4	70.0	33.1	100.7	86.9
	D	75.2	148.4	169.4	286.8	300.2	353.2	363.7	356.8	321.5	406.8	248.4
	E	47	36	48	49	73	69	59	60	73	51	51

Sources and Notes: See Table 33a.

for this trend can be suggested. The decline in the
bilateral component must have followed almost entirely
from the general decline in African commodity prices
which resulted in higher import surpluses (see Guinea,
Morocco, Nigeria, South Africa, the Sudan, and Tunisia)
and conversely higher export surpluses in the centrally
planned economies (Czechoslovakia and the Soviet Union)

Apart from this general influence, there were many
more specific ones at work and an examination of these
separately may be of interest.

In the past ten years trade between African and
the centrally planned economies has increased. However
relative to global African trade turnover, this particu
commodity exchange has declined. One of the reasons is
surely that as markets in the Eastern group become increasingly more developed, African products become less
attractive. There is clearly a limit to how much cotto
fibers, cocoa, and groundnuts the centrally planned ecor
omies can import from Africa, particularly when the fo
mer may want to accommodate export desires of other developing areas as well. Today the Soviet Bloc can prov
Africa with almost any kind of capital equipment the co
tinent might require. But, as a generalization, the o
products the Eastern trade area is genuinely interested
in importing from Africa are citrus fruits, tropical f
textiles, and minerals. Unless the African partners ca
adjust their commodity production to accommodate the Ea
ern group in this respect, one should not expect any i
mediate improvement in the degree of bilateral balanci
between the two areas.

The existence of surpluses of African imports fro
the centrally planned economies is furthermore a refle
tion of the nature of these imports. They consist--to
large degree--of Soviet and Eastern European deliverie
under programs of financial and technical assistance.
These projects are financed by long-term credits that
not be repaid before the projects have been completed.
Consequently, commodity deliveries for this purpose wil
not affect the degree of bilateral balancing for quite
few years to come.

PRICES

Having established the growth structure of trade
we may now be in the position to address ourselves to
the question of the prices which were paid for commodity exchanges in both directions. Starting with African
exports to the centrally planned economies, a tentative
deduction can be made: Commodity prices on goods received by Africa from the Soviet Union and Eastern Europe
were--after an initial bonus pricing--by and large on
par with "world market levels." Based on incomplete
statistics, there is little evidence that African prices
received in trade with members of the Soviet Bloc were
significantly worse, or better, than those received in
trade with Western Europe and North America.

This deduction was made on the basis of an analysis
of trade between three African countries and the Soviet
Union. For our purposes we chose Egypt, Ghana, and the
Sudan. Based on information from the country studies,
commodity exchange between these three nations and the
Soviet Bloc represented 74 per cent (over the 1958-65
period)--or close to three fourths--of total African
turnover of trade with the centrally planned economies.
Furthermore, the countries were selected so that, geo-
graphically, North, West, and East-Central Africa were
represented in the analysis. On the basis of volume of
trade and location of country, Egypt, Ghana, and the
Sudan will be considered "representative" African partners of the centrally planned economies.

As to commodities, in each instance we chose the
major products of the countries concerned: in the case
of Egypt and the Sudan, cotton; and in the case of Ghana,
cocoa beans. In each separate example these products
account for 80 to 90 per cent of the respective country's
trade with the centrally planned economies and, taken together they constituted, in 1964 and 1965, 75 per cent,
or again three fourths of all African exports to the
Eastern trade area. As such, cotton and cocoa beans will
be considered "representative" African export products.

TABLE 34

EGYPT (U.A.R.), GHANA, AND THE SUDAN

Comparison Chart of Prices Paid by the Soviet Union with Average Prices Received for
Egyptian Cotton, Ghanaian Cocoa Beans, and Sudanese Cotton (Sakel),
and Share of Soviet Purchases of Total Egyptian Cotton Exports,
Ghanaian Cocoa Beans Exports, and Sudanese Cotton Exports

EGYPT (U.A.R.)

(Egyptian Pounds^c thousand; exports f.o.b.)

Year	Total Egyptian Cotton Sales	Total Cotton Sales to the Soviet Union	Soviet Price (E.₤/Quantar)^a	Average Price (E.₤/Quantar)	Amount Variation (E.₤/Quantar)	Per Cent Variation	Soviet Rank as Buyer	Exports to the Soviet Union as Per Cent of Total Exports
1952	126,414,117	9,348,072	217.09	210.05	+ 7.04	+ 3.33	6	7.39
1953	116,347,650	4,142,131	159.83	150.88	+ 8.95	+ 5.93	9	3.56
1954	113,102,387	1,863,245	158.54	176.55	-18.01	-10.20	13	1.65
1955	107,437,735	5,765,245	177.51	174.02	+ 3.49	+ 2.00	8	5.37
1956	98,900,606	4,091,016	205.85	189.21	+16.64	+ 8.79	8	4.14
1957	124,156,364	28,413,031	194.02	211.20	-17.18	- 8.13	1	22.88
1958	109,860,423	27,733,498	164.93	175.37	-10.44	- 5.95	1	25.24
1959	110,153,729	28,331,322	165.36	155.71	+ 9.65	+ 6.20	1	25.72
1960	134,745,470	30,698,426	176.42	169.79	+ 6.63	+ 4.10	1	22.78
1961^b	91,069,910	25,409,316	176.50	180.36	- 3.86	- 2.14	1	27.90

Sources: Egyptian Government, Ministry of Finance and Economy--Statistical Department (After 1957: U.A.R., Presidency of
the Republic--Statistical Administration), Monthly Summary of Foreign Trade; Figures for 1952, Ibid., December,
1952, Table VIII, pp. 34-35; 1953, Ibid., December, 1953, Table VIII, pp. 34-35; 1954, Ibid., December, 1954,
Table VIII, pp. 32-33; 1955, Ibid., December, 1955, Table VIII, pp. 32-33; 1956, Ibid., Table VIII, December,
1956, pp. 28-29; 1957, Ibid., December, 1957, pp. 28-29; 1958, Ibid., December, 1958, Table VIII, pp. 30-31;
1959, Ibid., December, 1959, Table VIII, pp. 32-33; 1960, Ibid., December, 1960, Table VIII, pp. 34-35; 1961,
Ibid., September, 1961, Table VIII, pp. 36-37.

Notes: ^a 1 Quantar = 44.928 kg.

          ^b Cotton exports until September, 1961.

          ^c 1 Egyptian Pound 1952-61 = U.S.$2.84; 1962 = U.S.$2.30.

250

GHANA

(Ghanaian Pounds thousand; exports f.o.b.)[a]

Year	Total Ghanaian Cocoa Sales	Cocoa Sales to the Soviet Union	Soviet Price (G.£/Ton)	Average Price (G.£/Ton)	Amount Variation (G.£/Ton)	Per Cent Variation	Soviet Rank as Buyer	Exports to the Soviet Union as Per Cent of Total Exports
1955	65,358,937	4,095,476	319.9	318.4	+ 1.5	+ 0.5	5	6.2
1956	51,062,516	2,051,188	227.9	217.8	+10.1	+ 4.6	5	3.8
1957	50,873,407	6,249,339	172.5	195.5	-23.0	-11.8	5	13.9
1958	62,318,017	337,975	290.7	315.8	-15.1	- 4.8	14	0.7
1959	68,779,165	1,970,631	254.2	274.8	-20.6	- 7.5	6	3.1
1960	66,233,917	7,272,419	211.2	219.4	- 8.2	- 3.7	5	11.4
1961	69,274,169	3,047,951	157.1	169.4	-12.3	- 4.7	5	4.4

Sources: This table is based on Table 8, p. 77, in the article of A. Erlich and C. R. Sonne, "The Soviet Union: Economic Activity," in Brzezinski, Z., Africa and the Communist World. For our purposes, we have added a column for "Total Cocoa Sales to the Soviet Union," and also updated the table by one year. Figures for 1955: Ghana, Office of the Government Statistician, Annual Report on the External Trade of Ghana, and Report of Shipping and Aircraft Movements and Cargo Loaded and Unloaded, Vol. I, 1957, Accra: March, 1959, Table XIX, "Exports of Domestic Produce," p. 177; Figures for 1956, 1957, and 1958, Ibid., Vol. I, 1958, Accra: August, 1960, Table XIX, "Exports of Domestic Produce," p. 179; Figures for 1959 and 1960, Ibid., Vol. I, 1959, and 1960, Accra: 1961, Table XIX, "Exports of Domestic Produce," p. 191; Figures for 1961: Ghana, Central Bureau of Statistics, External Trade Statistics of Ghana, Vol. XI, No. 12, Accra: April, 1962, Table IX, "Exports of Domestic Produce," p. 193.

Note: [a]1 Ghanaian Pound - U.S.$2.80.

251

TABLE 34 (Continued)

Comparison Chart of Prices Paid by the Soviet Union with Average Prices Received for
Egyptian Cotton, Ghanaian Cocoa Beans, and Sudanese Cotton (Sakel),
and Share of Soviet Purchases of Total Egyptian Cotton Exports,
Ghanaian Cocoa Beans Exports, and Sudanese Cotton Exports

THE SUDAN

(Sudanese Pounds[a] thousand; exports f.o.b.)

Year	Total Sudanese Cotton Sales	Total Cotton Sales to the Soviet Union	Soviet Price (₤/Ton)	Average Price (₤/Ton)	Amount Variation (₤/Ton)	Per Cent Variation	Soviet Rank as Buyer	Exports to the Soviet Union as Per Cent of Total Exports
1957	21,264,980	996,949	499.22	386.68	+112.54	+29.09	6	4.7
1958	20,819,543	-	..	..	..	..	20	..
1959	36,524,763	1,498,742	274.49	230.88	+ 43.61	+18.88	6	4.1
1960	32,142,226	1,928,535	360.74	320.19	+ 40.55	+12.68	6	6.0
1961	28,901,808	2,889,963	294.17	302.43	- 8.62	- 2.80	5	10.0
1962	41,230,328	3,605,186	275.04	275.06	- 0.02	- 0.07	5	8.7
1963	42,791,950	4,268,970	275.20	259.52	+ 15.68	+ 6.05	4	9.9

Sources: The Republic of Sudan, Department of Statistics, H.Q. Council of Minister, Foreign Trade Statistics,
December,1957-December,1963. For each respective year: Tables on "Exports Classified by Commodity
by Country," SITC-Division 26, Commodity Group 263.1020: Cotton Fibers-sakel.

Note: a1 Sudanese Pound = U.S.$2.87.

Concerning the choice of Eastern trade partner we
selected the Soviet Union. There are many reasons for
this--the most pertinent is its predominant role as a
centrally planned trader with Africa, and more important, in view of the countries and products chosen, its
role as the major purchaser in the Eastern trade area.

Based on these facts: African partner, African
export product, and Soviet Bloc buyer, a comparison was
then made of Soviet prices paid for each commodity with
average prices received by the exporting African country in the initial stages of these trade relations.
The results of this exercise are set out in Table 34.

The preliminary conclusion remains valid, but re-
quires some qualifications. Clearly, bonus prices were
paid in the early stages of trade relations--in the
case of the Sudan as much as 30 per cent above average
levels, in the case of Egypt and Ghana, less. One reason for this--in the opinion of Erlich and Sonne--was
perhaps the Soviet Bloc's desire to gain a foothold in
African markets.[6] Their analysis, however, was based
on one country only--Ghana--where the bonus-pricing was
relatively slight. In the case of Egypt and the Sudan
where these took on more significant dimensions, the
Soviet Union would hardly be required to pay as much as
30 per cent above average to gain access to the markets.
Thus, it is necessary to seek other explanations. Soviet motives may have been partly noncommercial; substantial bonus-pricing is not the worst prelude to
closer establishment of economic and political relations. Also it is noteworthy that where the Sudan is
concerned, the Soviet Union did not buy anything from
that country in 1958, in which case the bonus should be
carried over two years. Accordingly, the motives behind
such bonus-pricing assume more reasonable proportions.

Apart from this, Soviet prices kept reasonably
close to average levels; moreover, in two of the three
cases mentioned above, they evened out to slightly
higher than normal market prices.

There is nothing surprising, or necessarily noncommercial in this. Whenever lower-than-average Soviet
prices were registered, it is possible that such de-
creases were due to isolated cases of low quality exports

from Africa; additionally, volume discounts granted
to a large customer might account for such pricing.
This conclusion might be plausible from the point of
view that the Soviet Union's purchasing policy has
generally not followed world trends. It appears from
Table 34 that not only were Soviet purchases maintained
at a reasonably stable level, with a slow rate of
growth, but also in poor marketing years the Soviet
Union, in some instances, increased its purchases, or
at least did not allow them to fall significantly below
levels established over previous years.

There is, however, one important reservation we
must make about the above conclusions. It concerns
price relationships between imports and exports. Trade
flows between any centrally planned economy and Africa
are--as is well known by now--purely bilateral in character. This permits the Soviet Bloc country to purchase large quantities of such items as cotton or cocoa
beans at higher prices than world market levels, as
long as the African seller must buy Soviet or Eastern
European exports at negotiated prices. If a centrally
planned economy were to enter the open market to purchase large quantities of primary products, this action
would probably increase average price levels, while
simultaneously exports sales of the centrally planned
economy would command a lower price than that obtained
under bilateral trading conditions.

As to the actual unit values of Soviet and Eastern
European exports to Africa, these are extremely difficult to assess. First of all, authorities in Africa
responsible for trade with the centrally planned economies appear to be cautious about giving out information about trade prices--for perhaps entirely justifi-
able reasons. On the other hand, it is equally as
difficult to arrive at valid conclusions by examining
figures from members of the Eastern trade area. For
one thing, intra-Soviet Bloc trade prices may include
a certain "customs union effect" from which the African
countries will not benefit. Furthermore, because of
the complete disparity which exists in the Eastern trade
area between domestic and foreign trade pricing, it is
of little value to try and apply unit values in the con
text of this study.

This is not to say that from Soviet and Eastern
European trade statistics it is impossible to calcu-
late unit prices. In 1962, for example, Egypt purchased 97 bulldozers from the Soviet Union at an
average price of $13,700, and 189 scrapers at $13,500
--but this information in itself is meaningless.[7] For
one thing, the statistics do not mention what type of
bulldozers and scrapers we are dealing with, and for
this reason it becomes useless to compare prices with
what is charged for equivalent Western equipment.

Compounding these difficulties is the fact that
most deliveries from the centrally planned economies
to Africa are made in conjunction with Soviet Bloc-
financed development projects. Thus, most probably
prices for individual pieces of machinery and equipment are estimated as part of total project costs.
But to determine the relative value of entire irrigation, hydroelectric power generating, or manufacturing
installations becomes an impossible task. Since no
two projects are ever alike, costs will depend on
materials used, completion-time, nature of amortization payments, etc., and any value judgment based on
comparisons would be entirely unrealistic.

TRADE CREATION OR TRADE DIVERSION?

One point to be raised at this juncture is
whether those African countries which have relatively
large trade flows with the centrally planned economies
have also experienced a generally faster growth of
their total trade.

An answer to this query would necessitate a more
thorough statistical investigation than available data
allow for--particularly since the swift growth of trade
between Africa and the Soviet Bloc is a recent phenomenon.

The following figures, however, may suggest some
correlation between the two:

	Percentage Share of Trade with the Centrally Planned Economies (Average 1957–63)		Average Annual Rate of Growth of Total Trade (1957–63)	
	Imports	Exports	Imports	Exports
Egypt (U.A.R.)	21.3	40.2	8.5	1.6
Ghana	4.7	6.4	3.6	-1.6
Guinea[a]	35.5	23.1	-1.9	9.2
Morocco	3.6	3.1	6.6	2.0
Sudan	7.8	8.5	8.2	7.9
Tunisia	3.2	3.8	6.7	-3.8
All Africa	1.2	1.4	3.9	2.8

Sources: See sources for Table 32; and U.N., Yearbook of International Trade Statistics, 1963.

Note: [a]Figures for Guinea from 1959 only.

Although we have chosen a period wherein African foreign trade underwent large yearly fluctuations, one could, in fact, argue that, if countries such as Egypt and the Sudan owe their higher than average rates of growth of total trade to the comparatively large share of the centrally planned economies in their total trade, the causes of this correlation might be manifold. On the simplest hypothesis one could argue that this is due to a fast-growing trade flow's pulling up the average rate. Alternatively, the economies most disposed to increase their trade with the Soviet Bloc may also be those bent on achieving the highest rates of expansion of production and trade.

	Imports				Exports			
	Value of Imports in 1963		Increment from 1957 to 1963		Value of Exports in 1963		Increment from 1957 to 1963	
	From the World	From Eastern Trade Area	From the World	From Eastern Trade Area	To the World	To Eastern Trade Area	To the World	To Eastern Trade Area
Egypt (U.A.R.)	916.2	133.2	319.9	20.0	521.6	207.2	28.9	19.5
Ghana	364.9	31.8	94.2	25.2	273.8	34.1	17.3	16.6
Guinea[a]	46.1	13.8	-3.9	4.8	55.4	12.5	19.3	7.3
Morocco	443.3	25.8	32.7	20.4	383.9	24.9	48.9	18.5
Sudan	245.3	26.2	51.3	20.2	205.9	30.3	58.2	23.7
Tunisia	221.8	13.5	46.5	10.7	126.0	7.6	-22.7	6.0

Sources: U.S. Department of Commerce, Value Series, "Exports and Imports of Free World Countries to and from the Soviet Bloc," 1957-63, and national trade statistics.

Note: [a]Guinea from 1959 only.

In no country--of those shown in the preceding
table whose trade has clearly been diverted to the
centrally planned economies from other markets--is
the association between growth of this trade and of
total trade evident. But for two countries, Egypt[8]
and Guinea, it is clear that part of the increment
of imports and exports alike can be attributed to
commodity exchange with the Eastern trade area.

For the remaining countries the effect of increased commerce with the Eastern trade area of their
total trade growth seems to have been negligible, and
this situation may persist for the next ten to fifteen
years to come. Furthermore, the net effect of the
growth pattern in cases where we have seen some trade
creation is questionable. While we lack detailed
commodity statistics for Guinea, in the case of Egypt
it does not appear that this "diversionary growth" has
stimulated exports of any "new" commodities, and in
that sense diversified the country's export structure.
Rather, sales to the centrally planned economies have
been centered on the country's traditional commodities
and growth of trade with the Eastern group has mainly
consisted of a step-up in production of these primary
products.

FUTURE OF AFRICAN-SOVIET BLOC TRADE

It is not the object of this study to provide any
detailed analysis of the future prospects of African
trade with the centrally planned economies, particularly
since the United Nations Economic Commission for Europe
and the Economic Growth Center at Yale University have
made available two authoritative studies of the problem.[9] However, we cannot in this context escape making
some broad conclusions and providing the reader with
some of the major conclusions reached in the works
mentioned. These conclusions, together with other information, may throw additional light on the future of
Africa's trade relations with the Soviet Union and Eastern Europe.

It was noted previously (in Table 7) that two
thirds of African exports to the Eastern trade area

consist of textile fibers--mainly cotton. On this point, former Premier Khrushchev noted toward the end of 1963:

> For a number of reasons, the socialist coun-
> tries are still dependent on non-socialist
> markets for some raw-materials at present
> in short supply. We believe the policy on
> this question should be to ensure ourselves
> reliable import sources of such items as
> copper, nickel, rubber, and cotton.[10]

On the face of it, this would appear to be very en-couraging for future African-Soviet Bloc trade, but then Mr. Khrushchev went on to say:

> Together with this, the new developments in
> science and technical progress make it poss-
> ible for us to arrange for the production of
> some of these items or their substitutes in
> the socialist countries. For example, the
> progress made by chemists in the U.S.S.R. and
> in the other socialist countries enables us
> to think in terms of undertaking, in the next
> few years, joint production of high-quality
> synthetic rubber which will completely re-
> place natural rubber, and of synthetic fibers
> which will replace cotton.[11]

Assuming that comparative cost considerations will play a relatively minor role in this commodity exchange, total imports of cotton into the Eastern trade area might decline relatively, or at any rate remain stagnant at levels observed in 1960, although the need to fulfill requirements for high-quality, long-staple cotton will probably remain, as will the desire for continued trade relations with cotton-growing nations like Egypt and the Sudan.[12]

Having established that trade in cotton products will probably not increase much above present levels, it appears that in only one commodity group--tropical beverages and fruits--do there exist possibilities for substantial expansion of imports into the Eastern trade area.[13]

Here it should be recalled, however, that at
present only five African countries have had any men-
tionable exports of these products, but in no case
did they account for more than 10 per cent of total
sales to the Eastern group.[14] Possibilities for
future development here will probably lie more with
the African countries than with the centrally planned
economies. Consumption in the Soviet Bloc of tropical
fruits and beverages is increasing fast. If it is
assumed that the Soviet and Eastern European Governments intend to raise consumption in this respect by
1980--at least to current levels in the Western world--
the U.N. study concludes that imports of foods, tropical fruits,and vegetables into the centrally planned
economies from developing areas might rise from their
present low levels--$150 million per year--to over $3
billion annually by 1980.[15]

Assuming that African growers can raise their output commensurately, they might, within the next fifteen
years come to account for about one third of the 1980
import estimates.

As to exports of mineral raw materials, prospects
here seem dim. It was mentioned earlier in this study
how practically the entire output of mineral products
is already tied up in trade with former metropolitan
countries. Barring any radical noneconomic policy developments, it must be assumed that these trade flows
will persist.

Where consumer goods and nonspecified manufactures
are concerned, exports to the centrally planned economies will probably not--at least in the next two
decades--take on any significant importance. In various
works on the subject it has been suggested that because
of their generally lower standard of living, the Eastern trade area might become customers for African-
produced consumer goods, which are assumed to be of a
more primitive standard than that currently turned out
in the developed world. Not wishing to pursue the
latter part of this argument, we shall confine our discussion to the former, which presents a view to which
we cannot subscribe. The supposition that Eastern
European purchasing standards were low might have been

valid ten years ago, but in the interval, not only
production standards in the centrally planned economies, but also the emphasis on the output of "soft-
goods" and--much more importantly--increase in living
standards and in the degree of consumption sophistication would seem to understate the above; African exports of nonfood consumer goods and manufactures to
the Eastern trade area will, accordingly, probably remain negligible for the foreseeable future.

So far, little has been said about imports from
the Eastern trade area into Africa. We established
earlier (in Table 7) that 75 per cent of these presently
consist of capital goods and manufactured equipment, the
remainder being mostly raw materials and food-products.
A reasonable assumption here would be that this structure is by and large likely to be maintained, with a
slight shift toward somewhat smaller food imports and
an increase in deliveries of capital goods and equipment.

The problem of what magnitudes these imports are
likely to attain is a different question. It has
been established that most "hardware" deliveries from
the Eastern trade area to Africa are intended for Soviet
and Eastern European development projects. An answer
to the question of magnitudes will be attempted in the
following chapter where the implication of the project
aid will be discussed, with some estimates of how this
is likely to develop over the next decade.

NOTES TO CHAPTER 8

1. U.N., Yearbook of International Trade Statistics,
1964, Table A, p. 12.

2. Ibid.

3. Ibid.

4. Ibid.

5. IMF, Direction of Trade, January, 1967.

6. A. Erlich and C. R. Sonne, "The Soviet Union: Economic Activity," in Z. Brzezinski, ed. Africa and the Communist World, p. 78.

7. See Chapter 4, Table 14.

8. In the case of Egypt, the strongest trade partner of the centrally planned economies in Africa, the increment in trade with the Soviet Bloc is less than could be expected. This is possibly due to the choice of period under consideration. Egyptian trade with the Eastern area increased radically from 1954 to 1957. Thereafter it remained on a stable level. In the past two years Egypt has sought to diversify her foreign trade, and the relative volume conducted with the centrally planned economies has undergone a slight decline. See Egypt: Monthly Summaries of Foreign Trade from 1954 onward, and also U.N., Direction of International Trade, 1963, and Yearbook of International Trade Statistics 1964.

9. See UNCTAD, Past Trade Flows and Future Prospects of Trade between the Centrally Planned Economies and Developing Countries (E/CONF. 46/35, February 13, 1964)(Geneva, 1964), pp. 24-68; and Bela Balassa, Trade Prospects for Developing Countries (Homewood, Illinois: Richard D. Irwin, Inc., for the Economic Growth Center, Yale University, 1964), Chapter 3, pp. 43-66, and Chapter 5, pp. 117-20.

10. Pravda, December 10, 1963, as cited in U.N. Doc. E/CONF. 46/35, op. cit., p. 40.

11. Ibid.

12. Bela Balassa, op. cit., pp. 16-17.

13. UNCTAD, E/CONF. 46/35, op. cit., pp. 42-47.

14. The main exporters are Egypt, Ghana, Guinea, Morocco, and Tunisia.

15. UNCTAD, E/CONF. 46/35, op. cit., p. 17.

9

AID COMMITTED AND AID DELIVERED

We established that by late 1966 Africa had received a total of $2.3 billion worth of development
loans from the centrally planned economies. This
amount accounts for about 20 per cent--or one fifth--
of all committed economic development aid received by
Africa from all sources in the 1954-66 period.[1] In
the country studies we detailed some projects toward
which this aid has been directed. The present chapter
will carry this analysis further.

It is obvious that, in this context, what is much
more important than a mere reporting on the purpose of
Soviet and Eastern European financial aid, is a determination of whether this has actually been utilized for
what it was intended, that is, when and in what manner
have funds been dispersed. For credits are not utilized
as soon as they are obligated. Allotment and obligation,
it should be noted, are only two of the steps in the aid
process. It takes time to plan projects, time for equipment to be built in the centrally planned economies, and
time for the structure to be erected in the recipient
country so that equipment can be installed.[2] Thus, in
no sense should lags between agreement and delivery be
construed as reflecting on the centrally planned economies' ability or willingness to honor their commitments.
Such delays are normal. The point is, however, important enough to warrant some estimate of the rate of expenditures, however rough. The question might be asked
in the following form: Supposing that all known commitments are obligated in full, what would be a reasonable
time schedule of the rate of disbursement?

An answer would have to be based on what little
is known about the actual flow of credits from the
centrally planned economies in Africa. Some quali-
tative and quantitative information provides certain
indications of the relationship between commitments
and disbursements of credits. The fact that most
credits are used for delivery of machinery and equipment indicates that the bulk of each credit is disbursed at the time when basic construction work is
sufficiently advanced to proceed with the installation
of machinery components. In the case of Algeria,
where aid has been primarily extended for projects of
an "industry-building" nature, this assumption gives
a clue to the disbursement rate. It can be assumed
that disbursement has gone faster in the case of
Algeria than, for example, in Egypt or Somalia, where
a major portion of credits has gone toward the construction of infrastructural projects. Here more local
work must be undertaken before major engineering components can be brought in; and even granting heavy construction costs, it would be fair to guess that Soviet
Bloc credits to Egypt or Somalia, at least for financing
dam or irrigation projects, have been disbursed at a
slower rate than have credits for purely industrial
undertakings.

The share of construction in the total investment
for a given project, and the time required for its completion, are obviously not identical for all undertaking
Consequently, the time span of a credit agreement will
vary considerably, depending on the size of the scheme,
delays involved in preparatory work and surveys, and in
many instances, on timing and the ability of the credit-
receiving country to organize the aspects of construction work which are to be executed with the use of internal resources. As will be seen from Table 35, in
most cases disbursement periods of Soviet and Eastern
European loans to Africa have lasted five to seven years
from first deliveries to the final project completion.[3]
This would include all "on-site" planning since the
credit agreement was signed.

In Table 35, we have based the estimates on the
above postulates, but also on others. Estimates are
drawn from such information as is available on anticipat

dates for the completion of various projects. In
those cases when such information is not available,
the assumption of a likely relevance of estimates is
based on the World Bank's experience with the rate at
which funds are disbursed under its loans.[4] In addition, it has been possible to get an idea of the length
of the disbursement period of Soviet and Eastern European
credits to Africa through information included in their
agreements with recipients.[5] Some credits are actually
allotted for a specific purpose in a specific period--
for example, the first stage of the Aswan project, of
which we know that it was to be completed in 1964, or
Guinea's three-year economic development plan, which
ran from 1960 to 1963.

We have also attempted, whenever possible, to follow export patterns of donor countries, through their
trade statistics, and aligning known groups of capital
equipment, identified by exporter, with relevant technical assistance projects financed by the same exporter.

It must be cautioned, however, that the figures in
Table 35 should be considered as representing only very
rough estimates, which can give only an approximate indication on the rate of disbursements.

We find that, while the Eastern trade area did extend some smaller credits to Africa in the early and
mid-1950's, the aid schemes did not really get under
way until the announcement of the $175 million Soviet
loan to Egypt in early 1958. From there on, however,
credits were extended at a rapid pace and reached a
peak in 1960-61, after which they declined somewhat.
Relatively few credits were granted in the latter half
of 1962 and 1963, but 1964 and 1965 have again wit-
nessed the award of large new development loans to
Africa.

The distribution pattern follows this cycle closely.
We see in Table 35 that any significant utilization of
credits began most likely two to three years after their
commitment. This would confirm the earlier assumption
of a two- to three-year project planning and preparatory
period for local work. Thus, credits have been most
heavily drawn upon from 1962 onward.

TABLE 35

AFRICA

Estimated Rate of Utilization of Soviet and Eastern European Credits, 1958-65

(U.S.$ million)

Recipient Country	Creditor	Amount	Estimated Period of Utilization (Years)	Date of Agreement
Algeria	Soviet Union	100	5	October 4, 1963
	Soviet Union	126.5	7	May 3, 1964

Estimated Annual Credit-Utilization

Congo (B)	Soviet Union	9	5	December 14, 1964

Estimated Annual Credit-Utilization

Egypt (U.A.R.)	Czechoslovakia	56	5	. . , 1957
	Czechoslovakia	23	5	June, 1960
	Czechoslovakia	172	10	. . , 1962
	Eastern Germany	100	5	March 1, 1965
	Hungary	14	4	. . , 1960
	Poland	15	4	. . , 1960
	Poland	20	5	. . , 1962
	Soviet Union	175	7	January 29, 1958
	Soviet Union	100	6	December 27, 1958
	Soviet Union	225	7	August 27, 1960
	Soviet Union	170	7	Summer, 1962
	Soviet Union	57	2	June 18, 1963
	Soviet Union	277	5	May 24, 1964

Estimated Annual Credit-Utilization

Ethiopia	Czechoslovakia	14	4	May 11, 1960
	Soviet Union	100	7	July 11, 1959

Estimated Annual Credit-Utilization

1958	1959	1960	1961	1962	1963	1964	1965	Total 1958-65	Remainder 196..
					0	10	15	25	75
						5	15	20	106.5
						15	30	45	181.5
						0	2	2	7
							2	2	7
0	0	0	0	0	0	0	0	0	56
		0	2	5	10	6	0	23	0
		0	0	0	0	0	0	0	172
							0	0	100
		0	0	2	2	4	6	14	0
		0	0	1	3	3	8	15	0
				0	0	5	10	15	5
0	0	5	8	10	20	25	30	98	77
0	0	2	10	20	30	30	8	100	0
		0	0	10	20	35	35	100	115
				0	10	25	25	60	120
						0	0	0	57
							10	10	267
		7	20	48	95	133	132	435	969
		0	0	2	2	4	6	14	0
	0	0	0	0	2	12	10	24	76
				2	4	16	16	38	76

Continued

TABLE 35 (Continued)

Recipient Country	Creditor	Amount	Estimated Period of Utilization (Years)	Date of Agreement
Ghana	Czechoslovakia	14	4	May 22, 1961
	Hungary	7	3	April, 1961
	Poland	14	4	April 20, 1961
	Poland	14	4	December, 1961
	Soviet Union	40	5	August 4, 1960

Estimated Annual Credit-Utilization

Guinea	Czechoslovakia	10	3	May 25, 1961
	Poland	4	2	. . , 1960
	Soviet Union	35	3	August 24, 1959

Estimated Annual Credit-Utilization

Kenya	Soviet Union	45	4	October 29, 1964

Estimated Annual Credit-Utilization

Morocco	Poland	12	4	October, 1962

Estimated Annual Credit-Utilization

Mali	Bulgaria	12.5	3	. . , 1961
	Czechoslovakia	10	3	June 13, 1961
	Poland	8	3	. . , 1962
	Soviet Union	45	4	May 18, 1961

Estimated Annual Credit-Utilization

958	1959	1960	1961	1962	1963	1964	1965	Total 1958-65	Remainder 196..
			0	0	1	4	6	11	3
			0	0	0	2	3	5	2
			0	0	2	4	4	10	4
			0	0	0	0	0		14
		0	0	0	2	5	10	17	23
					5	15	23	43	46
			1	2	3	2	0	8	2
		0	0	2	2	0	0	4	
	0	1	3	3	2	1	1	11	24
		1	4	7	7	3	1	23	26
						0	1	1	44
							1	1	44
				0	2	2	2	6	6
				2	2	2		6	6
			0	0	1	0.5	0.5	2	10.5
			0	0	0.5	0	0	0.5	9.5
				0	1	2	1	4	4
			0	1	1	2	3	7	38
			1	3.5	4.5	4.5	13.5	62.0	

Continued

TABLE 35 (Continued)

Recipient Country	Creditor	Amount	Estimated Period of Utilization (Years)	Date of Agreement
Somalia	Czechoslovakia	30	4	. . , 1961
	Soviet Union	44	5	June 2, 1961

Estimated Annual Credit-Utilization

Sudan	Soviet Union	22	4	November 21, 1961

Estimated Annual Credit-Utilization

Tunisia	Czechoslovakia	10	3	. . , 1961
	Poland	10	3	November, 1961
	Soviet Union	30	4	February 9, 1962

Estimated Annual Credit-Utilization

Uganda	Soviet Union	15.4	4	February 9, 1965

Estimated Annual Credit-Utilization

270

1958	1959	1960	1961	1962	1963	1964	1965	Total 1958-65	Remainder 196..
			0	0	0.5	2	3	5.5	24.5
			0	0	2	5	7	14	30
					2.5	7	10	19.5	54.5
			0	0	1	2	4	7	15
					1	2	4	7	15
			0	0	1	1	2	4	6
			0	0	0	1	1	2	8
				0	1	3	5	9	21
					2	5	8	15	35
							0		15.9
									15.9

Sources: H. G. Van der Tak and G. B. Baldwin, Disbursement Delays: An Analysis of the Bank's Recent Experience, IBRD Doc. EC-127 (Washington, D.C., 1964); Marcello Caiola, The Balance of Payments of the U.S.S.R., 1955-58, IMF Doc. DM-61/22 (Washington, D.C., 1961); UNCTAD, Financing for an Expansion of International Trade (E/Conf. 46/9), p. 114; Vneshnyaya Torgovlya, No. 3, 1961, pp. 42-44, and No. 6, 1961, pp. 29-30; Dengi i Kredit, No. 6, 1962; OECD, The Flow of Financial Resources to Less-Developed Countries in 1961 (Paris: OECD, July, 1963), Table 3, p. 17; IMF, Balance of Payments Yearbooks, 1962-63, and 1963-64; and National Import and Export Statistics.

In examining the commitment and utilization
pattern of Soviet and Eastern European development
loans to Africa, we see to a certain extent the same
phenomenon as the one found in the growth structure
of trade.[6] Credits seem to have been extended at a
time relatively close to the recipient's attainment
of independence. This tendency, however, is not as
clear-cut as it is in the case of growth of trade;
normally, the centrally planned economies appear to
have held out one or two years after independence before making any significant commitment to extend aid.

According to a rough estimate by the United
Nations Bureau of General Economic Research and Policies, total Soviet Bloc credit disbursements to all
developing countries between 1954 and 1962, ranged
between one quarter and one third of total commitments.[7] The rates of disbursement of Soviet and Eastern European credits to Africa are somewhat lower. On
the basis of conservative estimates in Table 35,
roughly one third or about 29.7 per cent of all commit
aid can be said to have been delivered by 1965-66.

Where individual centrally planned economies are
concerned, we find that by 1965-66, the Soviet Union
had disbursed about 31 per cent of its total committed
aid to Africa; the figures for Bulgaria, Czechoslovaki
Hungary, and Poland at that time were 16, 40, 90, and
per cent respectively. This points--very obviously--t
a fact that is not unexpected: The larger the donor a
the amount of his committed aid, the slower is the rat
of disbursement. Conversely, we find that the smaller
donors--Hungary and Poland--individually and totally--
account for a proportionately larger share of aid delivered than aid committed. There can be many reasons
for this. On the simplest hypothesis, smaller amounts
of aid facilitate faster disbursements and cause, to a
lesser degree, a strain on the internal economy of the
donors. This point is particularly important in view
of the continuously high level of demand for investmen
goods in the centrally planned economies. The extensi
of aid by directing scarce resources from domestic use
may have the consequence of affecting adversely the ra
of domestic investment and overall growth of output in
these countries. We have also found, in examining

available technical cooperation agreements and
"project-progress reports," that the Eastern European countries tend in general to direct their aid
effort to projects of an industrial nature. This
would require less preplanning and shorter completion periods than schemes of a more infrastructural
character, with which the Soviet Union has been heavily
involved.

The disbursement pattern is closely duplicated on
the African side, and we generally find that the smaller
the amounts of aid an African country has received, the
faster this has been utilized.[9]

TABLE 36

AFRICA

Economic Aid from the Centrally Planned Economies
Relationship Between Commitments and Receipts,
1958-65

(U.S.$ million and percentages)

Recipient	Aid Committed	Aid Received	Percentage of Aid Delivered
Egypt (U.A.R.)	1,404	435	31.0[a]
Ethiopia	114	38	33.3
Ghana	89	43	23.6
Guinea	49	23	49.7
Mali	75.5	13.5	17.9
Morocco	12	6	50.0
Somalia	74	19.5	26.4
Sudan	22	7	31.6
Tunisia	50	15	30.0

Source: Table 35, pp. 266-71.

Note: [a]Czechoslovakia's loan to Egypt of $172 million
         has been excluded from this calculation. The
         loan was not confirmed, nor does any record
         exist of its present status.

The reason for this may be analogous to the one
found for the centrally planned economies. The smaller
recipients have received mainly industrial projects for
which local costs are much lower than are those for infrastructural schemes.[10] Likewise, the recipients of
such projects may have been able to afford on-site preparation earlier and more easily than in the case of
countries on the receiving line of infrastructural aid.

INDIRECT AID

Before leaving the question of aid committed and
delivered, it may be useful to look briefly into Soviet
and Eastern European contributions to the various international multilateral aid agencies. The centrally planne
economies have extended aid to Africa, indirectly, throug
their contributions to the various United Nations branche
such as the Expanded Programme of Technical Assistance
(EPTA), the United Nations Children's Fund (UNICEF), and
the United Nations Special Fund (UNSF).[11] The contributions to other agencies are not directly related to finan
cial assistance, and the funds allocated to the United
Nations regular technical assistance program are financed
from global contributions to the regular United Nations
budget and cannot be broken down by contributing countrie
The contributions in the 1960-62 period from the centrall
planned economies to the three agencies mentioned above a
set out in Table 37.

SOVIET BLOC AID AND ITS IMPACT ON AFRICA

Although credits received by Africa from the central
planned economies represent only a relatively small proportion of total financial aid extended by all donor cour
tries to the continent, the impact of Soviet Bloc assista
on the economy of the recipients may be more significant
than the share in total aid would suggest, mainly because
of the concentration on a limited number of countries. F
thermore, the growth effect of these credits is enhanced
by the fact that they were directed toward the expansion
of investment goods industries and, moreover, they were

closely associated with extensive manpower training
with a view to enabling nationals of the recipient
country to take over construction and management of
future projects.

TABLE 37

Contributions of the Centrally Planned Economies to
EPTA, UNSF, AND UNICEF

(U.S.$ thousand)

Donor Country	1960	1961	1962
Bulgaria	36.8	36.8	24.9
Czechoslovakia	173.5	173.5	190.9
Hungary	98.1	108.8	108.8
Poland	250.1	285.0	285.2
Rumania	58.4	58.4	58.4
U.S.S.R.[a]	2,962.5	4,387.5	4,387.5
Total	3,579.4	5,050.0	5,055.7
of which:			
Per Cent of Total			
EPTA	39	52	51
UNSF	40	29	29
UNICEF	21	20	20

Sources: UNCTAD, Financing for an Expansion of International Trade (E/Conf. 46/9), p. 118, Table
28, as collated from U.N. ECOSOC, Official
Record.

Note: [a]Including contributions of the Byelorussian
and Ukrainian Soviet Socialist Republics.

So far, the estimates are too rough and warrant
no high degree of reliability, but it might be worth-
while at this point to glance at Soviet and Eastern
European financial aid and its total significance for
the economies of the African recipients. A full

examination of this question would require a detailed
consideration of the economic system and development
plans of each recipient, a task that ought certainly
to be undertaken, but which is beyond the information
available for this study. It is of some interest,
however, to compare the size of the credits from the
centrally planned economies with the "economic size"
of the African recipients. Tables 38a and b present
some crude estimates of Soviet and Eastern European
financial aid in proportion to national income of the
recipient countries in the same period.

What we have done here is to separate into periods
the time during which the African countries received
the largest amounts of aid from the centrally planned
economies, and then estimate the percentage share of
this aid of national income of the recipient countries
over the same periods.

Unfortunately, the figures--particularly in Table
38b--are too unreliable to warrant any precise relationships. From Table 38a we may, nevertheless, draw
the conclusion that, while no African country can be
said to be "dependent" on credits from the centrally
planned economies, in the case of Egypt and Ethiopia,
committed credits have accounted for a substantial
portion of these countries' national income.

As it could be expected, the delivered portion
of credits from the centrally planned economies was
greatly reduced in comparison with credits committed,
but here it should be noted that our calculation has
probably been undertaken too early. Most credits from
the Soviet Union and Eastern Europe to Africa will only
be utilized in the 1967-72 period; thus, Table 38b
would give a more realistic picture of the weight of
Soviet Bloc aid to Africa, if it were to be calculated
at the end of this decade.

The problem of measuring the impact of aid, however, is not as simple as all this. What we have done
is to compute credits, committed and delivered, in
terms of total national income, with a complete dis-
regard for national income distribution by sectors.

TABLE 38

AFRICA

Volume of Credits from the Centrally Planned Economies
Related to National Income of Selected Recipient Countries[a]
(U.S.$ million and percentages)

38a   Committed Credits and National Income

Recipient	Period Under Review	Estimated National Income	Committed Credits from the Centrally Planned Economies	Committed Credits as Per Cent of National Income
Algeria	1963	3,000	100	3.3
Egypt (U.A.R.)	1958-62	13,000[c]	970	7.3
Ethiopia	1959-60	1,530[c]	114	9.4
Ghana	1960-61	2,610[c]	89	3.4
Sudan	1961	1,000	22	2.2
Tunisia	1960-61	1,300[b],[c]	48	3.6

38b   Delivered Credits and National Income

Recipient	Period Under Review	Estimated National Income	Delivered Credits from the Centrally Planned Economies	Delivered Credits as Per Cent of National Income
Algeria	1964-65	6,150[c]	45	0.73
Egypt (U.A.R.)	1960-65	15,700[c]	435	2.77
Ethiopia	1962-65	5,430[c]	38	0.70
Ghana	1963-65	4,502[c]	43	0.95
Sudan	1963-65	3,110[c]	6	0.22
Tunisia	1963-65	2,260[b],[c]	15	0.56

Sources: U.N., Statistical Yearbook, 1965, Table 180, "Estimates of National Income,"
pp. 542-45. National income estimates in local currencies were converted to
dollars at prevailing IMF rates. For Algeria, Ghana, The Sudan, and Tunisia,
where no recent estimates are available, we have used base year estimates
provided in U.N., ECA, Industrial Growth in Africa (E/CN.14/INR/1/Rev.1)
(New York: U.N., 1963), Annex I: "National Income Estimates in Africa by Sector
of Origin," p. 85. On the basis of this information, and with assumed national
income growth rates of 4 per cent (Algeria, Ethiopia, and the Sudan), 5 per cent
(Ghana and Tunisia),and 6 per cent (Egypt, U.A.R.), estimates for the periods
under review were computed. See also Table 36, p. 273.

Notes: [a]Guinea, Mali, Morocco, Somalia, and the East African countries are excluded from
this calculation from lack of data.
[b]Gross domestic product at market price.
[c]Cumulative over period under review.

Apparently, Soviet and Eastern European financial aid
has been utilized faster in manufacturing or in construction projects than in agricultural or infrastructural schemes. But, no exact information as to sectoral
commitments or disbursements exists for credits from the
centrally planned group.

At any rate, it can be assumed that Soviet and
Eastern European financial aid to Africa has been more
important than figures in Tables 38a and 38b would
suggest. Some scattered information would seem to substantiate this. The available data on Soviet exports
of complete plants and industrial installations to
Africa in the period 1955-62 shows that Egypt absorbed
18 per cent and Guinea 3.4 per cent of all such exports
to the developing world. Ghana, Mali, and Somalia accounted for less than one per cent each.[12] In terms of
total aid committed to Africa, deliveries of complete
plants and installations amounted to 29 per cent of all
Soviet and Eastern European credit commitments to Guinea
and 20-22 per cent in Egypt.[14] In Mali such deliveries
of capital goods amounted to 7 per cent and in Ghana to
about 3 per cent.[15]

In further evidence of this, Eastern European sources
state that credit commitments of the centrally planned
group to Guinea amounted to 85 per cent of all credits
extended to that country in the period 1960-63, and those
offered by the Soviet Union to Egypt from 1958 to 1962
accounted for 30 per cent of total credits received.[16]

In all considerations of the impact of financial
assistance from the centrally planned economies to Africa
one must keep in mind, however, that this aid will not be
delivered in any single year but stretched out over a
longer period of time. In the final analysis, therefore,
any true measure of the impact can only be made when
projects have been completed and their total contribution
to the recipient economy can be assessed. Not the least
important of these contributions is the trade-creating
effect of technical and financial assistance agreements.
This can, however, not be quantified until committed
plant and equipment have been put into operation; but
here we may mention some preliminary effects. First of
all, the supply of initial factory installations and

equipment by the centrally planned economies obviously
assures a continuing trade flow of spare parts and re-
placements. Secondly, most Soviet and Eastern European
agreements on technical and financial aid to Africa
provide for repayments by means of exports of goods
produced by the enterprises which were constructed
with the aid of the credits. Not only is a provision
of this nature trade-creating, but it may also enable
the recipient country to achieve economies of scale,
especially if--as may be expected--exports to the
creditor country will not cease after the amortization
of the credits has been completed.

Consequently, the balance sheet of the financial
and technical assistance extended to Africa by the
centrally planned economies cannot as yet be drawn up,
but published facts permit some assessment of this aid.

It has consisted, in the main, of complete or
"packaged" projects--the external costs of which have
been financed by credits extended by the Eastern trade
area. The scale of these aid commitments reached a
peak in the early 1960's and is now stabilized at a
somewhat lower level. Since disbursements have been
made at a rather slow pace, a conservative estimate
is that only one third of all committed aid has been
delivered.

Over the period under review, 1958-66, there has
been a definite shift in the direction of Soviet and
Eastern European aid to Africa. Where Egypt and West
Africa were the predominant recipients in the early
years, East and North Africa are now the main bene-
ficiaries. Along with this development has gone an
increase in contacts on both sides. Thus, while in
1958-59, Czechoslovakia and the Soviet Union alone
extended aid to Egypt and Guinea, by mid-1967, all
members of the Eastern trade area were giving aid to
no less than twelve African recipients.

This assistance has been applied to almost every
conceivable facet of the African economies, although
most of it has been extended for industry or dam-
building purposes. Here it should be noted that
projects which this aid embraces are not all large-scale

(and by implication possibly uneconomic) undertakings. Many of them have not yet been formulated, but already at this stage it is apparent that several of the projects conform in exemplary fashion to development need of the recipients.

The question might be asked as to what extent the centrally planned economies have addressed themselves to solving specific obstacles to the growth or bottlenecks in the development process in those countries where they have operated. The problem is, of course, purely academic--in the sense that in a developing country the entire economic structure, resource allocation, production pattern, etc., constitute a bottleneck and any assistance--be this in the form of a football stadium or an irrigation project--will to some degree accelerate the rate of economic growth.

On a more practical and pragmatic basis, however, we might accept as a definition of a bottleneck any infrastructural impediment of a physical or a social nature that interferes with the development of agriculture or industry. If this is accepted, then the past few years have seen considerable improvements in the approach of Soviet Bloc aid to Africa.

It is safe to say that in the period 1958-62, little or no attention was paid by the Eastern group to specific obstacles to the development process in the aid-recipient African countries. Indeed, the early phases of deliveries of financial and technical assistance were often beset with poor planning, inadequate equipment quality, sloppy project execution, and more often than not, projects were planned with only scant attention to the impact these might eventually have on the recipient economy. In general, it could be commented here that whenever a centrally planned economy attempted to duplicate in Africa projects that had failed at home, these were frought with mishaps in Africa as well. This might possibly explain why agricultural undertakings have met with such little success.

The entire fault for this should not, however, be attributed solely to the centrally planned economies.

Apart from their relative newness in the field of
foreign aid, was the more important fact that up to
the early 1960's, very few African countries had
elaborated any coherent development plans and, in
many cases, it was not always easy for the Eastern
group (nor for that sake, for the West) to know at
what level of the economic structure external assistance could most effectively be placed.

The latter part of the period, from 1962 to the
present, has in this respect seen considerable improvements. A number of African countries have now
elaborated comprehensive development plans with
reasonably thorough surveys of their economies that
to some degree pinpoint major stumbling blocks to
economic growth; and the task of directing foreign
aid has become correspondingly simpler. Thus, prospective recipients now have a clearer idea of what
is required and donors can better adjust commitments
to their capacities.

The Soviet Bloc is, of course, making use of this
information in their prospective aid planning and,
from 1962 onward, financial and technical assistance
to Africa has improved both in terms of project selection and execution. It is no longer true to say that
Africa can expect to receive whatever it wants within
the framework of existing aid agreements with the centrally planned economies. It now appears that the
latter examine in great detail the usefulness of a
project to the recipient economy, with a view to finding
solutions to bottlenecks impeding the growth process.
The prime example may be said to have been the construction of the Aswan High Dam in Egypt, but the metallurgical industry complex in Algeria, the railroad development
in Guinea, irrigation projects in Ghana, and port construction in Somalia, must also be included. Needless
to say, all educational assistance rendered by the Soviet
Bloc would fall under this category. As a positive
side-effect of the more thorough aid planning we find
that prestige, or marginal income-producing schemes, no
longer figure as prominently as before in Soviet and
Eastern European development assistance to Africa. In
short, the quality of aid may be improving.

In spite of this, some aspects of the economic
aid from the centrally planned economies have tended
toward a negative--although possibly unwarranted--
effect on the African recipient.

We have noted that up to the early 1960's, this
assistance was extended purely on a project basis.
Since the Soviet or Eastern European donor provided
some--or in some cases all--of only the foreign exchange requirements of a project, the recipient has
had to finance local costs from his own budget.
Normally, these have amounted to as much as two to
three times the foreign exchange costs, and have im-
posed a heavy burden upon the recipient's economy.
The most frequent result here has been inflation, or
strong inflationary pressure. To the extent that
credits from the centrally planned economies have
financed unnecessary, or only marginally useful
projects the recipient economies have suffered, and
any benefits the credits may have conferred were more
than offset by losses through inflation and fiscal
and monetary dislocations.[17]

From an economic development point of view then,
the crucial question is not how specific funds are
used, but rather what effect the provision of these
funds has on the total disposition of resources in the
recipient country. If the country has a well articu-
lated development plan outlining a series of projects
to be undertaken in a particular sequence of time,
the financing of one of these projects through foreign
aid may not affect the recipient's investment program at
all. If the project falls within the country's scale of
priorities for the development of its own resources--
the consequence of providing foreign assistance for
the project is simply that it frees an equivalent
volume of domestic resources for some other purpose.
Although it may appear, therefore, that the donor is
financing the equipment for a cotton ginning mill, he
may in fact be permitting the recipient to step up his
volume of imports of consumer goods, or conversely,
the donor may free resources for financing projects,
e.g., in the infrastructural category, for which the
developing country may be less likely to obtain foreign
aid.

This is where--in the past four years--a definite
change can be detected in the approach of the centrally
planned economies to economic development in Africa.
Although there are no official statements to this effect
as yet, it is clear that loans extended by the Soviet
Union and Eastern Europe have over the last few years
been intended for use within the framework of the recipients' development plans.

This is not to say that the project approach used
so far has not been serviceable. In general, where a
country is in its early stages of growth and does not
possess an operative development plan, the case is
strong for following a project approach. This was the
situation with which members of the Eastern trade area
were faced when they initially began extending development credits to Africa. At that time, recipients had
only inadequate control of the use of their resources,
and any program support was quite likely to be dissi-
pated. Under these circumstances, project assistance
provided at least close control over a small portion
of available investment resources and foreign exchange.

This situation has now changed. Many African
economies possess today reasonably realistic development
plans, elaborated on a prospective basis from three to
seven years. Within the scope of these plans the centrally planned economies are now committing aggregate
credits for a number of years and their specific end-use
will be determined by the donor along with planners in
the recipient country. This kind of assistance is, of
course, particularly valuable since it is made prior to
the plan execution and can therefore be included in the
financial external-supply estimates as the plan is being
drawn up.

But in all its aspects, a quantification of implications of technical and financial assistance on the
productive capacity of any recipient country is an
elusive task. Neither the end-uses--even if these were
individually identifiable--nor the goods and services
to which aid resources are applied, can adequately indicate the net contribution of aid to productive capacity.

This depends, in the last analysis, on the overall
policies pursued by the recipient countries regarding
their total disposable resources rather than merely
on the form of specific aid utilization. Furthermore,
the impact of external aid on the capacity they help
create in the recipient country extends, of course,
far beyond the point of primary application. Obviously,
the creation of capacity in some lines may have a
greater growth potential than in others--and in such
cases a mere reckoning of the direct, or proximate
application does less than justice to its true contribution.

NOTES TO CHAPTER 9

1. OECD, The Flow of Financial Resources to
Less-Developed Countries, 1956-59, 1960, 1961, and
1956-63 (Paris: OECD, 1964). For our purposes we
define Soviet Bloc development aid as long-term soft
loans (see Chapter 3, pp. 72-74), and Western development aid as grants, loans repayable in local currencies, resource transfers, and hard loans at commercial
rates.

2. See below, p. 272.

3. We are here assuming that some project preplanning has taken place and gone into the protocol
of the credit agreement. See Chapter 3, pp. 75-79.

4. IBRD, Annual Reports 1958-63; and H. G.
van der Tak and G. B. Baldwin, Disbursement Delays:
An Analysis of the Bank's Recent Experience, IBRD
Doc. EC-127 (Washington, D.C.: May 12, 1964). See
also sources to Table 35, p. 271.

5. We understand this to mean credit agreements
for which the purpose is clearly and explicitly stated,
and for which some reports of utilization or completion
have been obtained. Credits for vaguely defined purposes such as "general economic development work" or
"vocational training" will not be utilized in this
analysis.

6.   See Chapter 8,   pp. 235-42.

7.   UNCTAD, Financing for an Expansion of International Trade (E/Conf. 46/9, March 10, 1964)(Geneva, 1964), p. 114.

8.   The Czechoslovak loan to Egypt of $172 million in 1962 is not included in the calculation.   No record exists either as to its confirmation or its present status.

9.   This conclusion would have been even more valid and clear-cut, had we not included in Table 36 figures for 1964 and 1965 commitments, which by 1965 had hardly begun to be utilized (Table 35).

10.   From a discussion on Soviet and Eastern European "aid techniques" (Chapter 3, pp. 75-79), we recall that the recipient will finance local costs, i.e., in the case of a factory it will put up the building, while the centrally planned economy will furnish and install the machinery.   In most developing countries the cost of putting up a building is much lower than the purchase and installation of machinery, whereas the opposite usually is the case for infrastructural schemes.   On an average, the developing country usually winds up financing two thirds of the project costs, the centrally planned economy the remaining one third.

11.   It should be noted, however, that these contributions have also been virtually bilateral in character, inasmuch as they have been made in nonconvertible currencies that had to be utilized in the donor country.   Because of this provision, United Nations aid officials have, in the past, had some difficulties expending these funds.

12.   UNCTAD, op. cit., p. 115.

13. $14 million.

14. $264 million.

15.   UNCTAD, loc. cit.

16.   Figyeloe, (Budapest), March 1, 1961.

17.   These comments can of course be applied equally well to the Western development aid to Africa, extended on a project basis.

CHAPTER **10** AFRICA AND THE CENTRALLY

PLANNED ECONOMIES--THE

PRESENT AND THE FUTURE

Ten years of African economic relations with the
centrally planned economies have now passed. In many
respects it has not been an easy period for either
partner, for its inception was marked by displays of
obvious political opportunism on the part of the Eastern group, and naïve African acceptance of these
overtures to help accelerate the pace of their economic growth.

Considered in a ten-year perspective, this period,
it becomes clear, can be divided into two parts: (1)
a sequence of trials and errors lasting up to 1961-62,
and (2) from then onward, more professional and refined
approaches on both sides. In the early part of the
period the centrally planned economies, in a headlong
drive to establish friendly relations with newly independent African countries more or less gave whatever
was asked of them, while the African recipients, for
their parts, were frequently less than realistic in
their demands. Poor planning was evident on both sides.
Indeed, the first six or seven years of African-Soviet
Bloc economic relations were cloaked with misunderstand-
ings, mistakes, and outright failures. Aid projects were
often hastily conceived of and badly executed. Commodit
deliveries from Africa to the Eastern trade area were of
poor quality, and occasionally--to the great dismay of
African exporters--dumped on world markets, with subsequent adverse effects on African commodity prices.

The unfortunate nature of these mishaps were compounded by political activities. Soviet and Eastern European foreign aid programs during this period were not, of course, any more humanitarian or altruistic in character than were those of their Western counterparts. In nature they may have been economic, but in motivation they were political--and immediate pay-offs on this account were frequently expected. When these were not forthcoming crude attempts were made to mix economic aid with political infiltration in the newly self-governing countries, doubly sensitive of their independence.

Results in almost all cases were wholly negative and, in a few instances, so deleterious that the African aid-recipient temporarily severed relations with the Eastern donor. These difficulties came to a head in 1961 with the expulsion of the Soviet ambassador from Guinea and the complete interruption of work on the Aswan project.

For all these reasons--initially faulty approaches by the centrally planned economies to their economic relations with Africa, misconceptions as to the nature of these relations on the part of the recipient countries, and the comparatively very small scale of trade and aid involved--relatively few results can be shown for the early efforts.

This is not to say that Western aid programs did not go through similar periods of difficulties, and in developed market and centrally planned economies alike there was an awareness of the fact that the entire approach to foreign aid must change.

Discussions of development aid from the Western world culminated in the spring of 1961 with President Kennedy's message to Congress on a long-term, program-approach to foreign aid.[1]

We have no record of any similar policy change in the centrally planned economies, but from information recently made available it is apparent that the whole question of the Bloc's relations with developing countries underwent a searching reexamination during

1962 and the years that have followed. Past programs
were put under scrutiny and new approaches considered.
While this soul-searching was in progress, Africa (and,
indeed, the entire developing world) received few or
no commitments on economic aid from the centrally
planned economies, although existing trade flows enjoyed a slight annual increase, or were maintained at
1960 levels.[2]

This discussion was particularly relevant in the
Soviet Union where clear indications of the need for
a more sensitive approach to the problems of developing
countries were manifested.[3] Thus, K. Ivanov says in an
article:

> This is an area where old recipes and plans
> will not work; the only ground here for
> political or theoretical reasoning is accumu-
> lated experience and intimate knowledge of
> the situation in each country and of inter-
> national relations as a whole.[4]

As a result of these realizations, the past four
years have seen considerably less friction in economic
relations between Africa and the centrally planned
economies.

This, however, does not mean that up to the early
1960's no benefits at all accrued from this economic
intercourse. From the African point of view trade with
the centrally planned economies, while not having attain
any major size, was still significant. Indeed, perhaps
the most important feature of relations with the Soviet
Bloc in the early period was precisely its willingness
to accept as repayment for goods and services local
products of the recipient countries. The attractive-
ness of this arrangement followed from the very natural
desire of the commodity producers to seek protection
from damaging price fluctuations on the world markets.
By virtue of their long-term trade agreements the centrally planned economies offered African primary producers an assured market for part of their output over
a number of years--a prospect that came to be recognized
as being of great assistance in foreign trade planning.

There is no question that this trade will ex-
pand--whether it will attain significant proportions
will depend partly on payments arrangements offered,
partly on the Soviet Bloc's willingness to continue
purchasing African primary products, but perhaps most
importantly, future expansion will be conditioned by
changes in the commodity composition of African exports.

On the first point little needs to be said here.
The development of new institutions for facilitating
multilateral trade within the Eastern trade area may
possibly result in some future degree of multilateral
payments arrangements in the trade between African
countries and the centrally planned economies, but there
are few indications that past or current bilateral arrangements have proved to be a major obstacle to growth
of commodity exchange between the two areas.

Rather, the more important impediments to trade
expansion must be sought elsewhere--in the desire to
reach self-sufficient production structures in the
planned economies--this is particularly relevant for
the Soviet Union--as well as in the very inflexible
African commodity export patterns.

As to Soviet Bloc willingness to continue purchasing African primary products, the past two years have
clearly shown that changes are in progress. Within
limits the Eastern group, and particularly the centrally planned economies in Eastern Europe, are now
increasingly taking comparative cost factors into
consideration in their foreign trade planning. Of
course, gains from such changes will be small in a
large, industrialized country like the Soviet Union
which has a relatively low dependence on foreign trade
in the first place. But advantages from "comparative
cost planned" foreign trade will be appreciably larger
in Eastern Europe which has a less provident natural
resource base. On this basis, there can be no question
that where African trade with the centrally planned
economies is concerned Eastern Europe presents a more
promising future market for African exports than does
the Soviet Union. However, willingness on part of the
planned economies to engage themselves more actively

in trade with Africa will have to be matched by the
latter with a much more complementary commodity structure of exports. It might, in fact, be stated that if
Africa is to hope for any greatly increased trade with
the Eastern group (or, indeed, with Western Europe and
North America as well), and for a reversal of the negative terms of trade experience over the past decade,
the continent must give more attention to production of
commodities which will have a chance of being marketable
in the Eastern trade area. Commodities in this category
must in the first instance include citrus fruits and
cotton textiles from North and West Africa, coffee and
tobacco from East Africa, and possibly some minerals
from the Central regions. The relative share of textile
crops must decline--as indeed it has since 1962--and the
Soviet Bloc must be willing to purchase increasing quant.
ties of semimanufactures within this commodity group.

True, authorities in the centrally planned economie:
have repeatedly stated their willingness to accept African traditional products in return for financial and
technical assistance. However, with increasing standard:
of living in the Eastern group and with higher levels of
consumer demands and consumer sophistication, the Africar
partners to this trade exchange should not expect that t
Soviet Bloc will be willing--or will forever require--to
continue importing African cotton, cocoa beans, and grou
nuts. Unless Africa evidences a serious intention to
restructure her commodity pattern of exports, trade with
the centrally planned economies will probably not expand
significantly beyond present levels, and it should here
be noted that relative to global African trade, commodit
exchange with the Eastern group has suffered a slight
decline over the past few years.

However, to some extent this trade will continue to
be conditioned by imports from the Soviet Union and East
ern Europe under their development projects. Here, we
have seen, the emphasis has been shifted from project to
modified program aid. While it is yet too early to indicate the implications of this change on the recipient
economies, it is clear that the new approach promises to
coordinate--in a more effective way than what so far has
been the case--financial and technical aid from the

centrally planned economies with the developmental
aspirations of the recipient African countries. As
aid committed under these programs leaves the blueprint stage we can expect an over-all expansion of
imports of machinery and other capital goods. This
will probably cause a relative increase in Soviet
Bloc hardware over fixed investment in the recipient
countries.

This conclusion would seem to be substantiated
by several Soviet statements regarding the future
course of foreign aid. While these are not official
policy declarations they can still be regarded as a
consensus of prevailing opinion. Generally, Soviet
economists now appear to be advocating economic development along a "balanced growth" program. A London
economist describes the idea thus:

> In order to overcome the limitations of the
> market created by low per capita incomes and
> to enjoy the internal economies of comple-
> mentary investment, it is necessary to start
> with a large-scale development programme,
> simultaneously trying to push forward over
> a wide range of economic activities.[5]

The Soviet endorsement of this view is given by
V. M. Kollontay who states that "the main thing is
now to put into operation a complex structure of
mutually complementary undertakings, and not an ob-
ligatory development of only light or heavy industry."[6]
Furthermore there is a growing tendency to recognize
the need for differentiation between the various basic
economic structures found in developing countries. A
sign of the growing sophistication in Soviet thinking
on foreign aid can be seen from a statement which un-
derlines the distinction that must be made, e.g.,
between small and large industries:

> Obviously it is not essential for every under-
> developed country to develop all or even the
> main branches of machine construction or heavy
> industry; for some such a task is beyond their
> resources, and for others it is not obligatory.

But it is very important that, in particular,
the big countries like India, Indonesia,
Burma, the U.A.R., and Pakistan should develop a national manufacturing industry and
begin to get a better share of the international division of labor. The actual character of industrial development will differ
in each country, according to its particular
resources of raw materials, of consumer
and capital goods, extracting and manufacturing industry, transport, power and the
various agricultural sectors. The effectiveness of any underdeveloped country's economic
policy depends on how far it succeeds in
strengthening and broadening the national
base of the economy (author's emphasis) as a
whole.[7]

Thus, it is apparent that the future character of
Soviet and Eastern European development aid to Africa
will change. One can expect improved planning, more
attention to local needs and conditions in the recipient countries, and concomitantly with this, increasing
elasticity and greater selectivity in the programs.

These conclusions would seem reasonable from the
point of view of present-day African and world politics.
In their ideological conflict with China certainly
neither the Soviet Union nor any of the centrally
planned economies in Eastern Europe can afford the
propaganda set-back that would follow from a mishandling of foreign aid projects. Coupled with this are
the sheer economic limitations on the outflow of
machinery and equipment from the Soviet Bloc. Mr.
Khrushchev admitted as much himself when he returned
from his 1964 visit to Egypt: "When the Soviet Union
helps the young developing countries and gives them a
part of the resources accumulated by its own labor, it
restricts for a certain time its own potentialities."[8]

This, however, should not be understood to mean that
the Soviet Bloc has gone back on, or is likely to go back
on aid already committed. Indeed, throughout the period
under review there is not a single instance of any centrally planned economy reneging on such promises of aid.

to Africa, no matter how adverse internal policies in
the recipient countries may have come to be to the
policy objectives of the donor.[9] But it appears likely
that Soviet Bloc aid to Africa will even off at a lower
level.

* * *

    Over the past decade much has been made of Soviet
and Eastern European economic penetration in the developing world. Often where economic aspects have strong
political overtones, the latter have been exaggerated
out of all proportion to the former.

    In the case of Africa even the most cursory exam-
ination of the economy of that continent will reveal the
many strong and intimate links that tie the newly independent states to their former metropolitan countries.
The centrally planned economies entered into this picture,
in many respects giving it a new perspective, and most
certainly affording the African states an alternative to
the economic relations maintained with their past masters.

    There is no doubt that old links will persist.
Neither the Soviet Union nor its Eastern European partners
realistically expect Africa to break completely away from
the West. What they do expect, of course, is a chance to
present and propagate their political philosophy and to
encourage the African states to follow a course of "positive neutrality" in the conduct of their external relations. It would be wrong, however, to interpret any
neutrality of the continent in foreign policy as a result
of its economic relations with the Soviet Bloc. The past
ten-year period has shown that Africa is determined to be
its own master and, while it may form coalitions, strike
up economic and political friendships (and break them
again), so far it has displayed a desire to remain free
from outside domination. From the African point of view
the centrally planned economies constitute useful partners
only to the extent that material assistance is provided

in significant volumes. If the Soviet Bloc should
fail to supply large-scale and satisfactory economic
aid, or do so in a way as to jeopardize help from
other sources, or take sides in internal disputes,
then the attraction will wear off quickly.

In the final analysis, whether Africa should go
the way of the centrally planned economies--or whether
it should become a stable member of the "third world"
in following the way to balanced economic growth,
political stability, and international respect--will
then depend, in no small measure, upon the caution and
intelligence African leaders exercise in the conduct
of their international economic affairs in the years to
come.

NOTES TO CHAPTER 10

1. The New York Times, March 23, 1961.

2. Cuba is excluded from this statement.

3. The author acknowledges that similar discussio
may well have taken place in Czechoslovakia, Hungary, a
Poland as well. Unfortunately, lack of access to the
local languages prevents him from reporting these (larg
untranslated) discussions here. In Eastern Germany the
question of foreign aid has been given relatively littl
attention.

4. K. Ivanov, "The National-Liberation Movement a
Non-Capitalist Path of Development," International Affa
(Moscow), No. 12, (December, 1964), p. 11.

5. H. Myint, The Economies of Developing Countrie
(London: Hutchinson, Ltd., 1964), p. 103.

6. "Socialism, Capitalism and the Underdeveloped
Countries," panel discussion in Mirovaya Ekonomika i
Mezhdunarodnye Otnosheniya, No. 4 (April, 1964), p. 127

7.   _Ibid._, statement by R. A. Ul'yanovskiy, p. 122.

8.   Interview in _Pravda_, May 28, 1964.

9.   As an addendum to the Sino-Soviet rift, it is interesting to note that while the Soviet Union tacitly seems to accept that even Soviet-favoring governments in Africa invite Western aid, the concept of "economic nonalignment," as professed by Tanzania (where the P.R.C. has been particularly active), is condemned by the Soviets as a "dangerous illusion." Source: _Mirovaya Ekonomika i Mezhudnarodnye Otnosheniya_, No. 3 (March, 1965), p. 141, and _International Affairs_ (Moscow), No. 4 (April, 1965), p. 62.

BIBLIOGRAPHY

BIBLIOGRAPHY

SOURCES

Official Government Statistics

ALGERIA
   Direction des Douanes. Le Commerce extérieur de
   l'Algérie, 1959, 1960, 1961, 1962, and 1963.

CONGO (B)
   Service de la Statistique. Bulletin mensuel de
   Statistique, Volume 5-6, 1961-62, Volume 7, 1963.

CONGO (K)
   Direction de la Statistique. Bulletin mensuel
   du Commerce extérieur de la République du Congo
   (Katanga et Sud-Kasai exclus). Volume 11, 1960;
   Volume 12, 1961; Volume 13, 1962.

EGYPT (U.A.R.)
   Electricity Commission. Electrical Power Projects
   in the U.A.R., Cairo: 1963.

   Information Department. Le Plan quinquennal pour
   le Développement économique et social, 1960-65.
   Cairo: 1960.

   Statistical and Census Department. Annual Statement of Foreign Trade, 1956, 1957, 1958, 1959,
   1960, 1961, 1962, and 1963.

   Statistical and Census Department. Monthly Summary of Foreign Trade, 1950-57.

EGYPT (U.A.R.) (Cont'd)
Statistical Administration. Summary of Foreign
Trade. December issues for the years 1958, 1959,
1960, 1961, 1962, 1963, 1964, and 1965.

Statistical and Census Department. Statistical
Yearbook of Egypt's Foreign Trade, 1957, 1958, 195
1960, 1961, and 1962.

Year Book of International Trade Statistics,
1953-57.

ETHIOPIA
Customs Head-Office. Import and Export Trade
Statistics, 1956/57 to 1962/63.

GHANA
Ministry of Commerce and Industry. Handbook of
Commerce and Industry 1962. Accra: Government
Printer, 1963.

Central Bureau of Statistics. External Trade
Statistics of Ghana, 1961, 1962, 1963, and 1964.

Office of the Government Statistician. Monthly
Accounts Relating to External Trade of Ghana,
and Report of Shipping and Aircraft Movements
and Cargo Loaded and Unloaded. December issues
for the years 1957, 1958, 1959, 1960, 1961,
1962, 1963, and 1964.

Office of the Government Statistician. Reports
on External Trade of Ghana, 1955/56 - 1960/61.

IVORY COAST
Service de la Statistique générale. Statistiques
du Commerce extérieur de la Côte d'Ivoire, 1956/57
- 1958/59.

Direction de la Statistique et des Etudes écono-
miques et démographiques. Statistiques du Commerce
extérieur de la Côte d'Ivoire, 1961, 1962, 1963,
and 1964.

KENYA
Government of Kenya.   Development Plan 1964-70.
Nairobi: 1964.

Treasury.   Economics and Statistics Division.
Economic Survey, 1963. Nairobi: 1963.

MALI
Ministère du Plan et de l'Economie rurale.   Rapport sur le Plan quinquennal et de Développement
économique et social de la République du Mali,
1961-65. Paris: Imprimerie Maubert, 1961.

MOROCCO
Solonitskii, Alexandr Sergeevich.   Marokko; Ekono-
maka i Vneshnyaya Torgovlya. Moscow: Vneshtorgizdat, 1962.

SOUTH AFRICA
Department of Customs and Excise.   Monthly Abstract
of Trade Statistics.   December issues for the years
1960, 1961, 1962, 1963, 1964, and 1965.

SOVIET UNION
Vneshnyaya Torgovlya SSSR za 1918-40 gody.
Moscow: Gostorgizdat, 1960.

Vneshnyaya Torgovlya soyuza SSSR za 1963 god.
Moscow: Vneshtorgizdat, 1964.

Vneshnyaya Torgovlya soyuza SSSR za 1964 god.
Moscow: Vneshtorgizdat, 1965.

THE SUDAN
Department of Statistics.   Foreign Trade Statistics.   December issues for the years 1957, 1958,
1959, 1960, 1961, 1962, 1963, and 1964.

TANZANIA (Tanganyika)
Department of Commerce and Industry.   Reports of
the Department, 1960, 1961, 1962, 1963, and 1964.

TANZANIA (Tanganyika) (Cont'd)
     The United Republic of Tanganyika and Zanzibar.
     Five-Year Plan for Economic and Social Develop-
     ment, 1st July 1964-30th June 1969.

TUNISIA
     Secrétariat d'Etat au Plan et aux Finances.
     Statistiques du Commerce extérieur de la Tunisie,
     1960, 1961, 1962, 1963, and 1964.

UGANDA
     East African Common Services Organization. East
     African Customs and Excise Department. Trade
     Reports of Kenya, Uganda and Tanganyika, 1961,
     1962, 1963, 1964, and 1965.

U.S.A.
     United States Department of Commerce, Bureau of
     Foreign Commerce, International Economic Analysis
     Division, Value Series. "Exports and Imports of
     Free-World Countries to and from the Sino-Soviet
     Bloc." Period covered: January 1, 1954-March 30,
     1965. Washington, D.C.: 1965 (mimeographed).

Statistical Material--International Organizations

UNITED NATIONS
     Statistical Yearbook, 1960, 1961, 1962, 1963,
     1964, and 1965.

     Yearbook of International Trade Statistics, 1961,
     1962, 1963, 1964, and 1965.

     Monthly Bulletin of Statistics, Volume 15, 1961;
     Volume 16, 1962; Volume 17, 1963; Volume 18, 1964;
     Volume 19, 1965; and Volume 21, 1967.

     Direction of International Trade, Series T, 1962,
     1963, and 1964.

     Economic Commission for Africa. Foreign Trade
     Statistics of Africa, Series A, Direction of
     Trade. Volume 1-7 (May, 1962-January, 1966).

UNITED NATIONS (Cont'd)
    Economic Commission for Africa. Foreign Trade
    Statistics of Africa, Series B, Trade by Commod-
    ity. Volume 1-10 (October, 1962-July, 1966).

INTERNATIONAL MONETARY FUND (IMF)
    International Financial Statistics, 1963-65.

    Direction of Trade, January, 1964-January, 1967.

    Balance of Payments Yearbook, 1962/63, 1963/64,
    and 1964/65.

 Official and Semiofficial Government Publications

CZECHOSLOVAKIA
    Státni Banka Ceskoslovenska. Bulletin.
    Prague: 1962, 1963, 1964, and 1965.

EGYPT (U.A.R.)
    National Production Council. Permanent Council
    for the Development of National Production.
    Cairo: 1955.

    National Bank of Egypt. Economic Bulletin.
    Cairo: 1958 to 1967.

FRANCE
    Banque centrale des Etats d'Afrique de l'Ouest.
    Notes d'Information et Statistiques. Paris:
    1958 to 1966.

    La documentation française, Notes et Etudes
    documentaires, Série économique et financière.
    The following reports: No. 2760: "L'Aide
    soviétique aux Pays sous-développés. Les Accords
    de Coopération industrielle et technique entre
    l'U.R.S.S. et les Pays sous-développés d'Afrique
    et d'Asie," March 13, 1961; No. 2833: L'Evolution
    de l'Economie tchécoslovaque en 1960," November 1,
    1961; No. 2972: "L'Evolution de l'Economie
    tchécoslovaque," March 13, 1963. Paris: Secré-
    tariat général du Gouvernement, Direction de la
    Documentation.

MALI
     Ministère du Plan et de la Coordination des
     Affaires économiques et financières. Comptes
     économiques de la République du Mali, 1959,
     1960, and 1961. Bamako: 1962.

MOROCCO
     Banque marocaine du Commerce extérieur. Bulletin
     mensuel d'Informations. Casablanca: 1964-66.

SOVIET UNION
     Gosudarstvennyi bank SSSR. Dengi i kredit.
     Moscow: 1960 to 1963.

     International Affairs. Moscow: 1961 to 1967.

     Mirovaya Ekonomika i Mezhdunarodnye Otnoshenie.
     Moscow: 1960 to 1964.

     Vedemosti Verkhovnogo Soveta SSSR. Moscow: 1959
     to 1963.

     Vneshnyaya Torgovlya. Moscow: 1958 to 1965.

     Voprosy ekonomiki. Moscow: 1961 to 1964.

THE SUDAN
     Bank of Sudan. Economic and Financial Bulletin.
     Khartoum: 1961, 1962, 1963, and 1964.

TUNISIA
     Banque centrale de Tunisie. Conjoncture. Tunis:
     1964.

  International Organizations--Reports and Documents

EAST AFRICAN COMMON SERVICES ORGANIZATION
     East African Statistical Department. Economic
     and Statistical Review, 1961, 1962, 1963, and 1964

EUROPEAN ECONOMIC COMMUNITY (EEC)
     Office statistique des Communautés européennes.
     Bloc oriental, 1965, No. 2. Le Commerce extérieur
     de l'U.R.S.S. par pays et par produits pour la
     période 1958-1963. Brussels: EEC, May 1965.

GENERAL AGREEMENT ON TARRIFS AND TRADE (GATT)
    International Trade News Bulletin, 1954-59,
    superseded by Developments in Commercial Policy,
    1960-65.

INTERNATIONAL BANK FOR RECONSTRUCTION AND
DEVELOPMENT (IBRD)
    Annual Reports, 1958-63.

    The World Bank Group in Africa, 1964. Washington,
    D.C.: 1964.

    Van der Tak, H.G., and Baldwin, G.B. Disbursement
    Delays: An Analysis of the Bank's Recent Ex-
    perience. Economic Staff Report 127. Washington,
    D.C.: 1964.

    Economic Growth: Foreign Capital and Debt Servicing
    Problems of the Developing Countries. Economic
    Staff Report 121 a. Washington, D.C.: 1963.

INTERNATIONAL MONETARY FUND (IMF)
    Caiola, Marcello, The Balance of Payments of the
    U.S.S.R., 1955-58 (DM/61/22) Washington, D.C.: 1961.

ORGANIZATION FOR ECONOMIC COOPERATION
AND DEVELOPMENT (OECD)
    The Flow of Financial Resources to Countries in
    Course of Economic Development 1956-59. Paris:
    OECD, April, 1961.

    The Flow of Financial Resources to Countries in
    Course of Economic Development in 1960. Paris:
    OECD, February, 1962.

    The Flow of Financial Resources to Developing
    Countries in 1964. Paris: OECD, July, 1965.

    The Flow of Financial Resources to Less-Developed
    Countries 1956-63. Paris: OECD, 1964.

    Domergue, Maurice, for OECD. Technical Assistance.
    Definition and Aims. Ways and Means. Conditions
    and Limits. Paris: OECD, 1961.

UNITED NATIONS

Economic Commission for Africa. African Trade
with the Centrally Planned Economies (E/CN.14/
STC/5), Addis Ababa: September, 1962.

Economic Commission for Africa. Economic Bulletin for Africa, 1962, 1963, 1964, and 1965.

Economic Commission for Africa. Les Accords
bilatéraux de Commerce et de Paiements conclus
en Afrique (E/CN.14/STC/24)(limited distribution),
Addis Ababa: November 14, 1963.

Economic Commission for Africa. Outlines and
Selected Indicators of African Development Plans
(E/CN.14/336), Addis Ababa: January 14, 1965.

Economic Commission for Africa. Aperçu du Commerce extérieur. Volume 1-13 (1962-66).

Economic Commission for Africa. Industrial
Growth in Africa (E/CN.14/INR/1/Rev. 1)(New
York, 1963).

Economic Commission for Europe. Economic Bulletin
for Europe. Volume 14, 1962; Volume 15, 1963; and
Volume 16, 1964.

Department of Economic and Social Affairs. Economi
Survey of Africa Since 1950 (E/CN.14/28) New York:
1959.

Food and Agricultural Organization. Agricultural
Commodities - The Outlook for 1970 in Eastern
Europe. Rome: 1963.

Technical Assistance Board. Technical Assistance
Activities in Ghana. Report of the U.N.-T.A.B.
Representative for the period January-July, 1964.
(Res. TAB/GHA/R.14), New York: September 29, 1964.

Technical Assistance Board. Report of the Resident
Representative in Mali (Res. TAB/MALI/R.2), New
York: October 30, 1964.

Technical Assistance Board. Report of the Resident Representative in the Sudan (Res. TAB/SUD/
R.9). New York: September 14, 1964.

UNCTAD. The Participation of Czechoslovakia in
International Economic Relations (E/CONF. 46/117),
Geneva: May 22, 1964.

UNCTAD. Financing for an Expansion of International Trade (E/CONF. 46/9), Geneva: March 10,
1964.

UNCTAD. Trade Problems between Countries Having
Different Economic and Social Systems (E/CONF.
46/34), Geneva: March 9, 1964.

UNCTAD. Past Trade Flows and Future Prospects
of Trade between the Centrally Planned Economies
and Developing Countries (E/CONF. 46/35), Geneva:
February 13, 1964.

Newspapers Consulted

AFRICA
L'Action (Tunis).

Afrique Nouvelle (Dakar).

Arab Observer (Cairo).

Daily Graphic (Accra).

East African Standard (Nairobi).

Egyptian Gazette (Cairo).

Egyptian Mail (Cairo).

L'Essor (Bamako).

Ethiopian Herald (Addis Ababa).

Evening News (Accra).

AFRICA (Cont'd)
    Financial Gazette (Cape Town)

    Financial Times (Johannesburg).

    Ghanaian Times (Accra).

    Horoya (Conakry).

    Le Peuple (Algiers).

    Nigerian Morning Post (Lagos).

    Rhodesian Herald (Salisbury).

    Somali News (Mogadishu).

    Tanganyika (Tanzania) Standard (Dar-es-Salaam).

    Uganda Argus (Kampala).

FRANCE
    Marchés Tropicaux et Méditerranéens, (Paris),
    1962, 1963, 1964, and 1965.

SOVIET UNION
    Izvestiya (Moscow), 1960 to 1966.

    Komsomol'skaya Pravda (Moscow), 1961 to 1965.

    Kommunist (Moscow), 1962 and 1965.

    New Times (Moscow), 1963.

    Sovetskaya Kirgiziya (Frunze, Kirghiz SSSR), 1963.

    Sovremennyy Vostok (Moscow), 1960 to 1965.

    Pravda (Moscow), 1958 to 1967.

    Pravda Vostoka (Moscow), 1961 to 1965.

    Trud (Moscow), 1961 to 1965.

UNITED KINGDOM
    African Research Limited (Exeter, England), 1964,
    1965, 1966, and 1967.

    Mizan Newsletter (London), 1964 to 1967.

U.S.A.
    The New York Times (New York, N.Y.), 1963, 1964,
    1965, and 1966.

WORKS

Books

Allen, Robert L. Soviet Economic Warfare. Washington,
    D.C.: Public Affairs Press, 1960.

Balassa, Bela. Trade Prospects for Developing Coun-
    tries. Homewood, Ill.: Richard D. Irwin, Inc.,
    for the Economic Growth Center, Yale University,
    1964.

Bauer, Peter T. West African Trade; a Study in Compe-
    tition, Oligopoly and Monopoly in a Changing
    Economy. Cambridge: Cambridge University Press,
    1954.

Berliner, Joseph S. Soviet Economic Aid. The New Aid
    and Trade Policy in Underdeveloped Countries.
    New York: Frederick A. Praeger for the Council
    on Foreign Relations, 1958.

Billerbeck, Klaus. Die Auslandshilfe des Ostblocks
    für die Entwicklungsländer. Hamburg: Verlag
    Weltarchiv G.m.b.H., 1960.

Brzezinski, Z., ed. Africa and the Communist World.
    Stanford, Calif.: Stanford University Press for
    Hoover Institution, 1963.

Cherviakov, P. A. Organizatsia i Tekhnika Vneshnei
    Torgovli SSSR. Moscow: Vneshtorgizdat, 1962.

Hance, William A. The Geography of Modern Africa.
    New York: Columbia University Press, 1964.

Handbuch der Entwicklungshilfe. Berlin: n.p., 1961.

Kaser, M. Comecon; Integration Problems of the
    Planned Economies. London: Oxford University
    Press for the Royal Institute of International
    Affairs, 1965.

Kodachenko, A.S. Sorevnovanie Dvukh Sistem i
    Slaborazvitye Strani. Moscow: Sotsekgiz, 1963.

Kovrizhnykh, et. al. Vneshnyaya Torgovlya Stran
    Narodnoi Demokrati. Moscow: Gostorgizdat, 1955.

Lavrichenko, Mikhail V. Ekonomicheskoe Sotrudnichestvo
    SSSR Stranami Azzi, Afriki i Latinskoi Ameriki.
    Moscow: Gospolitzdat, 1961.

Mikesell, Raymond F. and Behrman, Jack. Financing Free
    World Trade with the Sino-Soviet Bloc. Princeton,
    N.J.: Princeton Studies in International Finance,
    No. 8, 1958.

Morrison, David. The U.S.S.R. in Africa. London: 1963

Nove, Alec and Donnelly, D. Trade with Communist Coun-
    tries. London: Hutchinson and Co. Ltd., for the
    Institute of Economic Affairs, 1960.

_____. The Soviet Economy. London: George Allen and
    Unwin, 1961.

Pothekin, I.I. Afrika Smotrit v Buduschchee. Moscow:
    Izdatel'stvo vostochnoy literaturny, 1960.

_____. Afrika: Entsiklopedicheskiy Spravochnik.
    Moscow: 1963.

Pryor, Frederick L. The Communist Foreign Trade System
    London: George Allen and Unwin, 1963.

Rymalov, V. Ekonomicheskoe Sotrudnichestvo SSSR co
    Slabroazvitymi Stranami. Moscow: Gostorgizdat,
    1960.

Stalin, J. Economic Problems of Socialism in the
     U.S.S.R. Moscow: Foreign Languages Press, 1952.

The World Mark Encyclopedia of Nations. New York:
     Harper and Brothers, 1960.

U.S.S.R.-Ministry of Foreign Trade. Vneshnyaya
     Torgovlya SSSR, za 1918-1940 gody. Moscow:
     Gostorgizdat, 1960 (See also Section I.)

Wheelock, Keith. Nasser's New Egypt. London: Stevens,
     1960.

Yeshegodnik Bolshoy Sovetzkoy Entsiklopedii, 1963.
     Moscow: 1963.

                         Articles

Badawi, H.B. "Technical Assistance Programs. Their
     Role in Stimulating our Economic Development,"
     Egypte Contemporaine, Volume 42 (January, 1951),
     pp. 13-22.

Beck, C.F. "Czechoslovakia's Penetration of Africa,
     1955-62," World Politics, Volume 15 (April, 1963),
     pp. 403-16.

Bognar, J. "Economic Planning in Ghana," New Hungarian
     Quarterly, Volume 3 (July-September, 1962), pp. 3-31.

Bornstein, M. "The Soviet Price System," The American
     Economic Review, Volume 52, No. 1 (March, 1962),
     pp. 64-103.

_____. "The Soviet Price Reform Discussion," Quarterly
     Journal of Economics, Volume 78 (February, 1964),
     pp. 15-48.

Bykow, A. "UNCTAD, CMEA," International Affairs (Moscow),
     Volume 10 (February, 1964), pp. 68-72.

Byl, A. "Ghana's Struggle for Economic Independence,"
     Current History, Volume 43 (December, 1962), pp.
     359-65.

Castagno, Alphonso A., Jr. "The Somali Republic in
     Transition," Africa Report, Volume 3, No. 14
     (December, 1962), pp. 7-10.

"Czechoslovakia in the U.A.R.," Czechoslovak Foreign
     Trade, Volume 2, No. 9 (September, 1962), p. 9.

Daxey, G.U. "Economic Aid in Soviet Foreign Policy,"
     The Banker, Volume 112 (October, 1962), pp. 639-45

Domdey, H. "Die Welthandelskonferenz und die Stellung
     der DDR auf dem Kapitalistischen Weltmarkt,"
     Wirtschaftswissenschaft, Volume 12 (April, 1964),
     pp. 611-29.

"Economic Development in the U.A.R.," World Trade In-
     formation Service, Economic Reports, No. 59
     (1962), pp. 1-15.

"Economic Planning in Africa," Economic Bulletin for
     Africa, Volume 2 (June, 1962), pp. 29-44.

Economist, The, "Poor of the World Unite!," Volume
     211 (June 20, 1964), p. 1388.

Economist Intelligence Unit, "Three-Monthly Economic
     Review of the French African Community," No. 8
     (March, 1962).

El Serafy, S. "Economic Development by Revolution,"
     Middle East Journal, Volume 17 (Summer, 1963),
     pp. 215-30.

"Entwicklungshilfe der UdSSR," Ost-Probleme, Volume
     14 (July 27, 1962), pp. 469-73.

Frank-Ossipoff, Z. "Quelques réflexions sur le pro-
     gramme économique à long terme 1961-80, de l'Union
     Soviétique," Pays communistes, Volume 3 (July,
     1962), pp. 221-37.

Frisch, Ragnar. "Planning for the United Arab Republic
     Egypte Contemporaine, No. 85 (July, 1964), pp. 5-1

Gehlen, M.P.   "The Politics of Soviet Foreign Trade,"
    Western Political Quarterly, No. 18 (March, 1965),
    pp. 104-15.

Goldman, Marshall I.   "A Balance Sheet of Soviet Foreign
    Aid," Foreign Affairs, Volume 43, No. 2 (January,
    1965), pp. 349-60.

Grigorjan, O.   "Die Hilfe der UdSSR für die schwach
    entwickelten Länder," Deutsche Aussenpolitik,
    Volume 7 (July, 1962), pp. 767-72.

Hammond, N.J.   "Ghana on the Move," African Affairs,
    Volume 62 (July, 1963), pp. 249-56.

Hazelwood, A.   "Ghana's Second Development Plan,"
    Bankers Magazine, Volume 188 (July, 1959), pp.
    25-30.

Heim, P.   "Egypte 1963," Industrie, Volume 17
    (November, 1963), pp. 740-55.

Holzman, Franklyn L.   "Soviet Foreign Trade Pricing
    and the Question of Discrimination," Review of
    Economics and Statistics, Volume XLIV, No. 2
    (May, 1962), pp. 134-47.

Jonas, Josef.   "Czechoslovak Socialist Republic; An
    Exporter of Complete Industrial Plants,"
    Czechoslovak Foreign Trade, Volume 1, No. 10
    (October, 1961).

Kapranov, I.   "Die technische Auslandshilfe der Sowjet-
    union," Der Aussenhandel und der Innerdeutsche
    Handel, No. 1 (January, 1962), pp. 16-32.

Kerblay, B.   "L'Aide économique de l'U.R.S.S. au
    Tiers-Monde," Développement et Civilisations,
    No. 10 (April-June, 1962), pp. 37-50.

Kondrashov.   "Two Days in Asyut," Sovremennyy Vostok
    (now Aziya i Afrika Segodnya), No. 6 (June, 1960),
    pp. 19-24.

Koniewicz, G. "Nouvelle Politique soviétique en
    Afrique tropicale," Revue de l'Action populaire,
    June, 1962, pp. 690-96.

Kralova, H. "Prospects for Development of Czechoslovak
    Trade Relations with Cambodia, Indonesia and
    U.A.R.," Czechoslovak Foreign Trade, Volume 1,
    No. 7 (July, 1961), pp. 17-19.

Lamako, P.F. "Report to the Supreme Soviet on the
    1964-65 Plan," Current Digest of the Soviet Press,
    Volume 15 (January 8, 1964), pp. 3-12 and 27.

"La Roumanie et UNCTAD," Chambre de Commerce de la
    République populaire roumaine, Bulletin d'Infor-
    mation, Volume 10 (April, 1964), pp. 1-3.

"Mixed Economy for Ghana," Petroleum Press Service,
    Volume 31 (April, 1964), pp. 145-47.

Neuberger, Egon. "The U.S.S.R. and the West as Markets
    for Primary Products," Rand Corporation Research
    Memorandum, RM-3841 P.R., Santa Monica, Calif.: 19

Nove, Alec. "Soviet Trade and Aid," Lloyds Bank Review
    No. 51 (January, 1959), pp. 1-19.

Osipov, Yu. M. "Problems of Financing the U.A.R.
    Economy," Kratkiye Sooboshcheniya Instituta
    Narodnoy Azii, No. 79 (1964), pp. 87-108.

Polish Economic Survey, No. 14, 1963.

Prybyla, V. "The Economics of the Sino-Soviet Dispute,"
    Bulletin of the Institute for the Study of the
    U.S.S.R., Volume 10 (December, 1963), pp. 17-24.

"Recent Trends in African Trade," Economic Bulletin
    for Africa, Volume 1, No. 1 (January, 1961),
    pp. 10-33.

"Recent Trends in African Trade," Economic Bulletin for
    Africa, Volume 2, No. 1 (January, 1962), pp. A-9-3

"Recent Trends in African Trade," Economic Bulletin for Africa, Volume 3 (January, 1963), pp. 5-29.

"Recent Developments in African Trade," Economic Bulletin for Africa, Volume 4 (January, 1964), pp. 7-38.

"Review of Development Trends and Policies of Ethiopia," Ethiopian Economic Review, September, 1963, pp. 10-21.

Rosenstein-Rodan, P.N. "International Aid for Under-developed Countries," Review of Economics and Statistics, Volume 43, No. 2 (May, 1961), pp. 107-39.

Rymalov, V. "Soviet Assistance to Less-Developed Countries," International Affairs (Moscow), No. 9 (September, 1959), pp. 23-31.

_____. "The U.N. Trade and Development Conference," International Affairs (Moscow), No. 10 (April, 1964), pp. 80-85.

Sadek, G.H. "The Third Year of the Five-Year Plan," Scribe, Volume 7 (December, 1963), pp. 36-40.

Schilting, H. "Zur Rolle und spezifischen Bedeutung des Staatskapitalismus in der Republik Ghana," Wirtschaftswissenschaft, Volume 9 (1961), pp. 377-88.

Schonfield, A. "Trade as a Tool of Development," International Affairs (London), Volume 40 (April, 1964), pp. 219-31.

Schwarztraubor, J. "Soviet Bloc Economic Offensive. Ghana - a Case Study," International Commerce (supplement), March, 1963, pp. 63-65.

Sobolev, B. "Sovetskaya Pomoshch' Stranam Azii i Afriki," Finansy SSSR, Volume 38, No. 1 (January, 1964), pp. 33-41.

Stauffer, R.B. and Colebrook, M.J.   "Economic Assist-
     ance and Ethiopia's Foreign Policy," Orbis,
     Volume V, No. 3 (Fall, 1961), pp. 320-41.

Stepanovsky, J.   "Czechoslovakia and the Developing
     Countries," Pakistan Horizon, No. 17, 4th Quarter
     (1964), pp. 35-54.

Stolte, S.C.   "The U.S.S.R. and the World Trade Con-
     ference," Bulletin of the Institute for the Study
     of the U.S.S.R., Volume 11 (October, 1964),
     pp. 17-23.

Svoboda, Mirko.   "Experience of Czechoslovak Banking
     Passed on to Developing Countries," Czechoslovak
     Foreign Trade, Volume 4, No. 7 (July, 1964),
     pp. 3-5.

Symonin, N.   "The UNCTAD Problems and Prospects of
     Economic Cooperation," International Affairs
     (Moscow), Volume 10, No. 3 (March, 1964), pp. 62-67

"The Report on the Fulfillment of the 1963 Plan,"
     Current Digest of the Soviet Press, Volume 16
     (February 5, 1964), pp. 3-8.

"U.A.R. Industrial Revolution," Egyptian Economic and
     Political Review, Volume 5 (July-August, 1959),
     pp. 11-17.

Vanin, V. "Economic Cooperation of the U.S.S.R. with
     Countries of the Arab East and Africa," Problems
     of Economics, Volume 4 (April, 1962), pp. 54-62.

Vishnev, S.   "Sovetskoy Soyuz v Mirovoi Ekonomike,"
     Mirovaya Ekonomika i Mezhdunarodnye Otnosheniya,
     No. 2 (1962), pp. 16-17.

Wafa, Taher Abu.   "The Aswan Dam - Key to a Nation's
     Future," The UNESCO Courier, December, 1964,
     pp. 40-42.

Yurev, G.V.   "Shifting Emphasis in Soviet Foreign
     Trade Policy," <u>Analysis of Current Developments
     in the Soviet Union</u>, October 22, 1963, pp. 1-6.

Zauberman, A.   "Soviet and Chinese Strategy for Eco-
     nomic Growth," <u>International Affairs</u> (London),
     Volume 38 (July, 1962), pp. 339-52.

Zinger, H.   "Die Nationaldemokratische Entwicklung in
     Guinea," <u>Deutsche Aussenpolitik</u>, Volume 7
     (September, 1962), pp. 1060-63.

Zolberg, A.R.   "The Political Revival of Mali," <u>The
     World Today</u>, April, 1965, pp. 151-59.

INDEX

---

* Council for Mutual Economic Assistance; for brevity, "CMEA"
  in this index denotes all centrally planned economies, Soviet
  Bloc, etc.

ABOUT THE AUTHOR

Baard Richard Stokke is a development economist at Stanford Research Institute, Menlo Park, California. A native of Norway, he received his doctorate from the Graduate Institute of International Studies, University of Geneva, in 1967. Prior to joining the Stanford Research Institute, Mr. Stokke was an economic affairs officer at the International Trade Centre of GATT in Geneva, Switzerland.